P9-CAJ-113

Homilies for the Active Christian

By
Father Arnold Weber, OSB

Compiled by
Debera O'Leary, Pamela Patnode,
and Laurie Swing

CABIN SIX BOOKS
SAINT PAUL, MN

ISBN: 0-9728945-1-9

© 2006 by Fr. Arnold Weber, OSB

All rights reserved. Printed in the U.S.A.

Cover design by Linda Andreozzi.

Published by:

CABIN SIX BOOKS
157 BRIDGE STREET
SAINT PAUL, MN
651-765-1813

About this Book

This keepsake book of Fr. Arnold Weber's homilies was lovingly prepared by parishioners of Holy Name of Jesus Catholic Church, Wayzata, Minnesota for the family of Father Weber, OSB and the Holy Name of Jesus parish community. No portion of this book may be reprinted without permission. (Copyright 2006)

The parishioners of Holy Name of Jesus Catholic Church wanted a remembrance of the beautiful homilies Fr. Arnold delivered so passionately during his time as Pastor of Holy Name of Jesus. Fr. Arnold, when creating his homilies, relied upon many sources. He often said that he used the daily paper and the Bible every time he prepared a homily. In addition to these sources, Fr. Arnold relied upon other resources available to priests and ministers in the area of homilitics. Some of Fr. Arnold's thoughts evolved with influence from the various religious works, articles and books that he has read throughout his tenure as a parish priest.

We have noted these resources wherever possible. Some may have been missed. Fr. Arnold's tenure as a priest spans more than fifty years. Due to Fr. Arnold's age and his illnesses, not every source may have been recalled. Any omissions are not intentional. If you recognize a source that was not included, please notify Holy Name of Jesus Catholic Church in writing. They will contact the creators of the book, and make certain that the information is included in any future editions.

Please note, Holy Name of Jesus Catholic Church, St. John's University in Collegeville, MN and the Benedictine Abbey have no legal role in the preparation of this book, nor do they claim any responsibility to its production.

As the creators of this book, we lovingly pray that the words enclosed within will help you to remember Fr. Arnold Weber, OSB. And, most importantly, may they encourage you to walk closer to Christ and to strive to be an Active Christian.

May God Bless you!

A letter from Father Arnold

To Parishioners and Friends,

During the many happy years at Holy Name of Jesus, parishioners often asked me to publish my homilies. I responded that a homily was really part of the whole Eucharistic celebration that we share together, and that publishing it was not as necessary as putting it in your heart and bringing it home with you.

When the time came that I was to leave Holy Name and return to St. John's, numerous parishioners again asked me to publish my homilies.

Actually, I had not written on paper most of the homilies. In preaching homilies, I often used no notes. Other times I had a few notes jotted down, and occasionally I wrote out the homily entirely. Because I did not keep many of my homilies, it was difficult for me recall them, to publish them. I mentioned this to the people who asked me about preparing a book, but I continued to get requests.

Finally three parishioners urged me a little harder to publish some of the homilies. In discussing it with them, we decided to take my notes and see if they could compile them into a book. Because a great deal of time has passed since giving some of these homilies, I couldn't always remember what was mine and what I had gathered through my reading and my meditations and notes. I would want to give proper credit to all of the authors who have inspired me over the years, and whose materials I have used in preparing my homilies. In addition, it is my intention that this collection of homilies be for limited, private distribution only.

While I was still Pastor at Holy Name, I enjoyed visiting with parishioners in the gathering space before and after Mass. Often, I would overhear one parishioner ask another, "How did you like Father's homily?" And the other parishioner would respond, "Which one?" I was often kidded about giving three homilies at Sunday's Mass.

What actually happened, over the years, was that I carefully read and studied the Roman Missal called the Sacramentary. This is the large book you see on the altar that the priest uses to read from. The beginning of that book has many rubrics and instructions that really emphasize the importance of the instructions of the Second Vatican Council on the Liturgy—especially when it calls the members of the Catholic Church to full, active, and conscious participation in the Mass.

The instructions of the Sacramentary also say that the presider can give some instructions as the liturgy begins. This is what I did. I always gave a little "pep talk." I think this might have come from my coaching days. At the start of the game, we'd call the players together and we'd motivate them, give them a pep talk. I thought it was a good idea, and if we can do it for sports, why can't we do it for something even more meaningful like the Eucharistic celebration? I wanted to motivate people to have full, active and conscious participation. I believe people found it very helpful.

In coaching, when the game was over, I would usually call the players together again to let them know that, no matter whether they won or lost the game, if they had tried their best, then they were gainers. On Sundays, too, at the end of mass, I would again give a final pep talk. I wanted people to carry the word of God with them outside of the church walls and to remind them that when you put your heart into it, you will always be a gainer. So, the three homilies that the parishioners joked about, were not all homilies (two of them were pep talks, only one was a homily).

This book does not contain these pep talks from the beginning and end of Mass. I did not have any of that written down. These are the homilies that I gave after the Gospel. Many of the stories and anecdotes I shared are missing, because they were of the "off the cuff" variety.

Having said that, I want to mention that I always felt that humor was an important part of teaching. I felt people should really enjoy liturgy. By that, I do not mean entertainment. Stories and anecdotes, however, make people feel good about themselves and about worshiping God. They seem to enjoy it more.

Recently I found a quotation by Pope Benedict XVI. He said, "Humor is in fact an essential element in the mirth of creation. We can see how in many matters in our lives that God wants to prod us into taking things a bit more lightly, to see the funny side of it, to get down off our pedestal and to not forget our sense of fun." Somewhere along the line, I think it's important to have a joyful spirit in worshiping. It is not entertainment. It is true joy and true happiness.

Visiting with the Holy Name community in the gathering space on Sundays was a high point of the week for me, as I think it was for many of you. It was in the gathering space, often while visiting, that we began to prepare our hearts to celebrate the wonderful things of God: His creation, His redemption, and His sanctification.

I have so many happy memories of good worship at Holy Name and we all had our special parts. Because I was the presider for most of the masses for 23 years, the homilies were a very special part for me. But they were only one part of the whole worship experience.

The Sunday celebration was such a community celebration and the homily had to be given with that in mind—that we are all doing this together. Together we were to give praise to God, receive Jesus in the Eucharist, continuing to live the Mass.

I personally have such happy memories of the liturgies at Holy Name. There were so many people involved to make the liturgies truly come alive with full, active and conscious participation. Today, that continues at Holy Name, and it is a wonderful credit to the entire Holy Name parish community.

I took my role as presider very seriously. I hope these homilies will bring back some memories for you. My main duty to you was to share the word of God with you, and I miss it greatly.

God Bless You!

Fr. Arnold Weber, OSB

Foreword

After His resurrection, Jesus walked along the road to Emmaus where He encountered some disciples who did not recognize Him. Jesus explained the Scriptures to them and then joined them for dinner.

Upon the breaking of the bread, the disciples finally recognized that it was their Savior with whom they were dining. They asked themselves, "Were not our hearts burning within us while he spoke to us on the way and opened the Scriptures to us?"

(Luke 24:33)

For twenty-three years, the members of the Holy Name of Jesus parish community were blessed to have a pastor who walked with us on our faith journey and "opened the Scriptures to us" in a way that made our hearts burn.

During his time at Holy Name, Fr. Arnold Weber, OSB brought the members of this faith community closer to God—not just once—but week after week.

Fr. Arnold had a true love for the members of the Holy Name of Jesus parish community, a true love for children, and a true love for his vocation as priest. In addition to this love, Fr. Arnold had an amazing gift. His gift was the ability to deliver a homily with the power to open the Scriptures to each of us as individuals, as well as all of us together as a community. Through laughter, stories, tears and challenges, Fr. Arnold led us to a deeper love of Jesus.

As a community we will forever remember that our priorities should be: God, spouse, family and work—in that order. We will strive to become better in life rather than bitter. And most important, we will work to become Active Christians!

This collection of inspiring homilies is a testament to our community's love for Fr. Arnold Weber. The homilies themselves, however, are testimony of Fr. Arnold's love for Christ.

With great love, we present this treasured keepsake to you.

Sincerely,

Debera O'Leary, Pamela Patnode and Laurie Swing

Acknowledgements

This book is a collection of efforts and support by a number of people. We would especially like to thank Fr. Arnold Weber, OSB who humbly agreed to let us create the book. Our lives have been deeply enriched as we reviewed and worked with the many homilies from his years at Holy Name. For two and one half years, Fr. Arnold patiently met with us as we discussed plans, asked questions about homilies, and played an occasional game of Bingo. We are so very grateful to him for allowing us to create this book.

We also thank our families who gave us unfailing support as the project that we first thought would take months stretched out into years. Even our children stepped up to the plate to help. Becky Swing and Shannon Bullock helped their mothers with typing while the Patnode children helped prepare numerous mailings, made endless deliveries and hosted numerous events at their home. The patience and support of our husbands and children is forever appreciated.

In addition, many people from the Holy Name of Jesus community generously contributed time and talent to this project. A special thanks goes out to Rev. Mr. Sam Catapano, Brenda Coleman, Betty Conway, Dan Garry, Kathleen Hansmann, Fr. Jonathan Licari, Linda Meisinger, Don Prisby, Beth Prisby, Karen Richelsen, Jean Roozendaal, Bill Rose, Jim Sable, Sharon Sable, Greg Scherer and Diane Van Valkenburg.

Help also came from outside the Holy Name of Jesus Community. We thank Elizabeth Smith for her keen eye in proofreading and editing. We appreciate Jeff Cavins and the law firm of Lommen, Abdo, King and Stageberg, P.A. for helping us to obtain the answer to a legal question.

Finally, we thank Linda Andreozzi who designed the cover and layout of the book. Her deep faith and wonderful creativity helped to make this book the beautiful tribute to Fr. Arnold that it is.

Sincerely,

Debera O'Leary, Pamela Patnode and Laurie Swing

General Editors

Contents

Prologue

Section 1: Characteristics of the Active Christian

Section 6: Seasons and Special Events of the Active Christian

Section 7: Biography and Photo Album

●

Fr. Arnold and I have been good friends since he became Pastor at Holy Name in 1972. We have had the opportunity to share many good times together. We've traveled together, laughed together and leaned on one another more times than I can remember. We carried each other through major illnesses and deaths within our families and developed a brotherly bond.

Fr. Arnold loves the outdoors and is a very hard worker. He often had the snow shoveled from the sidewalks before the 6:45am weekday Mass. I do think, however, that Fr. Arnold enjoyed mowing the grass more. You'd often see him driving his shiny green John Deere lawn tractor, which seemed to have just two speeds: fast and faster.

Fr. Arnold has always enjoyed people and didn't shy away from the spotlight. I can remember many occasions when Fr. Arnold would put on his German hat and his lederhosen and lead a group in singing "Schnitzelbank".

I am grateful for Fr. Arnold's friendship and his leadership at Holy Name. Thank you and God bless you.

Bill Rudolph

What is a Homily?

✝

*Father Arnold's thoughts on
a definition of a homily.*

What is a Homily?

✝

When He was at the table with them, He took bread, blessed and broke it, and gave it to them. Then their eyes were opened, and they recognized Him; and He vanished from their sight. They said to each other, "Were not our hearts burning within us while He was talking to us on the road, while He was opening the Scripture to us?"

(Luke 24:30-32)

*I*n 1973 when I was appointed pastor at Holy Rosary in Detroit Lakes, I went to see the Bishop. He handed me a book that contained all the Catholic ceremonies, the Ten Commandments, the six commandments of the Church, and 16 sermons that were to be given over the next 16 weeks. I must say that they were correctly defined as sermons and not homilies! Sermons are topics of instruction; homilies are much more than that. It's true that education is part of their purpose, but mostly, homilies should offer inspiration that leads to a greater love of God, with emphasis on Scripture.

Some time ago a man stopped me after Mass, saying, "Father, that was a great speech." When I grinned, he said, "Oh, that's right, it's not called a speech. It's a homily." He was right. A speech is a talk delivered to a given audience for a particular purpose of some sort, but homilies are much more than that. They are meant to transform, rather than just inform or entertain. Homilies should persuade listeners.

The word homily comes from the Latin word *homo*, which means people and the ending *ly*, which means to share with. What is shared with the people in a homily is the Word of God. Homilies are an important part of the Liturgy of the Word, which, along with the Liturgy of the Eucharist, make up our Mass. Masses are inspiring when all the parts—prayer, readings, homilies, singing, Eucharist—are done well. A Mass that is done well encourages people's full, active, conscious, participation; promotes their faith; and leads them to successful social action.

Delivering a homily on Sunday is a privilege that should not be taken lightly. Good preaching is a primary way by which a congregation grows in both number and depth. It has a lot to do with how the people of a parish treat other people. After all, though we may come together as a parish family, when we leave church, each of us takes the Word of God, as we understand it, to everyone we meet.

So what is needed for a person to create and give a good homily?

Credibility

First, a good homilist needs credibility. As you might imagine, many a priest stands in front of a congregation shaking a little about that. For a homily to be really good, the priest must truly love God and want his parishioners to have His Word as part of their lives. Ultimately, we must know and relate to the Lord intimately enough to imitate Him. In other words, we need to have a personal relationship with Jesus Christ.

3

Jesus had a very attractive charismatic personality. All types of people flocked to Him, including many children. Everywhere that Jesus went, children surrounded Him because He allowed it. He loved them, and they loved Him. For the homilist, it ought to be similar. We should be aware that the congregation consists of people of many ages and stages. We ought to be preaching in a way that instructs and inspires everyone, not just the adults.

Jesus spoke with great conviction. No one else has ever talked with such authority. Of course, He got into a lot of trouble for this! Somehow or another in today's culture, homilists must also speak the Word with conviction. Otherwise our teaching gets watered down over time. At the same time great care must be taken to be compassionate. We need to have a kind enough spirit to look upon people sympathetically. The idea is not to scold, but to challenge. Homilists must embrace all types of people. Not just the loyal, hard-working, put-together, pleasant ones, but also those with negative attitudes, those who are puzzled and confused, and those who are not productive. That way people will be more inclined to accept the teaching and make any changes in life that are necessary.

Homilies must be relevant and meaningful. People should recognize themselves in the words of the homilist. When people would ask me after Mass on Sundays, "Were you talking about me today?" that was an indication that I had confronted the complexity of their experience and challenged them into conversion. When the homilist takes on the joys and sorrows of humanity, the homily has the right effectiveness. This type of preaching draws people together into community and motivates them into action. It's the type of preaching that challenges communities to offer hospitality to strangers.

Ability

Secondly, a good homilist does need some ability. Again, many a priest cringes at this one. Parishioners really do wish to be fed. They usually have heavy schedules, however, and time is at a premium.

Homilists have to be able to help ensure that the Sunday experience is powerful enough for people to want to return each week. They must give people something that will inspire them during the week and help them grow in their faith.

The homilist definitely has to provide good instruction. This should be the 'meat and potato' of every homily. Sound instruction requires a lot of study and preparation and prayer. For myself on Monday, I'd read the Scripture two or three times so I'd get a good feel for what the readings said. Then during the week I'd choose a topic and look at commentaries from a number of helpful sources. I'd try to find stories that were interesting and memorable. And it never hurt to add some humor to liven things up!

All homilists have their own personalities and ways of presentation. They must use whatever gifts God has given them and do the best they can in their delivery. Their message ought to be presented in a way that is inspiring. That demands a certain amount of enthusiasm and conviction about what is being said. Homilists should do more than just read their notes to the congregation. They should plan and practice, so the congregation feels a part of the homily and the homily feels a part of them. Jesus spoke in parables because it was an effective way to engage his listeners, so I think it's important for a homilist to present stories. Also it's good to make use of catechetical moments—naturally occurring times when a very good point can be easily brought out—whenever possible.

A challenge for today's homilists is to speak to the culture that we live in. There are so many issues that demand us to take a stand. Also, in a society saturated with success, sports, and sex, we have to find a way to make faith and religion meaningful and desirable to people. I used to keep a notebook in my pocket to write down phrases I heard or situations I came across that could be used in a homily. I always made it a point to view the notice boards that other nearby churches used to announce upcoming homilies. Another way to stay up to date on the culture would be to attend movies and read some of the current popular books.

Accountability

In addition to credibility and ability, a good homilist needs accountability. We homilists not only have to truly love the Word of God that we're preaching, we have to practice it. We need to speak the truth and challenge people towards the truth. To do this effectively, we must live in the truth ourselves. We need to call people to virtuous living and inspire them to want to be more like Christ. To do this we must be constantly looking to and living the higher values in life.

A Receptive Congregation

Finally, a good homilist needs a good congregation—one that is receptive to instruction on the Word when it's presented. A receptive congregation listens with an open mind and heart and spirit. They participate fully, actively, and consciously, so that the homily can have the best effect.

At some retreats the participants pray formally for the people giving the talks. I think it would be nice to have a ritual like that built right into the Eucharistic liturgy. Maybe the whole congregation could extend their hands over the homilist in blessing.

****

Friends, now that you know what a homily is and what it takes to create and deliver one, let me leave you with the finest example of a homily that I can think of. Right after the Resurrection a couple of disciples are on their way to Emmaus, which is about seven miles from Jerusalem. They are talking to each other when Jesus appears and asks, "What are you talking about?" They don't recognize Him, and answer, "Are you the only one in the world who hasn't heard about what's been going on around here the last few days?"

Anyway, the disciples fill Jesus in on what has happened and their uncertainty about it. After listening a while, He scolds them for their lack of understanding and begins to explain the Scriptures to them, starting with the book of Moses. The disciples are so intrigued that they invite Jesus to stay and eat with them, and as He breaks the bread, they finally recognize Him. At this point Jesus vanishes, but the instruction He gave them about the Scripture stayed with them. They said, "Were not our hearts burning within us while He was talking to us on the road, while He was opening the Scriptures to us?"

Their hearts were burning within them! That's the part that relates to what a good homily is. I've always been touched by the words *Mane nobiscum*, which are on a big sign as you come into Emmaus. Translated, the meaning is 'stay with us.' The hope is that after you hear the homily at Mass your heart will be burning, you will take the Lord home to stay with you, and you will introduce Him to everyone you meet.

Father Arnold's Guidelines for Good Homilies

1. Make the medium fit the message, and vice versa.
2. Use humor (not just joke-telling) to illustrate important points. It can be a really powerful tool.
3. Keep the newspaper in one hand and the Bible in the other. One tells you how things actually are and the other how they ought to be.
4. Talk about timely topics.
   Take a stand on the controversial issues.

> "For God so loved the world that He gave His only Son, so that everyone who believes in Him shall not die but shall live."
>
> John 3:16

> "This is what God asks of you: only this, to act justly, to love tenderly, to walk humbly with your God."
>
> Micah 6:8

These are Fr. Arnold's favorite quotes, and they are painted on the walls at Holy Name of Jesus.

> "That in all things God may be glorified."
>
> Rule of St. Benedict

Characteristics of the Active Christian

✝

Passion for Christ

Faith

Forgiveness

Truth

Compassion

Righteousness

The Beatitudes

Love

Generosity

The Active Christian

And some men brought on a stretcher
a man who was paralyzed;
they were trying to bring him in
and set him in His presence.

(Luke 5:18)

Friends, today we heard the story about Jesus curing the paralytic. I do not want to talk about the paralytic today, however, as much as I want to talk about the four people who carried him in on the stretcher. These four people cared enough for this paralyzed man to bring him to a place to be cured. They were four people who clearly had a love for the needy—who can surely be called "Active Christians."

What does it means to be an Active Christian? To help us understand this, we can use the letters that spell out the word ACTIVE.

A for "Awareness"

To be an Active Christian, we must have awareness. Probably one of the greatest scandals of our Christian existence is our lack of social consciousness—our failure to care about our brother.

Awareness demands that we know the world and the people around us. But knowledge is not enough. Our goal is to attain wisdom. Wisdom is more than intellectual savvyness. Wisdom is seeking the right answers. Wisdom is a largeness of mind that comes from understanding God, ourselves, and our neighbor. Wisdom is harder to attain than knowledge. To attain knowledge we simply need to be open to learning. To attain wisdom, we need to be open to learning and prayer. Wisdom comes through prayer as a gift of the Holy Spirit.

C for "Courage"

We need courage to speak out against the wrongdoings in our culture today. We also need the courage to forgive. Sin is a broken relationship. Forgiveness restores the relationship. Courage helps us do what is right, even when it's difficult or unpopular to do so.

T for "Time"

The most precious gift we can give another person is our time. Often, I hear people complain that they don't have enough time to be an Active Christian. These people are usually wrong. We are all given the same amount of time in each day. How we choose to spend that time illustrates what our priorities are. If Christ is a priority in our life, then we will make time to do His work and spend time with Him. We will realize that to be an Active Christian takes time.

I for "Individual"

Never underestimate what one person can do! The great movements that have shaped our country and our world are often initiated by a single person. The work of Mother Theresa in working with the poorest of the poor in India. Pope John Paul II, who received his seminary training in secret and began his works as a village priest in communist Poland. Locally, our own Mary Jo Copeland who founded Sharing and Caring Hands and Mary's Place which serve the poor of the Minneapolis area. All are examples of what an individual is capable of doing. They all started out small in their works. But through persistence, prayer and grace, their efforts grew to positively affect countless. We all have been given different talents. Together we can share our talents to become a community of charity.

V for "Vigor"

When I think of vigor, I think of John F. Kennedy. Do any of you remember how he delivered his speeches? Friends, he spoke with vigor! We need to have vigor like that. And living with vigor applies to our actions both inside and outside of church. The Catholic Church calls its members to "full, active and conscious participation during the mass." This is an example of vigor. If we come to mass to sit like a bump on a log, then we are not living with vigor. Our parish is blessed with many young families and a lot of children. People often ask me if the noise that children or babies make during mass bothers me. Do you know what I tell them? No. Squirming children don't bother me. Adults who are not participating in the Mass, however, now that bothers me! We need to sing to the Lord with vigor. Say "Amen" with vigor. Offer peace to our neighbors with vigor. Friends, live your lives with vigor.

E for "Example"

We need to be doers of the word. Our lives should serve as a witness to others as to what it means to be an Active Christian. The best example we have of this is Jesus Christ. Jesus was a doer. No question about it, He was an Active Christian. But His actions were not simply gestures. Everything He did was out of love. It was because of His love—His love for God and his love for us, that He did take action. We need to follow His example. With love in our hearts, we, too, need to take action, to be an example of Christ to others.

To be a Christian, a true follower of Christ, means that we need to become active. Like the four men who carried the paralytic to Christ, we too need to be aware, have courage, take time, recognize the importance of an individual, live with vigor, and be an example of Christ's love to others. I bought this spark plug at the hardware store the other day. The letters AC appear on the spark plug. I'd like to give this spark plug out to someone today. The AC on this spark plug stands for Active Christian. The person that I'd like to give this to has been a true Active Christian, a real spark plug within our parish community. Let us all try to live this way—like an Active Christian. Amen!

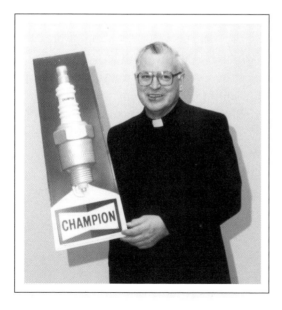

Father Arnold gave out many spark plugs throughout his years as Pastor at Holy Name of Jesus. Without a doubt, he inspired many people within the parish to become Active Christians.

Whatever It Takes

✝

I have become all things to all, to save at least some. All this I do for the sake of the gospel, so that I too may have a share in it.

(1 Corinthians 9:22b-23)

riends in Christ, we have that marvelous reading of St. Paul to the Corinthians in which he says he is under compulsion and has no choice but to preach the Gospel. If he doesn't, he's going to be ruined. Paul says, "I do it willingly, and I do it without charge." He also says, "I will make myself a slave to all so as to win over as many as possible. To the weak, I became a weak person, with a view of winning the weak. I have made myself all things to all men in order to save at least some of them. In fact, I do all things for the sake of the Gospel and the hope of having shared in His blessings." What a spirit!

Some time ago I was paging through my notes, and I found a Dear Abby column from a number of years ago. It was about a congregation that was looking for a new minister. As they say, "their pulpit was vacant." They had set up a screening committee, yet they just weren't making any progress. Someone or other objected to something about each candidate. One day one of the board members received this letter from an applicant:

Dear Ladies and Gentlemen,

I understand that your pulpit is vacant. I should like to apply for the position. I have many qualifications. I've been a preacher with much success and also have some success as a writer. Some say I'm a good organizer. I've been a leader at most places that I've been. I'm over fifty years old and have never preached in one place for more than three years. Some places I had to leave town after my work caused riots and disturbances. I must admit that I've been jailed three times, but not because of any real wrongdoings. My health is not so good, but I still accomplish a great deal. The churches I've preached in were small and have been located in big cities. I've not gotten along well with other religious leaders in the towns where I preached. In fact, some of them have threatened me, and one even attacked me physically. I'm not too good at record keeping, and have been known to forget to record certain events. However, if you can use me, I promise to do my best for you.

The board member turned to the committee and said, "So, what do you think? Should we call him?" One of the committee members was really appalled. He said, "Should we really consider a sickly, trouble-making, absentminded jailbird? Who signed the application?" The first board member looked the committee over and said, "Apostle Paul."

Although he doesn't have a perfect resume, Paul's spirit, attitude and energy toward his mission more than made up for anything that may have been lacking. St. Paul is a great example of how we, too, can spread the word of God and bring others to Christ. Let's take a look at how he did it.

First, Paul took his commission seriously. What was the great commission? Well, it's found in the Gospel of Matthew. "Therefore, go and make disciples of all nations baptizing them in the name of the Father and the Son and the Holy Spirit, teaching them to observe all that I have commanded you. And behold, I am with you always, until the end of the age." (Matthew 28:19-20)

St. Paul took those words seriously. He writes, "though I am free and belong to no man, I make myself a slave to everyone, to win as many as possible." (1 Corinthians 9:19) That is what Paul's life is about. To win as many people as possible to Christ and his church. St. Paul was on a mission—a mission to change the world.

You and I are in the church today, 2,000 years later, because St. Paul took the great commission seriously. And that quality of caring is what we all must strive to attain. People will not care what you know until they know that you care. No one gives us a better example of this than Paul.

Secondly, Paul was willing to do whatever it took to win people to Christ. This is what he says in the gospel today: "To the Jews I became like a Jew to win the Jews. For those not having the law I became like one not having the law, so as to win those not having the law."

I think there are two types of people in the world today. Those who say "whatever" and those who say, "whatever it takes." We all know people who, when asked to do something that we think is really important, simply shrug their shoulders and say, "whatever." Some people are like that even with their faith: "Whatever."

Right now I'm going to make some statements, and after each one, I want you to all say together, "whatever" with a little shrug. Okay? Here we go:

Jesus said to love your neighbor.

"Whatever."

Jesus said there's more rejoicing over one sinner who has been found than 99 who stayed within the safety of the fold.

"Whatever."

Jesus said that what you have done for the least of these, so too, you have done for me.

"Whatever."

Now, let's change our response from "whatever" to "whatever it takes." Here we go:

Jesus said to love your neighbor.

"Whatever it takes!"

Jesus said there's more rejoicing over one sinner who has been found than 99 who stayed within the safety of the fold.

"Whatever it takes!"

Jesus said that what you have done for the least of these, so too, you have done for me.

"Whatever it takes!

Are you and I like St. Paul? Are we willing to do whatever it takes to bring the world to Christ? Shouldn't we think like Paul? Whatever it takes. Shouldn't we take on Paul's spirit?

The final point I'd like to make about St. Paul is this: As far as I can tell, Paul understood that to minister to people in Christ's name, we must meet them where they are at—not where we are at. Let me tell you a story about that.

There was a sales trainer who asked his audience if they liked strawberries. "Yes," they all said, "They are delicious." Then the sales trainer suggested they go fishing and use strawberries as bait. One of the trainees pointed out the fact that fish don't like strawberries. "But you do," replied the trainer. "Yes," said the trainee, "but I want to catch fish." The lesson the trainer was trying to make is this: When we go fishing, we need to offer the bait that the fish like—not what we like.

How often in our apostolate do we go fishing with strawberries? The question we need to ask is this: "What are the needs and preferences of the people I am trying to reach with Christ's message?" We must acknowledge that these needs and preferences might be different from our own.

When Paul was speaking to the Greek-speaking Jews (who were not familiar with the word "Messiah"), he used the Greek word

"Christ." When speaking with the Gentile audiences who were not familiar with the term "Messiah", Paul used the Roman word, "Lord." Paul was not trying to change the Romans into Palestinians. He was trying to change them into Christians. He understood people's needs and preferences, and brought Christ to them on that level.

Paul is a great example for us. Do we have the same passion for our faith that he did? Do we take our great commission seriously? Have we even thought about it lately? Do we try to bring others to Christ by meeting them on their turf instead of our own? Like Paul, let's live for Christ with a new attitude. Whatever it takes.

Sunday mornings became our favorite time of the week… we were eager to receive the challenge of our beloved pastor, Father Arnold Weber. Week after week, God used Father Arnold's extraordinary gift and love of preaching to teach, inspire and form us. We were touched by the practical relevance of the gospel which he carefully and prayerfully prepared and preached. With new conviction, we went home each week, determined to do better.

His influence has extended beyond the years we shared at Holy Name. His passion has become our passion and the spirit of Fr. Arnold lives on. We are most grateful to have shared our faith journey with him. Praise God! Thank you Father Arnold!

Brenda Coleman, Parishioner of Holy Name of Jesus

Unbelievable

✝

As a result of this, many of his disciples returned to their former way of life and no longer accompanied him. Jesus then said to the Twelve, "Do you also want to leave?" Simon Peter answered him, "Master to whom shall we go? You have the words of eternal life."

(John 6:66-68)

At the start of the 1987 baseball season, the Minnesota Twins were listed as a 150-1 long shot. Then they clinched the American League title. The headline in the St. Paul Pioneer Press read: "Unbelievable."

For two weeks, it was unbelievable. And then, the final game of the World Series. The Minnesota Twins beat the St. Louis Cardinals.

People all over Minnesota were saying, "Unbelievable, it must be a dream." What they really meant was, "this is too good to be true."

It's strange. We are willing to believe all sorts of bad news and catastrophe. But along comes some good news and we say, "Ah, go on now. You're kidding me. It can't be."

That's what happened with Jesus. For the last five Sundays, we've heard from the Gospel of John. Jesus has been telling us, "I am the bread of life. He who eats of this bread will live forever." The people, however, are saying, murmuring, "Ah, go on. You're kidding. How can this be?"

Why are they saying this? Because it's unbelievable. It seems too good to be true. And yet, it IS true. And we'd better believe it if we know what's good for us.

Today's readings focus on the issue of fidelity, and the choices we make to remain faithful. The people in all three readings were given choices. In Joshua, the Israelites are asked to choose whom they will serve. In Ephesians, we learn about fidelity between spouses. And in the gospel, Jesus challenges his disciples to believe in Him and His message.

In the reading from the book of Joshua, the Israelites chose to remain faithful to God. But, Jesus' disciples were more divided on that issue. One group simply could not come to terms with what Jesus said. The thought of eating Jesus' actual flesh to have eternal life was too difficult for them to understand or believe. So they left. Jesus asked the second group if they, too, wanted to leave. For once, Peter got it right. He said, "Lord, to whom shall we go. You have the words of everlasting life."

The story in the Gospel dramatizes an important point. The point is this: there are times in life when we are pushed to the wall. There are times in life when we are ready to quit. There are times in life when we need something to hold on to. In today's Gospel the disciples are pushed to the wall. Their faith was challenged by what Jesus said. They responded in two ways. One group found it too difficult to understand, and they parted company. The second group met the challenge and remained faithful to Jesus.

Why did the first group fail and the second group succeed? The Gospel doesn't really answer this, but it does leave us a clue. When Jesus asked the second group if they, too, wanted to leave, Peter said, "Lord to whom shall we go? You have the words of eternal life." When pushed to the wall, they kept their eyes on Jesus. They didn't let a problem distract them. When pushed to the wall, they fell back on their personal faith in Jesus.

The other group focused on the problem. "How can he give us his flesh to eat?"

This is the lesson for all of us to learn. When changes in life, in family, in the church take place, we need to remember to keep our focus on Jesus. Keeping our focus on Jesus will require us to make some tough choices—just like the Israelites and the disciples did.

I have said, many times, that our priorities in life should be God, spouse, children, work—in that order. To keep our priorities in this order, however, requires us to make choices during the week. It's easy to say that God is a priority in our lives. But if we skip mass on Sunday to get to a hockey practice, then, by our choices, we can see that we have lost our focus on God. I often tell people that I can figure out what everyone's values are—just show me your calendar and your checkbook.

Christ has made us an amazing offer. He has promised us everlasting life. To receive this gift, however, we will be asked to make some difficult decisions. What he promises sounds as though it is too good to be true. But I tell you, it is true. Let us all try to be like the Israelites and the second group of disciples in today's readings. Let us choose to follow Christ.

Faith and
the Storms of Life

They came and woke him saying,
"Lord, save us! We are perishing!"

(Matthew 8:25)

riends, there's a story about a couple with six children who decided to take a day for relaxation and go boating on a lake. While they were out on the lake, a violent storm came up. They each grabbed a safety cushion and tried to hold on to one another as they were tossed from the boat into the water. They prayed together and held on as long as possible, but eventually, let go of each other and drifted apart. The man began calling out his wife's name, but there was no answer. Then he remembered Psalm 50, which says, "Call upon me in time of distress. I will rescue you and you shall glorify me."

The man began to pray and call on the name of God for help. Soon, a rescue boat came by. All of the children were on the boat, but not his wife. Then, all of a sudden, she appeared in the water. The couple and their children had a joyful reunion, followed by a prayer of thanksgiving.

They thanked God for rescuing them. They also thanked God for drawing them closer to Him and to one another as a result of the storm.

That story is very much like today's gospel story. Both stories involve frightened people caught in a storm at sea and afraid for their lives. Both stories involve people who, in their fright, call out to God for help. Both stories involve people whose prayer is heard and whose faith is greatly increased as a result of their experience.

These stories have an important message for us today. It's a two-fold message that we need to be reminded of again and again.

The first message is that the storms of life are often occasions that draw us closer to God and to one another. Notice I said often, because this is not always the case. As a matter of fact, the storms of life can do just the opposite, they can widen the gap between us and God.

And that's where the second message is for each of us. The difference between a storm that draws us closer to God and one that does not is prayer.

But it is not just any kind of prayer. It's the kind of prayer that Jesus taught his followers to pray. It's the kind of prayer in which we place all of our trust in God and in God's will for us. It's the kind of prayer that Jesus prayed in the Garden of Gethsemane when he said to his Father, "Not my will, but yours be done." (Luke 22:42)

A prayer that is not prayed in the spirit that God knows what is best for us is not really a prayer at all. A prayer that is not prayed in this spirit treats God as a servant and not a loving Father. It portrays our own basic selfishness and a complete lack of trust that God knows what is best for us. As St. Augustine said, "What we ought to pray for is in the Lord's Prayer; what is not in it, we ought not pray for."

The Wayzata Community Church bulletin had a prayer in it that I like. It said, "Father, may I have enough happiness to keep me sweet; enough trials to keep me strong; enough sorrow to keep me human; enough hope to keep me happy; enough failure to keep me humble; enough success to keep me eager; enough friends to give me comfort; enough faith and courage to banish depression; and enough determination to serve God better today than I did yesterday?" I especially like the last line of this prayer.

Friends, the Chinese word for crisis consists of two characters. The first character means danger. The second character means opportunity. A Christian crisis is both, and it offers us the opportunity to choose what we will become as a result of what life has dealt us: bitter or better.

When we are experiencing a crisis, we must remember that we are never alone. Jesus is at home in chaos. He was born in a stable. He grew up in Nazareth, which had a terrible reputation. He spent time with people who had many mental and emotional problems. And, of course, he suffered on the cross. Sometimes when you are going through a crisis you may be tempted to call out to Christ, "Don't you care?" Know that He cares. Christ is above the storm. He steadies the storm.

When thinking along these lines, you may ask, "Why doesn't God intervene to stop the suffering of people?" Many people have asked this question. Rabbi Harold Kushner wrote a book titled, *When Bad Things Happen to Good People.* His own young son died from a disease. So he addresses this question in the book. You may have asked this question yourself.

In the readings today others are also asking God this same question. In the first reading, Job is crying out for answers. Likewise, in the gospel, the disciples, in the boat in the storm, call out to the sleeping Christ, "Don't you care?" Paul's letter to the Corinthians looks at it in the larger picture.

What it boils down to is trust. If we could answer the question, we would have no need for faith in God. Faith is accepting what we don't understand.

We can find help, though, in Jesus. He took our flesh and died on the cross. He did not promise us that we would not suffer. He promised us that He would be with us during our suffering.

Throughout history the church has been referred to as a ship. The "bark of Peter." There are people in this ship, and at times, they are as frightened as the disciples were today in the gospel reading. Since Vatican II, the ship has been a bit rocky, and people are wondering if Jesus is asleep. Some have even jumped out.

What I say to you today is this: Stay in the boat! Jesus is in the boat. Sometimes there are lots of waves. People have a tendency to make waves, but stay in the boat.

I'll close with this familiar poem.

"Up in a quaint old attic,
as the raindrops pattered down,
I sat paging through an old schoolbook—
Dusty, tattered and brown.
"I came to a page that was folded down.
And across it was written in childish hand:
'The teacher says to leave this for now,
'tis hard to understand.'
"I unfolded the page and read.
Then I nodded my head and said,
'The teacher was right—now I understand.'"
There are lots of pages in the book of life
That are hard to understand.
All we can do is fold them down and write:
"The teacher says to leave this for now,
'tis hard to understand."
Then someday—maybe in heaven—
We will unfold the pages again,
Read them, and say,
"The teacher was right—now I understand."

Annie and I, along with our three kids, Dan, Tim and Kerry, have been members of Holy Name Parish for the past 30 years. When we joined Holy Name, we were pretty normal parishioners attending Sunday mass and going about our busy lives. Then we met Father Arnold and our lives changed forever. We could not wait to get to church to celebrate the Mass with him. You could always tell how much he loved to be there, how much children made him happy, and how he loved to teach us how to be "Christ-like." He motivated us and made us want to teach Sunday School, expand God's kingdom, help the poor and be good parents... even when It's hard. The fruits of his teachings have blessed our family many times over. His love and lessons filter through our hearts and souls. Arnie instilled in us a sense of family, community, and giving back. I'm sure he's done the same for many, many other families that he has touched.

Anyone who has met Father Arnold knows that he is a great spiritual leader, known for his heart-warming homilies, great liturgies and German wit. As a pastor, Father Arnold has taught us how to be stewards of God's word, how to be grateful and generous with our time, talents, and treasures. For us, he has been a mentor, a teacher, someone to turn to and to rely upon, a leader, a spiritual director and a close personal friend. He has taught us how to be part of a community, how to be a family, how to be generous, loving, caring, and kind to those in need and to each other. We will be forever grateful to Father Arnold for these invaluable life lessons.

We all know Arnie for his quotes, stories, and anecdotes, all of which we fondly refer to as "Arnieisms." We all have our favorites. Here are a few of ours:

• Accept him as he is. Accept him as he is. Accept him as he is.

• John 3:16...God so loved the world that he gave us his only begotten son, so that everyone who believes in him shall not die, but shall have life everlasting.

• Keep your priorities straight—God, Spouse, Family, Work.

• That in all things God may be glorified. (Rule of St. Benedict)

• When you sing, you pray twice. (St. Augustine)

• The best thing a father can do for his children is love their mother. (Rev. Theodore M. Hesburgh, C.S.C.)

• Bitter or better.

• You can't get to heaven by writing a check, but you may want to give it a try.

• Act justly, love tenderly, walk humbly with your God. (Micah 6:8)

Arnie, his stories, and his homilies will live on in our family forever. We are grateful to have been blessed with his presence at Holy Name.

Doug and Annie Cooley

A Visible Kind of Faith

When Jesus returned to Capernaum after some
days, it was reported that He was at home.
So many gathered around that there was no
longer room for them, not even in front of the
door; and He was speaking the word to them.
Then some people came, bringing to Him
a paralyzed man, carried by four of them.
And when they could not bring him to Jesus
because of the crowd, they removed the roof
above Him; and after having dug through it,
they let down the mat on which the paralytic
lay. When Jesus saw their faith, He said to the
paralytic, "Son, your sins are forgiven."

(Mark 2:1-5)

*T*ucked away in today's Gospel reading is a very unusual statement. I have read this story many times before, but for the first time, the clause—"when Jesus saw their faith"—captured my attention and started me wondering. What does it mean? Ordinarily we do not think of faith as something that can be seen. Our ideas on the subject tend to be considerably more abstract than that. Faith is something that can be felt with the heart or accepted with the mind, but it would seldom, if ever, occur to us that faith could be seen with the eyes. Yet that is exactly how it is stated in our reading.

Jesus was teaching in a house somewhere in Capernaum. The word got around, and soon the house was filled. Outside people surrounded it, hoping to get in. Among the crowd was this special group of five men—one who was paralyzed and four friends who were carrying him. When they got to the house where Jesus was, it was too late to get in. In fact, they couldn't even get close to the door.

Most people would have given up and gone home at this point, but not these determined men. They climbed up to the top of the house, cut a hole in the roof, and lowered their paralyzed friend through the opening into the presence of Jesus. Just picture it: the paralyzed man on his pallet slowly descending to the floor near Jesus. Above Him, his four friends peering expectantly at the Lord through a hole in the roof, obviously awaiting a miracle. Then it is that we read: …Jesus saw their faith…

I like this idea because it tells me that faith is something real. It tells me that it's solid; it's substantial; it's tangible. To Jesus it was actually visible. He could look at it and see it with his own eyes. I wish that we all could have this visible kind of faith. What kind of faith would that be?

A Faith in People

For one thing visible faith would be a faith in people. When Jesus looked at those five men, He saw people believing in people. It was evident in their attitudes and actions. The four healthy men believed that their friend was important. It made no difference to them that he was paralyzed and had to be carried from place to place. He was a friend in need. They saw him as someone worth their concern, time, and efforts to help. The paralytic showed some faith of his own. He must have had a great deal of confidence in his friends to allow them to carry him into a crowd, take him up on the roof, and lower him through a hole. In a very real sense he placed his life in their hands. Had anything gone wrong, he wouldn't have been able to save himself. Even for a person who could walk, it would have been a frightening experience, but the paralyzed man had enough faith in his friends to risk it.

That was a large part of what Jesus saw—people who cared for and believed in other people. We need to give special attention to this, because I'm not at all sure there is any such thing as real faith without it. We're fooling ourselves if we think that we can exercise faith in God, and at the same time be bitter and cynical toward people. That would be like believing in Mozart without believing in music. How can the two be separated? By the same token, how could we believe in God and not believe in the people He created in his own image? How could we believe in Christ and not believe in the men and women for whom He died? How could we believe in the Gospel and not believe in the sinners for whom the good news is intended?

There is a little wall poster you sometimes see in business establishments that has a brief two line message. The top line says: In God We Trust. The bottom line says: All Others Pay Cash. I realize the poster is intended to be humorous, but it illustrates the approach some people take to life: to believe in God with all their heart and to believe in people very little, if at all. I would say that's impossible. Faith in God cannot be sustained in some sort of religious vacuum. It has to live and work and grow in a real world of real people. If I read the New Testament correctly, believing in God and believing in people are two sides of the same coin. There is absolutely no way to tear the two apart. If you hold on to one, you hold onto the other. If you give up either, you give up both. So that is what Jesus saw: a group of people actively involved in a loving, caring, giving and sharing relationship. They believed in each other and it showed.

A Faith in God

That isn't all He saw. These people also believed in and counted on a power beyond their own. They were realistic enough to recognize that human needs often exceed human resources. We humans can't do it all. This was clearly the case with the paralyzed man. He had friends who were willing to help but needs that far exceeded the power of any human to meet. His friends could carry him from place to place and were willing to do so, but they couldn't give him the ability to walk. There were those who cared for him very deeply, but they could not lift from his heart its load of guilt. They could not convince him that his sins were forgiven. Only God could do those things.

We're all faced at some time or another with similar situations— circumstances of life that are beyond our control. We do our best, but our best is not enough. There are problems we cannot solve, questions we cannot answer, heartaches we cannot heal. There are burdens too great to be borne by human strength alone. When such a time comes, our options are:

- Give up in despair, and allow fear and resentment to move in and take charge.
- Grit our teeth, set our minds, and with stoic courage seek to ride it out to the bitter end.
- With quiet, calm, determined faith, bring our burden and place it at the feet of the Lord, trusting Him to do for us what we cannot do for ourselves. Just like the men in our story!

How the Lord will meet our needs, we don't always know. That He will meet our needs, we can rest in absolute confidence. He will either lift our burden or give us the help and strength to carry it.

Yes, friends, we need to believe in God and believe in our fellow human beings. Then we might have a faith so real it can be seen by others.

Forgive 70 x 7

Then Peter came up and said to him,
"Lord, how often shall my brother sin
against me, and I forgive him?
As many as seven times?"
Jesus said to him, "I do not say to you
seven times, but seventy times seven."

(Matthew 18:21-22)

Friends, one of the most crucial problems today is finding the meaning in life! So many people are disappointed because they say life has no meaning. Well, what is the meaning in life? Can I decide that for you? Most would say not. So how then do you find the right answer?

I think we have to start by asking the right questions. Some get the right answers to the wrong questions and then wonder why they're missing out on a meaningful life. For example, a young man goes to college and tries to decide on what area to focus his studies.

So he asks himself "What career will give me the most money?" He might get the right answer to that question and make millions but be disappointed in the end.

A lot of unhappy people today would eagerly trade their success for peace and happiness. What goes wrong? They find the right answer to the wrong question. They get rich but not happy. They find no meaning in a life dedicated to the pursuit of money.

Let's look at another young person. She goes off to college too, and asks, "How can I make the greatest contribution where I will find the deepest satisfaction?" Now if she gets the right answer to that question, she may or may not make a lot of money, but one thing is certain: She will discover meaning in life. She'll find a lot of good living, she'll be fully alive and develop a spiritual life as part of the whole.

Do you see what I'm saying? You must ask the right questions, then find the right answers.

We're not alone in asking the wrong questions. Peter does that in the Gospel today when he asks the question: "When my brother does me wrong, how often must I forgive him?" Peter wanted Jesus to give him a specific number. His theory was that seven times would be enough. But Jesus said, "No, seventy times seven."

But Jesus wasn't actually saying that you must forgive a person only 490 times, and after that you can resent them, hurt them back or hate them. Jesus didn't give a specific answer because Peter was really asking the wrong question. The fact that Peter would even ask the question shows that he didn't understand the nature and meaning of forgiveness. Any answer with a specific number would have been inadequate. Suppose Jesus had been specific and said a thousand. Imagine that a bride and groom agree to forgive 1000 times and no more. Imagine the bookkeeping! And what a way to stop a loving relationship!

The real question is not "How many times must I forgive?" But "Why should I forgive even one time?" If you know that answer, you won't need to ask other questions. If you understand the nature and necessity of forgiveness, you can apply it in all ways. If forgiveness is a valid approach to human relationships, surely it is as valid the hundredth time or the thousandth time as it is the first.

Looking again at Peter's original question, let's rephrase it and ask "Why should we forgive at all?" There are two definite answers. One is we should forgive because we need forgiving ourselves. We are all involved on both sides. Sometimes we do the wrong, and sometimes we are wronged. I find it interesting that Peter asked, "How often must I forgive my brother?" I wonder why he didn't ask "How often should my brother forgive me?" The reason is that Peter was human just like we are. Most of us are more sensitive and conscious of being wronged than of wronging someone.

Notice how Jesus has this subtle way of pointing out to Peter the inequity in his thinking. He tells the story about a servant who owed his master more than he could pay. The servant asked for mercy and received it from the master. The same servant was owed a small amount of money by another fellow and demanded his money on the spot. I think Jesus is telling Peter you can't place a limit on your forgiveness of others.

That's how it is with you and me. We can't afford to block the channels of forgiveness. I can tell you how often I want to be forgiven by God and by people I know and love. It's not seven times, it's not seven times seventy, it's every time.

With forgiveness there are no enemies, no opposing sides. Imagine a Christian saying "I can't forgive." This is such a basic part of being a Christian. Christians who can't forgive are missing out on a huge part of Christ's teaching. When he says "Love your neighbor" there's no room in that for withholding forgiveness.

The second reason we need forgiveness is because if we don't forgive, it will hurt us more than anyone. Others will be hurt also, and not just the one we don't forgive. Suppose you seek the forgiveness of a friend and he flatly refuses. What would that do to you? It could break your heart; that's what it would do. But eventually your hurt would heal, and at some point you would say, "I have done my best. I have sought reconciliation. There is nothing more I can do. Now it's time to get on with life."

But resentment and an unforgiving spirit never heal. It's like a pus pocket in the soul, spreading poison in your life. Refusing to forgive leads to a sour, cynical, and sad personality. If you've been holding out on forgiveness for someone, now is the time to give up that resentment and anger. You've hurt yourself far more than anyone else. Christ calls for us to love one another. Remember that it's not the ones who you find easy to love that He had in mind. It's the hard ones, the ones who may have hurt and angered us. We need to forgive them and love them. We don't need to even understand them. Love them. Love yourself. Forgive.

As with many other things Christ calls us to do, we can't do this alone. Pray and ask for Jesus' help in developing a forgiving heart. It may not happen overnight. If this has been a trouble spot for a long time, you'll need to be patient with yourself. Pray for the person you're trying to forgive. You just can't continue to be angry with someone after you've prayed for them a while.

I'd like to share one of my favorite stories about forgiveness as a conclusion.

There was a young fellow looking down and out sitting by the side of the highway. He was tired—not a car in sight. He wanted to write a letter that he had put off for a long time. He took some stationery out of his suitcase, sat on the highway, and using his suitcase as a writing board, he wrote this letter:

Dear Mom,

If Dad will permit it, I would like to come home. I know there's little chance he will. I'm not going to kid myself. I remember he said once if I ever ran off I might as well keep on going. All I can say is that I felt leaving home was something I had to do. Before even

34

considering college, I wanted to find out more about life and about me, and the best way for us (life and me) to live with each other. Please tell Dad—and I guess this will make him sore all over again—I'm still not certain that college is the answer for me. I think I'd like to work for a time and think it over.

You won't be able to reach me by mail, because I'm not sure where I'll be next. But in a few days I hope to be passing by our place. If there's any chance Dad will have me back, please ask him to tie a piece of cloth to the apple tree. I'll just be going by on the train. If there's no cloth in the tree I'll just quietly, and without any hard feeling toward Dad—I mean that—keep on going.

Love,

David

Evening came. The young man hitchhiked. Car after car came, nobody stopped. Finally, a man passed him when it was dark. He noticed taillights get brighter as the man slapped on his brakes, so he ran to the car. The door swung open and a voice said, "Hop in, boy. I almost missed you. You ain't easy to see out there."

"Thanks, Mister," David responded as he climbed in the car.

"Forget it—I used to thumb a lot myself," the man said.

"How far are you going?" asked David.

"Ames, Iowa, about 200 miles away. Where are you heading for?" the man said.

"Home," David said with a grin. "I'm heading home."

"Where's home?" asked the man.

"Maryland—we have a farm 30 miles from Baltimore," David explained.

"Where have you been?" the driver inquired.

"West Coast, Canada, and a little of Mexico," responded David.

"And now you're heading home again?" the man asked conversationally.

"Well," the man said, "I know how it is. I was out on that same old road when I was a kid. Bummin' around. Letting no grass grow under me. Sometimes, though, I was wishin' it would."

"And afterward," David asked, "did you go home?"

"Nope. I didn't have a home to go back to like you do. The road was my old home. Lost Ma and Pa when I was young. Killed in a car wreck.."

"That's rough," David said with such feeling the man looked at him.

"Bet you could do with a little sleep," the man suggested. And at that David let himself doze off.

Later on David woke up, remembered that he had to mail the letter in his pocket. "Excuse me, sir, would you mind stopping at a mailbox so I can mail this?" David requested. "I want to make sure that it gets home before I do."

As they stopped at the next mailbox, the man said, "Bet your folks will be tickled to hear from you."

"I hope so," David said and went back to sleep.

The next day, hitchhiking was slow. He finally jumped a slow-moving freight train. For 60 miles he rode along as the rained started dripping from the sky. The train stopped, and David went back to the highway. When cars quit coming, he walked. Finally he jumped another train.

The landscape started to look familiar; he was getting closer to home. Through a dusty window he would soon be able to see his father's fields. Two different picture tortured him—the tree with the cloth—and the tree without it. His throat closed and he could hardly breathe.

He tried to fortify himself with the idea that whether or not he was still welcome, at least he would see the place again.

The field was sliding closer, one familiar landmark at a time. Nothing could postpone the moment of knowing. The trees would be around the next bend.

He couldn't look. He was too afraid the cloth would not be there—too afraid of what would be staring at him—just another tree, just another field, just another somebody else's strange place, the way it always is on the long, long road, the nameless staring back at the nameless. He jerked his head away from the window.

Desperately, he nudged the passenger beside him. "Mister, will you do me a favor? Around this bend on the right, you'll see an apple tree. I wonder if you'll tell me if you see a cloth tied to one of its branches?"

As they passed the field, the boy stared straight ahead. "Is it there?" he asked with an uncontrollable quaver.

"Son," the man said in a voice slow with wonder, "I see a piece of cloth tied on every branch."

○

We have had the privilege of teaching the baptism class at Holy Name of Jesus for the last nine years. One evening we were sharing stories with Fr. Arnold of the funniest questions or comments that we had heard regarding baptism. The gem came from Fr. Arnold. One couple wanted to know if they had to bring the baby to the baptism!!! We couldn't top that one.

Fr. Arnold has been a wonderful mentor for us in many areas but especially in the area of pastoral care. We have been blessed to have worked with him.

Deacon Terry and Sue Schneider

Spin-Masters
Need Not Apply

You are the salt of the earth . . .
You are the light of the world.

(Matthew 5:13,14)

The text of Matthew says, "You are the salt of the earth; you are light to the world." Friends, Jesus is talking about us. Notice, He didn't say, "You should be the salt of the earth." He said, "You are the salt of the earth." That's a big difference. "Should be" is a suggestion. "Are" is a fact. It sounds to me like we have no choice. We must be eager to turn the world upside down. If we do not add seasoning or give a ray of light to our society in some way, then we are good for nothing except to be trampled underfoot.

The great medical missionary Albert Schweitzer was once pushing a wheelbarrow as he helped to build a new road in a poor village. A visitor saw him and was shocked that the famous doctor was doing such a menial task. He said, "Doctor, why are you doing that? How is it that you push a wheelbarrow?" With a twinkle in his eye, Schweitzer answered, "It's very simple. You pick up a shovel, use it to fill the wheelbarrow with dirt, then take hold of the handles, and push."

That's the way it is with the Lord's work. There are many wheelbarrows to fill, and many workers needed to fill them. Who are the ones appointed to do God's work? The people who are the salt of the earth, the people who are lights to the world, those are the ones who will fill and push wheelbarrows. *Spin-masters need not apply.*

Salt of the earth people know how to be active Christians. People who are rays of light to the world reflect positive values like joy, optimism, goodness, and beauty. These people understand the concept of truth. *Spin-masters need not apply.*

You may have noticed that, nowadays, instead of facing the truth straight on in a given situation, many people like to put a little spin to it. For example, politicians who get in trouble get their publicists to sugarcoat the truth a little to make it more palatable to the public.

This reminds me of a story. A woman comes back from a visit with her doctor and says to her husband, "Honey, I'm in very poor condition. The doctor says that to get better I must go to Hot Springs, Arkansas, and then to Aspen, Colorado, and then I must buy myself a new mink coat." The husband, of course, was confused and upset, so he went to the doctor and said, "What exactly is my wife's problem that you told her go to Hot Springs and Aspen and buy a mink coat?" The doctor said, "Sir, I just recommended to your wife a regimen of hot baths and some fresh air, and told her to be sure to dress in warm clothing." The wife in this story put more than a little spin on her medical condition.

It seems the problem is that today there's a notion that everything is relative and nothing absolute. According to a recent Gallup poll, 70% of American people reject the notion of moral absolutes. In the past most Americans did accept standards and absolutes. They understood right from wrong. Nowadays, we have a lot of spin-masters.

Is truth a personal choice? No. When we talk about things of the faith, we shouldn't look to the spin-masters. Truth is from God. God is real. The truth of the good news of Jesus Christ doesn't need to be changed to fit the spirit of the times. We may not like hearing the truth, but our moral weaknesses do not change the validity of Christ's message.

In contrast to the twists of the spin-masters, we Christians have the sincerity of St. Paul. In his letter to the Corinthians, he says, "When I came to you, brothers and sisters, I did not come proclaiming the mystery of God to you with lofty words of wisdom. I came to you in weakness and in fear. I was trembling my speech and proclamations were not with plausible words of wisdom but with a demonstration of the spirit of power, that your faith might rest on the power of God."

St. Paul is one of the wisest and most talented men who ever lived. He's also quoted more than just about anyone in history, even Shakespeare. But Paul spoke simply and directly when he taught the truth of Jesus Christ. He wanted people to experience the power of God, not the power of his oratory. He knew that the Corinthians loved big words and complex logic. He also knew there were others who gave them just what they wanted. Paul decided that if he did that, it would undermine the message he brought. It would be wrong to alter the truth of the message to please that particular audience. Paul wanted converts, not compliments.

In addition to the example of St. Paul, these three quotations from Scripture can help us focus on the truth of the Christian message.

1. From Genesis: "In the beginning, God created the heavens and the earth."

2. John 3:16,17: "God so loved the world that He gave His only begotten Son, so that whoever believes in Him shall not die, but live. For God did not send His Son into the world to condemn the world; but that the world might be saved through Him."

3. From Luke: "Love God with your whole heart and mind and soul and strength, and love your neighbors as you love yourself."

These statements from Scripture are true, and their truth is powerful. Our Christian faith gives us authority and confidence and purpose. When we believe that we are the children of the living and loving God who created this world, a God who is involved with us every day, it does something to us. It invigorates us and gives us a sense of meaning and direction. When we believe deep down that God loves us, we can do wonderful things. We can learn and achieve most anything. People with a strong Christian faith don't need the services of a spin-master.

Teachers and parents, beware of the spin-masters on TV and elsewhere. Our culture is filled with them. We need to be clear when we talk to our children about truth. That doesn't mean to be unsympathetic. But if we believe the Scriptures, we know that ultimately it is the truth that sets us free. Let's be the salt of the earth; lights to the world. Let's speak the truth. *Spin-masters need not apply.*

○

What always comes back to me whenever I am reminded of Fr. Arnold's homilies is love. "The greatest gift a father can give to his children is to love his wife." "Accept them as they are." Even his manner of speaking to us was loving, especially when he would call us to action or to change. I remember these moments the most, when his love for us was so great that he would raise his voice and become passionate about whatever it is that needed to change in the parish. He wouldn't allow us to be apathetic, but he didn't shame us either. He gave us hope that we could love more.

Amanda Weldon, former parishioner of Holy Name of Jesus

Called to Compassion

✝

"And who is my neighbor?"

(Luke10:29)

"A man fell victim to robbers . . . they stripped him and beat him and went off leaving him half-dead. A priest going down that road . . . passed by on the opposite side . . . a Levite . . . when he saw him, passed by on the opposite side. But a Samaritan traveler who came upon him was moved with compassion at the sight . . . he lifted him up . . . took him to the inn and cared for him."

(Luke 10:30-34)

*F*riends, if I asked you to name the ten most famous Bible stories, I think almost all of you would include these two: the Prodigal Son, and the Good Samaritan. Most of us would know that the Good Samaritan stopped to help an injured man on the side of road when no one else would. This is a parable, which is a story that has meaning in multiple layers.

Jesus told the Good Samaritan Story in answer to a lawyer who asks, "What must I do to inherit eternal life?" That sounds like a good question. However, Jesus figured the man actually knew the answer and understood the principle of the law, but realized that something must be bothering the man. So Jesus, as He often did, answered with another question. He turned the question around and said, "What is written in the law?" The lawyer answered by quoting from Deuteronomy (6:4), "You shall love the Lord, your God, with all your heart, with all your being, with all your strength, and with all your mind, and your neighbor as yourself." Jesus affirmed His answer and added "do this and you will live."

But the lawyer still wasn't satisfied and pressed Jesus further in asking Him, 'And who is my neighbor?'" Here we have this fellow who obviously knew many Jewish laws and the technicalities. He probably abided by all of the laws and tried to be a good man, but he wasn't sure how far he had to go to satisfy the law. So he asked Jesus, and he probably expected a simple definition. Jesus could have just said, "Your neighbors are all the Jews, the Gentiles, the sinners, prostitutes and so on." But He wanted the lawyer to draw his own conclusions, so Jesus told a story. And that's how we get this marvelous Good Samaritan story.

The story begins with a man going from Jerusalem to Jericho. In those days this was a dangerous road, with thieves who'd kill you just to see if you had anything worth taking. Back then most people traveled in groups with armed men to protect them. But this poor fellow, for some reason, was traveling alone. And, of course, robbers attack him, beat him severely, and leave him for dead. Along comes a priest on his way to worship at the temple, but he goes over to the other side of the road, to avoid this bloody, beaten body. Next comes a Levite, a member of the tribe of Israel from which the priests come. You'd certainly expect him to stop to help, but he does the same thing! Then a third man comes by. He's a Samaritan. The other Jews don't think highly of Samaritans because they'd intermarried with Gentiles and acquired some of the Gentile culture while the other Jews were off in exile. So here comes this despised Samaritan and what does he do? He stops to help the poor man. Not only does he clean his wounds and bind them up, he picks the man up, puts him on his donkey, and takes him to an inn where he feeds him and takes care of him. The next day he talks to the innkeeper, gives him a few silver coins, and asks him to look after the injured man until he's well enough to move on.

Jesus looked at the lawyer and said "Which of these three, in your opinion, was neighbor to the robbers' victim?" The lawyer answered, "The one who treated him with mercy." Jesus said to him, "Go and do likewise." Notice that Jesus didn't ask which was the better neighbor. He used "neighbor to." There's action involved in that. It's not a passive effort. It means you have to do something; take action.

The lawyer can see in Jesus' story the principle and the practice of the law. From a strictly legal point of view, were the priest and Levite operating within the terms of the law? It's likely they were because they didn't know the injured man, they had probably never seen him before, so they didn't consider him a neighbor. But Jesus is saying that being legally correct in principle is not as important as being loving in practice.

How we treat our neighbor is very important business to us as Christians. You know that I like to say that as Christians, we're in the Mercy business, the Love business and the Compassion business. Love is "out there" not just here in church. Let's go out and be moved to compassion and "neighbor to" those we meet in life.

To be compassionate, we need to be open to newness. The priest and Levite were not prepared to deal with anything out of the ordinary. Seeing their fellow countryman beaten and lying by the side of the road, they didn't know what to do, so both make the decision to become blind. Both of them actually crossed over to the other side of the road to avoid getting too close to this person in distress.

Their own narrow view of life will not allow them to enter into the pain of another person… to be a good neighbor. It would be too disturbing to their daily routine to reach out in compassion to the unknown injured man on the other side of the road. As you heard this story, perhaps you shook your head in disbelief. How could two religious persons, such as the priest and the Levite, be so closed to the pain of another person? At times we ought to do some head shaking about our own blindness to the distress of other people. It is not easy to allow ourselves to see something that we would rather not see. In fact, it can be a very disturbing experience to allow the pain of another person into our safe and protected worlds. The priest and Levite were not willing to deal with the consequences of discovering in any detail the pain of the man lying by the side of the road. If they went over to the man, leaned down and looked closely at him, talked to him, asked him how he felt, they would then have had to respond to what they discovered.

There is a cost to this increased sensitivity. It cost the Samaritan time, inconvenience, and money. There's always a cost when we make the decision to let others into our own small world. But when we continually refuse to do so, our world becomes even smaller. Our personal insulation becomes thicker and stronger. After turning away from the distress of others many times, we can arrive at a point where we hardly even notice that others are in pain. If we find ourselves in that position we should be very disturbed.

I have a story that will give you something to think about. It was a cold day in December in the big city. Standing barefoot and shivering in front of a shoe store was a boy about eight years old, peering through the window. A lady coming down the street noticed him, and approached the boy asking, "Why are you looking so earnestly in that window?" "I was asking God to give me a pair of shoes," was the boy's reply. The lady took him by the hand and went into the store and asked the clerk to get a half dozen pairs of socks for the boy. She then asked the clerk if he could give her a basin of water and a towel. He quickly brought them to her. She took the little boy to the back of the store and removed her gloves, knelt down, washed his feet and dried them with a towel. By this time the clerk had returned with the socks. Placing a pair upon the boy's feet, she then purchased him a pair of shoes and gave him the remaining pairs of socks. She patted him on the head and said, "No doubt you feel more comfortable now."

As she turned to go, the astonished boy caught her by the hand and looking up into her face, with tears in his eyes, asked her a question, "Are you God's wife?"

No, she was not God's wife, but she certainly was one of God's children herself, and she was able to see and respond to another child of God. The Good Samaritan and this woman showed their love in a very concrete way. Love is not general; it is always specific.

It seems to me that the most important question here is this one: What are the obstacles that prevent me from seeing and responding to the needs of other? It's true that we can't respond to all the needs that we come across; however, there is quite a difference between not responding to all the needs we see, and not responding to any of the needs that we encounter. If our first response is always to turn away, or to cross to the other side, then we have a serious spiritual problem—one that we need to thoughtfully look at.

Aren't we all God's children? We need to see one another this way and respond with compassion and love when we see someone in need. May the Lord open our eyes and our hearts and give us the courage to reach out in love to all whom the Lord sends our way.

*My husband Bill and I had the privilege of having
Fr. Arnold down to Florida with us for four days. When Fr.
Arnold arrived, the fun immediately began! We enjoyed the Fort
Myers area—swimming in the ocean and sun bathing on the
beautiful sandy beaches. We spent the days sight seeing and the
evenings watching the beautiful sunsets. The highlight of this
visit was when Bill took Fr. Arnold to see the Twins at spring
training. Bill was able to get Fr. Arnold into the locker room
where he had a chance to meet many of the players. To top it all
off, when Corey Koski saw Fr. Arnold, he said, "I know you! You
just baptized my baby!" Fr. Arnold really got around!*

*The grand finale of the trip was gathering close to 50 people
at a restaurant, with Fr. Arnold as the guest of honor. That was
a wonderful evening for all who attended. My favorite saying of
Fr. Arnold's is to become better and not bitter. This saying has
helped me through some difficult times lately. Fr. Arnold, we
thank you for your life and for your love for our family.*

Betty Conway, parishioner of Holy Name of Jesus

One Life to Live

✝

"I am the Lord, I have called you in righteousness and will hold your hand and keep you and give a covenant to the people, a light to the Gentiles,"

Isaiah 42:6

I, the Lord, have called you…

Did you hear what the Lord says in today's reading? He says, "I, the Lord have called you." He's talking to us. We have been called by God. So, stand up a little straighter and puff out your chest a little. We have been called by God!

Some of us can remember when, as children, we were out playing and suddenly we'd hear our names called so we'd come in for dinner. "Joe, Beth, Samantha, it's time to come home." Strangers rarely call out our names. Only the people to whom we are important call our name. Being addressed by name when we're talked to adds so much, don't you think? It makes what a person says so much more personal. What a magnificent idea, Isaiah, saying that God will call us by name. Using our names says we are known. We are loved. No one can say then that his or her life does not matter. The Lord of Creation calls the name of each one of us.

. . .in righteousness. . .

But notice, the prophet does not stop with "I, the Lord have called you." He goes on to say "in righteousness." We are not simply called, we are called into righteousness. What in the world could these words mean: "Called in righteousness"?

Imagine that we would each be given a pair of white overalls marked "righteousness" that would make each of us a symbol of God. What would we be like wearing these overalls? Wouldn't we all be more loving, more disciplined, and more responsible? Probably so. We would be honest yet compassionate, hard working, yet relaxed. We would be tender with little children, role models for youth, and a friends to all who know us. In short, we would be more Christ-like in our character. All of these good attributes belong under the heading of "righteousness."

But here is what we need to see. We cannot obtain righteousness just by working for it. You know those resolutions you made to change something for the New Year? I hate to tell you, but it is very difficult for us to change any part of our character by merely resolving to do so. What we need is a new heart and a new spirit. Righteousness comes from being joined with Christ. Christ does not call us because of our righteousness. Christ calls us, and then righteousness comes because of our relationship with Him. We must be touched by Jesus. There must be a commitment to the person of Jesus. He provides the overalls; you and I don't stitch them by hand.

Friends, this is an important truth. People who believe that righteousness comes from an act of will have a tendency to move beyond righteousness to self-righteousness. We have much of this in religion including some in the Christian community. When we're self-righteous, we are then prone to condemn those we judge as not having enough willpower, character, and personal discipline. We become the older brother refusing to welcome the prodigal son; we become the priest or the Levite who did not help the traveler left to die on the roadside; we become the Pharisee who exalts himself over the tax collector; we become the rigid, reactionary Jews stoning the apostle Stephen.

Righteousness is a gift from God. It is not something we simply have or do.

There's a story I heard a number of years ago, but it's a good one and worth listening to again even if you've heard it before. When Paul Powers was seven years old, his mother died of pneumonia. After his mother's death, Paul's father became an alcoholic and began beating Paul on a regular basis. Paul joined a street gang for protection. Soon he spent all his time stealing and in street fights. By the time he was 12, he accidentally killed a woman. He spent the next four years in a prison.

At 17, he was removed from the prison and was put in the care of an elderly couple called Mom and Dad Adams. The Adams loved Paul in spite of his wild temper and rough ways. They were always ready to forgive him and give him a second chance. Through their influence and an evangelical crusade, Paul gave his life to Jesus. A few years later, Paul met and fell in love with a young woman named Margaret. Margaret loved Paul, but after hearing about his rough background she wasn't sure about marrying him. One day Paul took Margaret for a walk on the beach. Margaret remarked just as the tide was washing away her footprints, that maybe their relationship would soon be washed away, too. Paul assured her that he was fully committed to her for life. That night they became engaged. After their romantic walk, Margaret returned to her room and wrote a poem based on trusting God, even when you can't see Him working.

It's a poem that describes millions of us. You may know the poem. It's called "Footprints." It's been around for while, but it's still poignant. Paul did not become the kind of man that Margaret could love only because he made up his mind to do so. Paul was changed by the power of Christ's love. Sometimes we have regular church-goers who never get touched in this way by Jesus. They believe they can transform themselves, and you know what? No change ever comes.

...and I will hold your hand...

Let's go back to our verse from Isaiah. "I, the Lord, have called you into righteousness and I will hold your hand and keep you…" Our lives are an open book to God. Not out of the desire to keep us in line, but out of the desire that our feet shall not stumble. God does not hold our hand to control or manipulate us. God does not keep watch over us so we never have an opportunity to express our own freewill. No, God stays close to us and watches over us that we might find comfort when we are in pain, direction when we are lost, and hope when we are in despair. "I, the Lord, have called you into righteousness and I will hold your hand and will keep you."

...and give you the covenant of the people as a light to the Gentiles."

Finally, let's look at the climax to the passage where we find the ultimate purpose. Isaiah writes, "… and give you for a covenant of the people as the light of the gentiles." We have been called to be a blessing, God's blessing, for all. The need for Christ's followers to be a light for the people of the world is as great now as it was when He walked this earth. We are God's people—called for a purpose—to be God's instrument for the gentiles in the world. This mission, by the way, friends, is not optional. Either we are God's people or we are not. Either we claim our responsibility to be God's light in the world or we do not. Friends, there really is no middle ground.

Dr. Graham Scroggie was a very famous Bible teacher. He was once counseling a young woman who knew that God was calling her, but she wasn't sure if she wanted to do it. The doctor picked up a piece of paper and wrote two words on it. "No" and "Lord." This, the doctor explained, is not a complete sentence. If Jesus is truly our Lord, then we can't possible say no to Him. He is our master and our lives belong to Him. But if we say "no" to Jesus' calling, then He must really not be our Lord. So, the phrase, "No, Lord" won't do. One of the words has to go, he explained. The doctor handed her the piece of paper, told her to think about her decision and to mark out one of those words, either the "no" or the "Lord." Then, finally, he stepped away.

He began praying for the young woman. As he prayed, he heard the woman crying. In a few seconds he heard her whisper, "Jesus is Lord. Jesus is Lord. Jesus is Lord. Jesus is Lord." He turned and looked at the paper in her lap. She had crossed out the word "No."

Many of us want to claim Jesus as Lord, but we want to do it privately and act as if it has nothing to do with our witness to the world outside. Dr. Scroggie is right. Either Jesus is Lord of our lives or He is not Lord at all. We have been called by God. God has filled us "in righteousness." We have not earned it on our own.

God is with us, holding our hand to keep us from falling. God has called us to be a light for a dark and dying world.

So, go, wear those overalls, live in Christ, let Him fill you with righteousness and be a light to the world.

●

Fr. Arnold baptized me. He is good at doing speeches. And he plays Bingo! We've played with him at our house, and he even wins!

Claire Patnode, 8 years old, member of
Holy Name of Jesus

52

The "Be" Attitudes

✝

When Jesus saw the crowds, he went up the mountain; and after he sat down, his disciples came to him. Then he began to speak and taught them, saying . . .

(Matthew 5:1,2)

How many genuinely happy people do you know? That's not an easy question to answer, because happiness isn't a quality that's easy to measure. We can't just separate people into two groups—happy and unhappy. However, we do know that there is a universal longing for happiness, and that many people aren't as happy as they'd like to be, and that's too bad. A closer look at the beatitudes can give us the key to being happy. But first, let's start with two assumptions:

God wants us to be happy.

Just think about the creation story in Genesis. Man and woman were made in the image of God Himself and placed in a garden, surrounded by beauty, with the idea to love life and live it well.

However, there are also many stories in the Bible that speak of mistrust between God and man. For example, the fall of Adam and Eve after they were deceived by a serpent that promised them greater happiness than they already had. Maybe that's why so many people today don't believe that God desires our happiness. Their vision of God is similar to this schoolboy's: "God is like the principal of our school. He walks around with a scowl on his face, and if He finds anyone having fun, He puts a stop to it." I hope that I can convince you that God really does want you to be happy.

God can make us happy.

One way is through the beatitudes, which describe attitudes about the way to be, qualities that allow God's will to be accomplished in us and through us. The beatitudes tell about characteristics that God develops in our lives, not what we can achieve on our own. They not only give us a picture of true happiness, or joy, but each is a promise of what God can make us into if we let Him.

There was a boy in the hospital whose face became disfigured in an explosion. A doctor holds up a photo of what the boy looked like before the accident and tells him, "I can make you look like this again with plastic surgery, if you will let me."

That's how I see the beatitudes. God holds up a picture of a happy person, the kind we are all meant to be, and says to us, " I can make you look like this, if only you let me. It might take a long time and be painful at times, but I invite you on the journey to Christian happiness." The question is: Will we let Him?

Now let's look at the beatitudes one at a time.

Happy are the poor in spirit,
for theirs is the reign of God. (Matthew 5:3)

First, what does it mean to be poor in spirit? Probably humble and open to growth. If we aren't poor in spirit, we might be self-satisfied, or filled with what the Bible calls pride, the first of the deadly sins. Look around a bit. Disaster often comes when we think we know it all, because pride gives us a false sense of security. Proud people see no need to change because they're so satisfied with the way they already are. Think about the Pharisee and the tax collector praying in the temple. The Pharisee's prayer was filled with pride that kept him static – without growth or movement—while the tax collector, in humility, begged for God to be merciful to him, a sinner.

Humility helps us to realize that whoever and whatever we are is only possible because of God. It makes us dissatisfied with ourselves where we are and allows God to keep us moving the way He wants us to go. If we can be like this, we inherit the kingdom of God!

Happy are the sorrowing,
for they shall be consoled. (Matthew 5:4)

This beatitude might seem like a contradiction because gladness and sadness are opposites. But we have to remember the capacity that enables us to experience happiness is the same one that enables us to experience sorrow. To have true joy, we have to open our hearts, and that makes us vulnerable. Genuine happiness always includes the possibility of sorrow.

There are types of sorrow, however, that don't lead to consolation and growth, such as self-pity. The song *Paper Doll* tells about this man who lost his girlfriend to another guy. He made a big paper doll of her so she'd always seem to be there when he came home. His way to avoid a broken heart was to never move forward and love again. What a price to pay!

But remember, sorrow and suffering can lead to happiness. Sometimes it is in our times of deepest need that we allow others the opportunity to give. The second beatitude asks this question: How much of life are we willing to experience? The more we hold back and protect our hearts, the less is the possibility for joy.

The dangerous road of love is the only path that leads to genuine happiness.

Happy are the lowly,
for they shall inherit the land. (Matthew 5:5)

The key word to understanding the third beatitude is "lowly," which can be translated as meek, gentle, or patient. The Philippians said it this way: "Happy are those who claim nothing, for the whole earth will belong to them." Lowliness doesn't seem to be a very desirable quality to have, until we remember that Jesus Himself claimed to be meek and humble. We have to realize that lowly does not mean weak. In fact, it's almost the opposite. The Greeks used lowly to describe a powerful wild horse that was captured and tamed to be under control, so lowliness can be thought of as the strength to control brute forces. You might also think of it, in part, as anger management. The lowly or gentle will only get angry at the right time over the right things and express their anger in the right ways.

The word "inherit" in the second part of the beatitude brings to mind the concept of things being handed down within a family. St. Francis of Assisi preached that there are two main questions in life: 1) Who is God? 2) Who am I? The Bible gives us the answer to both. God is the father and we are the children. Lowly people are the ones who understand and accept this relationship to God. They see themselves as individuals who are members of God's family. They are willing to carry a burden to help meet the needs of other family members. They don't get jealous over other's fortunes; they rejoice. They appreciate others and their gifts. Thus, they become a part of the inheritance.

Happy are they who hunger and thirst for holiness;
they shall have their fill. (Matthew 5:6)

This beatitude reminds us that not all human desires are bad to fulfill, although many are, such as the desire many of us have for fast food that smells and tastes good but gives us very poor nutrition. However, strong desires can be very good. Our souls, as well as our bodies, can hunger and thirst. In this case, the desire is for holiness.

How many people do you know who hunger and thirst for holiness? Probably not too many. We might be confused by what holiness means. Some might think it means to be super-religious, to live in a cave with other strange people and spend all our time in contemplation. Here what it means is completeness or fullness that we not only think is nice but also that we long for, believing it is the way to happiness. As St. Augustine said, "Our hearts are restless until they rest in God." Do we long for holiness in this way? Or do we believe that we are happier when we ignore moral rules?

Of course, none of us will ever reach perfection or completion here on earth, but this beatitude tells us that eventually we will have our fill.

Happy are they who show mercy;
mercy shall be theirs. (Matthew 5:7)

The key to understanding this beatitude is the word "mercy." Not everyone understands the meaning of this word. Many think that it's the opposite of justice, in that justice gives an offender what he or she deserves, while mercy lets him/her off the hook. That's not true. The opposite of justice is injustice, and mercy is not at all about laxity or permissiveness or indifference to evil. In fact, mercy is an extended form of justice. It wants not only to correct a wrong deed, but also to redeem the wrongdoer.

Consider the case of a teenage boy who robbed three stores. In court, the owners of the places that he robbed confront him.

Store #1 Owner (to the Judge): "Aww, he's just a kid. Since he's never been in trouble before, I'm not going to press charges. Let's just drop it."

Store #2 Owner (to the Judge): "That's crazy! This kid is dangerous. Besides, he took my stuff. Throw the book at him so he won't see the light of day for a long time."

Store #3 Owner (to the boy, making no attempt to excuse the crime): "I'm as concerned about you as I am about the theft." (Then to the Judge): "Please give this boy a suspended sentence and parole, and have him make restitution."

The first solution here is indulgent, and the second vindictive, while the third is the merciful one that fulfills this beatitude. As you can see, mercy comes into play when something goes wrong. It is the invincible hope and belief that human nature is redeemable. And this leads to happiness.

Happy are the single-hearted,
for they shall see God. (Matthew 5:8)

Most of us would like to see God some day. In his poem *Crossing the Bar*, Alfred Lord Tennyson says:

"I hope to see my Pilot face to face

When I have crossed the bar."

The sixth beatitude tells us how we can see God. We must be single-hearted; in other words, pure in heart, as most Biblical translations say. Pure means unmixed with anything, and heart is the part of us that responds to truth, beauty, goodness, and mystery. Therefore, a pure heart is a heart that does what it is supposed to: it opens up and responds fully to the deepest realities of life. When we open our hearts in this way, we can see with them. In order to see God, we must let our heart be a heart.

Happy are the peacemakers,
for they shall be called sons of God. (Matthew 5:9)

The seventh beatitude about peacemakers seems to make sense. We would certainly expect peacemaking to go along with happiness.

A happy person would probably be at peace with himself and others; however, peace is much more than the absence of strife. It also has to do with actively choosing to do whatever is needed to stay in right relationship with God, others, and ourselves. Many times this means making amends and seeking reconciliation. If we want to be peacemakers, there are three ways to pursue this ministry of reconciliation:

1) We can practice preventive peacemaking; that is, we can be careful in what we say and do, and always try to draw people together.

2) We can resolve not to return evil with evil. When insulted or injured, we can choose not to strike back in kind.

3) We can overcome evil with good. We can look at the example of Jesus on Calvary, praying for those who hurt Him.

To be a peacemaker, though, we must first have peace within ourselves. But how? It's a product of faith in God as our loving father. Peacemakers are God's children. They have no enemies, and want only to work for the redemption of all.

Happy are you who are persecuted for righteousness' sake, for yours is the kingdom of heaven. Happy are you when they insult you and persecute you and utter any kind of slander against you because of me. Be glad and rejoice for your reward in heaven is great.
(Matthew 5:11,12)

These also seem to be strange beatitudes. We tend to link happiness with pleasure and are a bit shocked to see it linked to suffering. But let's face it. Righteous living in an unrighteous world can be a risky business. Jesus was really upfront about this. He let us know that his kind of happiness can trigger persecution. He looked upon the world as a great battlefield between the forces of good and evil and never played it safe on the sidelines. So if you are feeling persecuted, remember that your reward in heaven will be great.

This brings us to the end of our pilgrimage through the beatitudes. Maybe looking back on the journey, you're surprised to learn that to an active Christian happiness must be different than it is to the average person on the street, whose the beatitudes might be something like these:

Happy are the hard-boiled, for they never let life hurt them.

Happy are the complainers, for they eventually get their way.

Happy are the blasé, for they never worry about their sins.

Happy are the slave drivers, for they get results.

As you can see, these have no resemblance to the beatitudes of Christ. Which set of "be" attitudes will you choose?

○

Although we both love to sing, neither Fr. Arnold nor I will ever be invited to sing at Carnegie Hall. My wife Linda and I were on the first of two trips to the Holy Land with Fr. Arnold. In the Church of St. Anne, our guide invited us to sing a song together because the acoustics in the building are incredible. We sang and were awed by the rich, soaring notes that came back to our ears. I told Arnold, "This is amazing! Even you and I sound good." He responded, "With you it is amazing. For me, it is miraculous."

Greg Scherer, parishioner of Holy Name of Jesus

The Answer is Love

You shall love the Lord, your God with all your heart . . . and you shall love your neighbor as yourself.

(Matthew 22:37a, 39b)

Friends, last Sunday people asked Jesus if it was lawful to pay taxes. This week, He's asked another question: "What is the greatest of all God's commandments?" (Matthew 22:35)

Jesus' answer is simple and direct:

"You shall love the Lord, your God, with all your heart, with all your soul and all your mind. This is the greatest and the first commandment. The second is like it: You shall love your neighbor as yourself. The whole law and the prophets depend on these two commandments." (Matthew 22:36–40)

Jesus quotes one law from Deuteronomy and one law from Leviticus. You might think that the rabbis would have given him a round of applause for this answer. But they did not. And the reason is that Jesus' answer was NEW. He tied these two laws together for the first time, saying that you can not separate them. To love God AND your neighbor—this was a new concept.

In the first letter of John, he tells us, "If anyone says he is in the Light but hates his brother, this man is still in darkness." (1 John 2:9-10) To be a follower of Christ, we must love both God and our neighbor.

People often come to me in need of spiritual direction. They thirst to grow more in holiness. They want to be more perfect. "Any programs you recommend?" they ask me.

I tell them that a day of reflection, retreats, fasting, daily mass and tithing are all good, but they are only means. To have true spirituality, we need to have love, because God is love. We need to love God, love our neighbor and love ourselves.

In fact, I find that love is the answer to many of the questions I am asked. For example:

Would you like to know what it means to be a follower of Jesus Christ? The answer is in today's gospel. The answer is love.

Do you want to know how to relate to your neighbor? The answer is in today's gospel. The answer is love.

Are you wondering how to respond to your enemies? The answer is in today's gospel. The answer is with love.

How do we improve our parish's spirituality? The answer is in the gospel. The answer is love. This is my biggest job description—LOVE.

So how do we get started? By learning to love ourselves. Self-love is the foundation for all our other loves. Loving ourselves does not mean we are selfish and self-centered. Rather, it means we recognize that we have value in God's eyes. We are valued and loved for who we are.

The first person I deal with in the morning is myself. The last person I deal with each night is myself. Someone once said, "I may not be much, but I'm all I've got." We need to remember that God accepts us as we are—and we should do the same.

Three steps to self-love are to:

1. *Accept ourselves as we are.* It's hard to love anyone more than we love ourselves. Before we can truly love and appreciate our neighbor, we need to have a healthy love and acceptance for ourselves.

2. *Forgive ourselves.* We all sin. Jesus died on the cross to save us and forgive us for our sins. God forgives. We, too, must forgive.

3. *Improve ourselves.* Self-improvement is our personal responsibility.

There is a children's hymn that I would like for us to sing together, one you've all sung many times before. This hymn reminds us that Jesus loves us. To be more like Christ, we, too, need to love. This is our greatest commandment. It is also one of our greatest challenges. We must love God, love our neighbor, and love ourselves.

Jesus loves me this I know
For the Bible tells me so
Little ones to Him belong
They are weak but He is strong.
Yes, Jesus loves me.
Yes, Jesus loves me.
Yes, Jesus loves me,
The Bible tells me so.

You Can't Take it With You

†

And He said to them, "Take care!
Be on your guard against all kinds of
greed; for one's life does not consist in the
abundance of possessions."

(Luke 12:15)

ast week the point of the homily was "Ask and You Shall Receive." This week it's "Hoard and You Shall Lose." In other words: "You Can't Take It With You." Have you ever seen a hearse with a U-haul attached to it?

When Jesus was around a crowd, people asked Him a lot of questions. Usually they were upset about something and wanted answers or help. In today's gospel, there's a man like this. He comes to Jesus and gets right to the point: "Teacher, tell my brother to give me my share of our inheritance." Obviously, this man thinks he's been cheated out of something important.

Often when questioned, Jesus asked questions in return. He does that today. "Friend, who has set me up as your judge or arbiter?" Maybe Jesus knew what was really going on with the two brothers and their inheritance. Anyway, He decided not to get involved in

64

the dispute. Instead He turned to the crowd and gave them this teaching, right to the point: "Avoid greed in all its forms. A man may be wealthy, but his possessions do not guarantee him life." Then He told the story of the rich fool who wanted to tear down his grain bins and build larger ones to store all his surplus grain.

This rich man planned to relax and enjoy life after those large new grain bins were built and filled with his stuff. He thought he would have blessings in reserve for years to come. Then he could eat well, drink well, enjoy himself, and, best of all, relax. Only one problem; it was too late. The rich man died that night. He should have relaxed earlier.

If he'd decided he'd worked long and hard enough when the harvest was finished, if he'd chosen to share his surplus with the poor and needy instead of hoarding it, what a difference that would have made. Instead of being a bad example of greed, the rich man would have been a good example of generosity, stewardship, and sharing. At his death God would have said to him, "Well done, good and faithful servant!" instead of "You fool!" If only he'd told himself to relax earlier, the rich man would have been on the way to growing rich in the sight of God instead of growing rich for himself.

The rich man was a fool because he lost his relationship with the Creator. He forgot that his land and crops were divine gifts. He talked about "my" crops, "my" gain, "my" goods, when they should have been shared with the community. Maybe he was like Ebenezer Scrooge, the Charles Dickens character whose name has become a synonym for "greed." Scrooge's only purpose was to make money and hoard it. He was grouchy and heartless, even to the point of denying money to a crippled child. No one admires a cranky, selfish, cruel man like Scrooge. We all would probably agree he was a fool.

In fact, none of us are off the hook when it comes to greed. Remember, Jesus said, "Avoid greed in all its forms." That means we need to look at all of the ways a person can be greedy.

Maybe the rich man in Jesus' story wasn't like Scrooge at all. Maybe he was a nice guy. Jesus doesn't say anything about his disposition, just his greed. The rich man doesn't really sound like a grouch. After all, his long-range plan was to eat, drink, and be merry. He could have simply been someone who had plenty and wanted more. Someone just like many of us today.

Jesus saw this as dangerous—wanting more just for the sake of having more. Nowadays this is considered a virtue. We call it ambition. We call it success. We say, "That man's got drive. He's going places." We pay him big bucks to give motivational speeches. It appears we can be greedy without being grouchy. In fact, we can be greedy pleasantly.

We can also be passively greedy. For example, we might not take what belongs to others. We might not rob or defraud anyone. But maybe, like the rich fool, we hold back what we've got stacked up from others who need. Maybe we have money to invest and ignore people that can't pay their bills. Maybe we have a chance to help someone and we don't, like the priest and Levite in the story of the Good Samaritan.

There's evidence that some people are interested in abandoning greed as a way of life. They're saying to themselves " relax" and choosing voluntary simplicity —taking less stressful jobs, down-sizing their homes, and getting rid of stuff. In other words, "living simply so that others might simply live."

Robert Foster, in the book *Celebration of Discipline*, lists some ways that people can reduce their urge to acquire more stuff:

1. Buy things for usefulness rather than status.
2. Reject anything you find addictive.
3. Develop a habit of giving things away.
4. Enjoy things without owning them.
5. Appreciate all creation.
6. Avoid "buy now, pay later" schemes.

Now is the time for each of us to take an honest look at our own personal "harvest." Do an inventory of the clothes, utensils, knickknacks, books, art objects, and collections of stuff that create bulges in our personal storage bins, such as closets, attics, spare rooms, file cabinets, and garages. But, instead of having another neighborhood garage sale or flea market, just GIVE the useful items to a local Good Will or parish St. Vincent de Paul Society. And for other extra things that aren't worth giving away, the motto might as well be: "When in doubt, throw it out."

According to one of author Ernest Hemingway's biographers, on the first day of each new year, Hemingway gave away some of his most treasured possessions. When asked why he did this, he answered, "If I can give them away, then I own them. If I can't give them away, they own me."

Parable from Father Arnold "Accept Him As He Is"

Father Arnold often repeated the story of the monkey, the dove, and the python. It is a story about accepting and valuing differences in others. The story goes like this:

A monkey, python, and dove were friends. One day the python invited them to dinner. Not much time had passed before the python noticed dirty spots on the table from the monkey's hands (which he used for walking). The python got upset and asked the monkey why he couldn't keep his hands clean. The dove began to repeat, "Accept him as he is."

(Father Arnold asked the congregation to help with the story and we had to repeat this part. We all repeated this phrase three times, "Accept him as he is. Accept him as he is. Accept him as he is").

Soon after that dinner date, the monkey invited the python and dove to dinner and the python kept sliding off the chair. The monkey asked him to sit up straight, and of course, he couldn't. Then the dove said, "Accept him as he is."

Once again we all repeated this part. "Accept him as he is. Accept him as he is. Accept him as he is."

At the time, the story taught me a lot about accepting limitations in others as well as in myself. It was a practical application to some of the relationship issues I faced at work, as well as with our family. Years later, I am now a teacher and these words have been invaluable in helping me to accept the beauty in each child I teach. Instead of trying to fit each one into a mold, I accept them as they are and try to impart knowledge and love in the way they can best take it in. I mean this sincerely. Fr. Arnold also said it was important to let people feel your love more than anything you teach. I have followed that advice and have had some great experiences with the children. He often joked about the loud music of teenagers and said he didn't like the music, but he loved being with the teens. I am trying to practice that same mind set in my life in working with children and young people. I love you, Father Arnold, and I thank God for all your goodness and wisdom.

Claudith Washington, parishioner of Holy Name of Jesus

Practices of
the Active Christian

✝

Focus on What's Inside

Have a Positive Outlook

Pray Without Ceasing

Rest in Christ

Practice Social Justice

Practice Stewardship

Respect All Life

Looking Good
versus Being Good

✝

Everything they do is for men to see.
They make their phylacteries wide and the
tassels on their garments long. They love
the places of honor at banquets and the most
important seats in the synagogues. They
love to be greeted in the marketplaces and
have others call them Rabbi . . . The greatest
among you will be your servant. All who
exalt themselves will be humbled, and all who
humble themselves will be exalted.

(Matthew 23:5-8, 11,12,)

*I*s there anyone in this church who doesn't enjoy looking good? We all do, whether we admit it or not. Anyone who says that looking good isn't important is deceiving him- or herself. If we don't look good, it really does affect how we feel about ourselves. Some time back researchers at Yale University did a study on what we call "bad hair" days. They found out that on days when our hair doesn't cooperate, we tend to feel more embarrassed and less smart, sociable, and capable. Surprisingly, men are more likely than women to be affected by bad hair days. Of course, some men don't have to worry about this problem any more.

An internet poll a few years back asked this question: Which member of your family is the best looking? A majority of the respondents named themselves as the best-looking family member. Another poll question was: Which member of your family is the smartest? Again, the top-rated answer was "me." However, when the poll question asked which member of the family was most likely to tell a lie, "me" ranked ninth out of ten possible answers. Looks like most of us think that we are better looking, smarter, and more honest than the rest of the family!

This is just like the Pharisees that Jesus knew. The Pharisees were a group of Jewish scholars who were experts in the Law of Moses. In some ways they were the best people in the land. Following God's commands was the focus of their lives. There's nothing wrong with that. Somehow, though, the Pharisees missed the point. In their desperate desire to be obedient to God's laws, they created more and more rules. Soon they had compiled more than 50 volumes of rules and laws that had to be followed for a Jew to be considered righteous.

It's no wonder that the Pharisees didn't get along with Jesus. They differed from him significantly in how they viewed the life of faith. They emphasized rules over relationships. Jesus, on the other hand, valued relationships. He taught about loving God and loving one's neighbor. He told the Pharisees and anyone else who would listen that faith was primarily about falling passionately in love with God. Then, once a person knew and loved God, he or she would be inspired to love others and live a pure and holy life. Any necessary rules would follow naturally.

The Pharisees, following directions laid down in the book of Deuteronomy, wore on their wrists and foreheads small leather boxes called phylacteries that contained Scripture verses and tassels or fringe on their robes to remind themselves to follow God's commandments. Unfortunately, a fierce competition developed among them. They began wearing larger and larger phylacteries and longer and longer tassels to show that they were more religious than their colleagues. This would be similar to modern-day Christians fighting about who had the most WWJD clothes in their closet or the biggest fish symbol on their car.

The Pharisees wanted everyone to know how important they were. They used their religious position as a status symbol and as a means of showing their superiority. They valued respectability over righteousness. Pride and position were more important than sacrifice and service. What other people thought of them became their primary concern.

There's a Jewish folktale that illustrates humorously the desire that we all have to look good to others. It goes like this:

The men of the city of Chelm decided that they wanted to do something that would let everyone know of their town's importance. They decided to choose the wisest man in town and name him their chief sage. None of the other towns around had a chief sage, so this would prove Chelm's importance. To distinguish their chief sage from everyone else, the men of Chelm decided that he would wear a pair of golden shoes. That way when anyone saw him, they would know he was the chief sage of Chelm.

The trouble was, though, when the chief sage was tramping through the streets of Chelm in the golden shoes, he stepped into a mud puddle, and the mud covered up his golden shoes completely. The men of Chelm decided that wouldn't do, so they crafted a pair of leather shoes to protect them from mud. But the leather shoes covered up the golden ones. What a problem! How would anyone know who was the town's chief sage if they couldn't see his golden shoes? Finally the men came up with a solution. The chief sage would wear the golden shoes on his hands! That way if any outsider wanted to know who was the wisest man in Chelm, they could point to the fellow wearing the golden shoes on his hands.

If you laugh at that story, then do so cautiously. We live in what is arguably the most appearance-conscious nation on earth. From a young age, we are bombarded by messages proclaiming that appearance is more important than substance. And many of us fall into that trap. We want to avoid "bad hair" days at all costs.

We can't really condemn the Pharisees too much because we are often guilty of the same twisted thinking that they had—valuing rules over relationships, appearances over authenticity, and respectability over righteousness. In other words, we, like the Pharisees, often consider looking good more important than being good or doing good.

What's the difference between a Christian who looks good and one who is good? Between a respectable Christian and a real one? Jesus made that distinction when He said, "The greatest among you will be your servant." He took the lowest place at the banquet table and washed the feet of His disciples. He didn't wear fancy robes with long tassels. He hung out with outcasts, sinners, and tax collectors (considered the worst of the worst), not with the movers and shakers. Respectable members of society got nervous when He entered the room. He didn't play by their rules.

But Jesus wasn't trying to abolish the Law of Moses. He was trying to go beyond it, to show people the abundant life that flows from living in true relationship with God and others.

In closing, let me say that the saddest secret in most churches today is the number of people who sit in the pews week after week, year after year, and never develop a true relationship with the living God or with the people around them. They keep all the rules. They dress up and look good. They are very respectable. But they are spiritually dead.

Friends, don't be one of those people. There is abundant life waiting if you are willing to seek God's face and look into the heart of your neighbor.

I have been blessed by many people in my life who have influenced me by their love and the way they lived their lives. Over the years my parents, teachers, coaches and spiritual directors have helped me to discern what is really important in life. But there is only one person who affected my life in such a way that it altered the direction of my life. That man is Fr. Arnold Weber, OSB. Fr. Arnold, by his life, and by his love for the priesthood, raised awareness in me of what it meant to be a priest and gave me the courage to leave the business world and enter the seminary. Without his guidance and support, I doubt that I would be a priest today. Thank you Fr. Arnold for coming into my life! With deep love and affection.

Fr. Al Backmann

Following Jesus Without Embarrassing God

✝

...But in your hearts sanctify Christ as Lord. Always be ready to make your defense to anyone who demands from you an accounting for the hope that is in you; yet do it with gentleness and reverence. Keep your conscience clear, so that, when you are maligned, those who abuse you for your good conduct in Christ may be put to shame.

(1 Peter 3:15,16)

Baptist Tony Campolo wrote a book called *Following Jesus Without Embarrassing God.* In my opinion, he hit the nail on the head. Many Christians are most certainly an embarrassment to God. Their views and their actions in no way, shape, or form resemble those of Jesus. Unfortunately, many of these non-Christian Christians are very vocal and very visible. And the damage they cause is incalculable. They are to Christianity what the Taliban has been to Islam.

75

How do we practice our Christian faith in a way that contributes more to this world than it detracts? How do we follow Jesus without embarrassing God?

In today's reading, the apostle Peter gives some advice on this. Here are three things we can do to ensure that our faith comes across appropriately to others:

1. Be a positive Christian.

Notice that Peter says we are to give an account for the hope that is within us. Christians who embarrass God do not communicate hope. They communicate anger, fear, and despair. They are down on the world, down on their neighbors, and down on the governing authorities. They are sarcastic, cynical, and sometimes even cruel. And all while wearing the name of the gentle man from Galilee who preached hope.

It's easy to be cynical about life. It's the popular thing to do. There's even a book called *The Cynic's Guide to Life,* which contains familiar sayings with a negative twist. Here are a few of them.

a. This land is your land. This land is my land. So stay on your land.

b. Always take time to stop and smell the roses, and sooner or later you'll inhale a bee.

c. Do not walk behind me, for I may not lead. Do not walk ahead of me, for I may not follow. Do not walk beside me, either, just leave me alone.

Yes, it's so easy to be a cynic and see the dark side of human nature. The question is, can you also see the hand of God?

2. Do things with gentleness and reverence.

Like Jesus did. Use deeds rather than words. Once a pastor was preparing a funeral service for a man named Herbie. The funeral director had told him that Herbie had no family, so the pastor figured it would be a very brief ceremony for a small gathering. Herbie had been a door-to-door salesman of household items. Many of his customers bought things from him out of habit. Some bought out of pity. Herbie made a modest living and kept mostly to himself. Occasionally, he did small favors for his neighbors, such as raking their leaves or bringing their papers in to them. When customers and acquaintances throughout the city read Herbie's obituary in their morning papers, each reflected on the unassuming man they had known. Neighbors swapped stories about his small acts of kindness. Housewives recalled the dependability with which he made his rounds. "He has nobody," many said. "That's so sad. I think I'll go to his funeral." So that is how it came to be that on a cold February morning more than 1,000 people crowded into the pastor's small church for the funeral of a modest door-to-door salesman. Herbie never would have imagined how many people he had influenced. Neither will we, if we do things with gentleness and reverence.

In 1969 British journalist Malcolm Muggerdde traveled to Calcutta, India, to do an interview with Mother Teresa. Muggerdde was required to film the interviews in Calcutta's Home for the Dying, which Mother Teresa had established and run. His camera operators protested that the home was too dark for proper filming and insisted that the film would not turn out. However, this was the only place where Mother Teresa felt comfortable doing the interview, so they gave it their best shot. Later, Muggerdde and his crew were astonished to find that the film turned out beautifully. In fact, in the film, the small dark room appeared to be filled with a bright glowing light. Muggerdde came to believe that this light was the light of God's love glowing from Mother Teresa to all those around her. He was not the kind of man to get carried away with exclamations of praise, but that was how he felt about Mother Teresa. Do you think that Mother Teresa ever embarrassed God? I doubt it. She was a soul of gentleness and reverence. We have heard it said: "What you are speaks so loud that I cannot hear what you say." And it's true.

You follow Jesus without embarrassing God by living a life of love, concern, and sensitivity to others.

3. Keep a clear conscience.

We should be able to assume that this will be done as a matter of course, but unfortunately, we cannot. Many contemporary Christians, without even being aware of it, follow the dictates of 1960's morality, and separate their personal consciences from their social consciences. They think that as long as they care about the poor, as long as they fight bigotry, or as long as they seek to be peacemakers in a world of strife, then it really doesn't matter what is done in their personal lives. And they turn blind eyes to the personal indiscretions of many prominent individuals who have been elevated to prominent positions. Let's keep our standards high and strive for both.

****

Jesus is looking for positive people who are gentle and reverent and who have clear consciences. Our testimony of faith rings hollow if we do not possess all of these attributes. Peter has written this advice to people who respect Christ in the world. Hey, that's us! He's saying, "Look, you are special people. Be positive, be reverent, be gentle. And for Heaven's sake, don't do anything that would embarrass God."

●

My favorite saying by Fr. Arnold is this: "I AM NOT IN THE JUDGMENT BUSINESS, BUT THE MERCY BUSINESS."

Rev. Mr. Sam Catapano, Holy Name of Jesus

Grumble, Grumble, Grumble

And do not complain as some of them (the Israelites) did, and were destroyed by the destroyer.

(1 Corinthians 10:10)

There's a resort in Colorado with a hot spring and a cold spring side by side. People can wash up comfortably in one and get a refreshing rinse in the other. "Do you know how wonderful this is?" a tourist marveled to a Colorado native who worked at the resort. The native replied, "It's not so great. Notice there isn't any soap."

Grumble, grumble, grumble.

In Corinthians, Paul lists many things to avoid as sins, and grumbling is one of them. Wow, is grumbling really a sin? Well, Paul reminds us about what happened to the Israelites in the Book of Exodus. Remember, they were constantly complaining to Moses and Aaron. They said:

"We're starving. You brought us out of Egypt to watch us die of hunger." "We're really sick of bread. Why don't we ever have meat?"

"Now we're thirsty. Where will you get water for us? Out of the rocks?"

And so on.

Grumble, grumble, grumble.

What is a grumbler, anyway? Is it just a discontented person? I don't think so. We all have a little discontent in our lives—at home, at work, in our parish, and in the Catholic Church. Some discussion about our discontent can be normal and good. It helps us let off pressure, like a safety valve. I think a grumbler, though, is a person who doesn't know how to properly handle or express disagreement or discontent. Many grumblers have good intentions, but their grumbling can stir up unhealthy conflict and cause trouble or even disaster. Grumblers are like termites that chew away at the foundation of a house.

Here are some characteristics of grumblers:

1. They tend to communicate indirectly and anonymously; for example, with unsigned complaints.

2. They have difficulty expressing their dissatisfaction in a clear way. They hint and use innuendos. Perhaps they don't really know what they're unhappy about, they just know they are. "I'm fed up!" they say.

3. They focus on problems without offering solutions.

Case in point: In one church there was an elder who got up in front and spoke to the congregation for three years in a row. Every year he said the same things:

"There aren't any young people in our church."

"We should be doing more for the young people in our church."

"Young are the future of our church."

"If we don't get the young back to church, our church will die."

During those three years, this elder who was so concerned about the young never once invited any youth to his home. He never chaperoned a youth activity, did not offer youth a scholarship for school or camp, and did not suggest setting up a church youth group.

Grumble, grumble, grumble.

How should we deal with the grumblers around us? They usually aren't really bad people. Most even think they're being helpful. But unchecked grumbling can lead to big problems.

Maybe we can learn from Moses. He certainly had to learn to deal with grumbling. In fact, the Israelites grumbled so much that Moses began complaining to God about them. You know what God told him? "Toughen up, Moses, criticism is part of the job!"

We all want everybody to like us, even Moses did. But that isn't how it works. The truth is, we are never going to please everyone. If we take criticism and grumbling personally, that just makes things worse. Don't let your own behavior be governed by grumblers.

On the other hand, don't automatically dismiss grumblers and their complaints. Listen carefully and try to figure out if their concerns are legitimate.

Case in point: Once a young father was driving his kids and their friends home from a sporting event. The six kids were rowdy and boisterous, and the dad was tired from working all day. He could hardly wait to get home and relax, so he was very impatient when they began complaining that they needed a bathroom right now. He pulled into a gas station to let them use the restroom, and, of course, they wanted money for candy and really complained when he wouldn't give it to them. Finally, they came out and got in the car, and the dad took off for home. At this point the kids really began to put up a ruckus, but he ignored them. Complain, complain , complain! He thought. "Quit whining!" he told them, but they kept it up. About five miles down the road, he finally heard what they were saying. "Dad, Dad, you forgot Peggy!" Then he roared, "Why didn't anybody tell me?"

Friends, the last point I'd like to make today is that we must try to help grumblers learn an appropriate way to deal with their dissatisfaction. Get them involved in working with others toward a common goal. Working for a good cause helps everyone feel needed. Doing something worthwhile usually helps people get rid of their discontent.

Healthy people notice the same problems as grumblers, but they try to do something about the problems. If they notice there's a need, they try to fill it. If they see something broken, they try to fix it. Healthy people are like Isaiah, who said, "Here I am, Lord, use me."

Don't be a grumbler.

○

Spending time with Father Arnold was a special treat, but he is in high demand and there were not always many opportunities. However, I had ten days to share with him when my mother and I went to the Alps on one of his trips. My ancestors are from Germany as are his, so we were interested in many of the same things. My mother and I learned so many things on that trip, and the visits to the monasteries and beautiful churches, and the German meals and songs were very special. One of the last times that I danced with Father Arnold was at the beer garden in Munich, and as I remember that happy time, I also remember what a wonderful friend he has been to me.

Sunny Scott, Director, Music and Worship, Holy Name of Jesus

How to Pray

He was praying in a certain place, and when He had finished, one of His disciples said to him, "Lord, teach us to pray . . ."

(Luke 11:1)

Many years ago, Norman Vincent Peale, the famous protestant minister, author and inspirational speaker, told a story about a man named Jim Johnson, whose job was to save a bankrupt hotel in a large city. Every night Jim drove to the top of a hill and prayed for twenty minutes for the hotel, the employees, the customers, and the city. Soon business began to pick up. There was a new spirit. The employees and the management felt better, and there were more customers. Jim Johnson credited the rebirth of the hotel to prayer. Just think if the prayers of one man could save a hotel, imagine what the prayers of a nation could do! They could transform the world.

As far as I know, the only thing the disciples ever asked Jesus to teach them was how to pray. We heard them ask Jesus in today's gospel. Why did they ask Him how to pray? Didn't they know already? Didn't many of them come from a Jewish religious background?

When the disciples watched Jesus pray, they noticed something different about His way of praying in comparison to their own. Prayer was a source of strength and peace for Jesus, and it made a real difference in His life. When Jesus went into prayer, He came out of it changed. "Teach us to pray," they asked Him. They weren't looking for more words to memorize. They wanted the strength and peace and transformation that Jesus found through prayer.

As we heard in today's Gospel from Luke, Jesus did tell His disciples how to pray. First, He gave them a model for prayer. Next, He emphasized the importance of persistence in prayer. Both concepts are important for us today.

The Model for Prayer

Jesus gave us the Lord's Prayer as a model for how to pray. It is not called The Lord's Prayer because Jesus prayed it, but because it is the only prayer He ever gave to His disciples or to us.

When we pray, it is important that we focus. The word "focus" comes from the Latin word for "hearth" or "fireplace." When we think of a hearth or fireplace, we think of the fire—its warmth and power—as a focal point. God must be the focal point in our prayers. When we pray, we join in fellowship with Him, so that His will can be done through us. What a joy this is!

St. James once said, "If you ask and you don't receive, then you have asked wrongly." This happens quite often. When the focus of our prayers is our will, then we turn God into an errand boy or mail service catalog.

Often our lives become cluttered—sometimes even with beautiful things—and we lose our focus on God. Once a church purchased a beautiful statue of a saint. The environment committee found a place to put the statue. Then they purchased some beautiful flowers to place around the statue. The flowers were in full bloom and smelled lovely. A couple of candles were also added to the display. The committee continued working to enhance the display.

When the pastor walked by, they asked "What do you think?" "It's great," he said, "but where's the statue?"

The environment committee lost their focus. Their display became cluttered. The flowers were good and beautiful. The candles were lovely as well. But they added clutter, rather than focus. Our prayers need to remain focused on God as modeled in the Lord's Prayer.

The Gospels tell us that there are four types of prayer:

1. Prayers of adoration acknowledging that God is Almighty and our God.

2. Prayers of contrition acknowledging that we are all sinners and need mercy.

3. Prayers of thanksgiving for all of our blessings we have received.

4. Prayers of supplication or petition asking God for something.

The Lord's Prayer contains all four types of prayer. Let's take a close look at each line.

Our Father, who art in heaven

The first line of the Lord's Prayer gets right at the heart of what it's all about. Prayer is rooted in relationship with God. By saying "Our Father," we enter into a relationship—and not just any relationship. We enter into a loving relationship with our Father, Abba. We acknowledge that we are His children.

Hallowed be Thy name

This line shows our humility and our recognition that God is Almighty, and that His name is to be spoken with complete respect.

Thy kingdom come

Jesus Christ needs to be within us; the kingdom has to become a part of our own lives. But, we can't stop here. We need to extend the kingdom. It is both a vertical and a horizontal relationship.

Thy will be done

The Blessed Virgin Mary said this prayer when the angel Gabriel announced that she would be carrying the Son of God. Jesus himself prayed this prayer in the Garden of Gethsemane. Not my will, but Your will be done. This is what faith is all about. It's about conforming our will to the will of God.

Give us this day our daily bread

This line focuses on our needs. We are asking God to provide, not just nourishment for our bodies, but nourishment for our souls. The Word of God, the Eucharist, and the food we need for our bodies, God provides it all.

Forgive us our trespasses as we forgive those who trespass against us.

Forgiveness is the key. Oh, how Jesus wanted us to forgive. Actually, this could be a dangerous prayer if God really believed us. We're asking Him to "forgive us as we forgive others." Lucky for us, God is in the mercy business and is capable of perfect forgiveness time and time again.

Lead us not into temptation, but deliver us from evil

With this statement we admit we need help. Don't put us to the test. We know we are weak and need to rely on His strength and mercy.

At Mass we say the Lord's Prayer. Did you ever notice when we say it? We say it right before communion. Before we receive Christ, we glorify God, we thank God, we ask God for forgiveness and we ask Him to provide for our needs. We prepare our hearts to receive Christ in the Eucharist. What reverence we should have for this prayer. This prayer truly has it all. It flows from love and leads to love.

Persistence in Prayer

Now, let's talk about the importance of persistence in prayer. Jesus thought this was important. In the Gospel of Luke, Jesus tells the story of the man who asks his friend, in the middle of the night, for three loaves of bread. The friend says no. Jesus says, "I tell you, if he does not get up and give him the loaves because of their friendship, he will get up to get him whatever he needs because of his persistence." "Be persistent," Jesus told the disciples. He said to keep on asking, knocking and seeking. Stay at it. Don't give up. Persistence in prayer leads to intimacy and love.

Friends, there have been changes in thought over the years with regard to prayer. In the past, prayer was looked at as an obligation. You said your prayers before and after meals, in the morning, and at bedtime. It was not something you looked forward to or enjoyed, but you understood that it was good for you. Kind of like dieting. No wonder some people considered prayer to be boring. Today, there seems to be a new, more positive spirit to prayer. There is more joy. People are doing more than just saying their prayers; they are communicating with God.

The key reason for this is responsibility: the ability to respond. Anyone can react. Animals and even plants can react to outside stimuli. But only people can choose how they respond. Now if we have the choice to respond, we also have the choice to not respond. Friends, we need to choose to respond. We need to pray. Having a sense of responsibility means having a sense of love. Spouses, pray for each other. Parents, pray for your children. Pray alone and pray as a family. When there is prayer in the family, there is strength in the home.

Persistence in prayer was a message that St. Paul, like Jesus, hammered home time and time again. He told the Thessalonians to "pray always, never ceasing, render constant thanks to God. Such is God's will for you in Jesus Christ." He told the Romans, to "Rejoice in hope, be patient under trial, persevere in prayer." To the Galatians He said, "Pray perseveringly, be attentive to prayer." And to the Ephesians, He said, "Pray in the spirit of thanksgiving."

When people ask me, "How do we learn to pray?" I tell them, "One way is to do it." Get started. Try it out. Follow Jesus' example. Say The Lord's Prayer, and stay at it; pray always, don't give up!

What a wonderful feeling to be in the constant presence of God! Keep your focus on God, and be persistent in prayer—pray always in this way.

○

It was my privilege to have Fr. Arnold as my supervisor from 1982-1998, while I was director of worship and music at Holy Name. I had contact with him almost daily. His many fine attributes left a lasting impression on me in many areas.

Foremost was his hospitality. It was edifying for me to witness first hand his ability to accept people wherever they were, sinners and saints alike. His spirit of gratitude was very inspiring. It has helped me to have a thankful heart for all of my blessings, large and small. His words, "better not bitter" have influenced my ability to carry the crosses that each of us receive.

I was introduced to Fr. Arnold's spontaneity before I even began working at Holy Name. After I was hired, I decided to come to Holy Name to worship so that I could get a feel for their liturgy. The first time I came to Mass, after communion, Fr. Arnold had me stand, introduced me to the community and then proceeded to invite me to come to the sanctuary to speak to the assembly. I will never forget my initiation to Holy Name!

Rosemary Gleason, Holy Name of Jesus

Come to Me

Come to me, all you who are weary and find life burdensome. I will refresh you. Take my yoke upon you and learn from me, for I am meek and humble of heart; and you will find rest for yourselves. For my yoke is easy and my burden is light.

(Matthew 11:28-30)

Friends, our story today is a very profound one because it's about an invitation Jesus has for us. I don't know what I'd rather hear from Him than the words He says today, "Come to me." Jesus said this often. He said, "Come and follow me." It's an invitation we can't pass up. We all need restful spirits, inner peace, calm.

Then He asks us to take up his yoke. What kind of rest and refreshment is Jesus talking about here? Remember us, the weary ones, the ones already burdened by this hard and demanding life? Is

He asking us to take up a yoke and pull like we're in a team of oxen? Or is He asking us—inviting us—to lay our burdens on Him, and work through Him and with Him, to pull together?

He is asking us to surrender to Him and to submit to Him, but not in a mindless way. He wants us to think and to learn from Him, so that with His help, we can carry our burdens calmly and with peace of mind. When we submit ourselves to Him, we can give up all the fretting and worrying about the little things that bother us. By following Jesus, we learn about the important things in life to focus on and can let the little things go.

Jesus says, "Learn from me." He also says that He will give us direction and life abundantly. To learn from Him we all need to sit at his feet and listen to what He says. As Light of the World, He has some important things to tell us. He can shed light into those dark, worrisome corners in our minds where the anxiety builds and the restlessness grows.

In the 1985 book *Habits of the Heart* by Robert N. Bellah and others, it says that the longest trip that a person can ever take is the nine-inch one from the head to the heart. Without making that trip, it's impossible for us to change. We can only confront issues with attacks and arguments. Attitudes are stubborn and negative or downright belligerent.

Our religion—our faith—resides in the heart. When Jesus said, "Come to me," He was inviting us to take on His heart, go His way, and live in His love. When we come to Jesus, when we let Him into our hearts, then change becomes possible. When we put Jesus at the center of our lives, then our own behavior can change, our family lives can improve, and even our attitudes toward money and work can be different.

Let me tell you a story about a business man that I came across in Fortune magazine some years ago (April 27, 1989). This man owned two businesses, a personnel agency in New York and a pizza business in New Jersey. He said, "I have everything: four houses, three cars and great businesses." He also said, "I don't have what I really want: a good marriage and children. My wife doesn't want children because I'm too volatile." He acknowledged that his temper got in the way of his dealings with his employees and with his family. He smoked three packs of cigarettes a day, took three sleeping pills at night, and fought with his wife constantly. He knew all this about himself, so he decided to make a few changes. He slowed down and went to marriage counseling. But still, his wife left him.

Finally, this man turned to the Lord. He answered Jesus' invitation to come to Him. He changed. Notice that I said this time he changed. I did not say he made a few changes. He really changed because he turned to the Lord. In doing so he was able to reconcile his marriage, and he and his wife had their first child. His employees even recognized that he had changed.

Jesus' invitation of "Come to me," was as powerful for a successful American businessman in 1987 as when Jesus originally said it 2000 years earlier by the Sea of Gallilee.

When we are feeling anxious: *"Come to me."*

When we are hurting: *"Come to me."*

When we are confused by life: *"Come to me."*

When we feel hopeless: *"Come to me."*

Accept the invitation.

"Come to me, and I will give you rest."

Rest Awhile

✝

*And after He had dismissed the crowds,
He went up into the hills by Himself
to pray.*

(Matthew 14:23)

The Apostles traveled with Jesus through Judea and Galilee, and as they walked, Jesus instructed them on how to live their lives to please God. Eventually, of course, Jesus would leave the Apostles. In the time following the Resurrection when Jesus was no longer with them, they relied on the instructions Jesus gave them during their travels in Judea and Galilee. In living and spreading the words of Jesus, the Apostles realized that they were pastoring others as Jesus had pastored them. We continue that work today.

Jesus imparted four great lessons in His teaching. These particular lessons create guiding principles for us. They are called pastorals. The word "pastoral" comes from the idea of a shepherd in the hills watching over his sheep. A pastoral gives guiding principles to the shepherd, or pastor, and by extension, individual Christians, as we minister to each other.

The first pastoral came at the time when, after a period of teaching them, Jesus sent the apostles out to preach repentance to the people and to heal the sick in body and soul. The word "apostle" means "one who is sent out". The Apostles were authorized by Jesus to act in His name and with His authority. They were also given the Great Commission in the Gospel of Matthew to spread the teachings of Jesus. We are all given this authority.

The second pastoral called for the Apostles to answer and be accountable to Jesus. They were to report all they had done and taught. This instilled them with integrity. We are all held accountable to Jesus.

The third pastoral came when Jesus told the Apostles to rest. "Come by yourselves to an out-of- the-way place and rest a little." Not only did He say this, but we also know from Scripture readings throughout the New Testament that He tried to put this into practice Himself. It's part of our ministry to rest a while. It helps us to be retooled and refueled.

For us Christians, an important part of this resting and renewing process is prayer. Jesus, again, gave us many examples of this. And like Jesus, through prayer, we too can get charged up, and let God light our fire. It helps keep the salt fresh in us as we strive to be the salt and light to others. You could say we have a religious responsibility to goof off from time to time. I imagine that seems a little strange to hear from the pulpit—that we have the responsibility to rest, relax, take off our shoes, loosen our ties, and as people say, "let it all hang out." That's a real healthy attitude to have. God didn't create any of us to work all the time—not even His apostles.

And, of course, we have the Judeo-Christian idea of Sabbath—to rest. It's even a commandment—remember the Sabbath and keep it holy. It goes back to the creation story—God worked for six days and rested on the seventh. The Sabbath was created for *our* benefit;

it wasn't created for God's benefit. As Jesus says in Mark (3:27) "Sabbath was made for man and not man for the Sabbath."

You've heard me talk before about growing up on a farm in central Minnesota, and you probably know that on a dairy farm, or any farm with animals, there are some chores that need to be done every day, even on Sunday. But in our house, these chores were kept to a bare minimum, and for the most part we stayed home and played, maybe had some company drop in, or went visiting ourselves. But the important part of the day was Mass and time and fellowship with God. We took time to relax, visit, and worship.

I have a poem here that says it all so well.

Take time to laugh, it is the music of the soul.

Take time to think, it is the source of power.

Take time to play, it is the source of perpetual youth.

Take time to read, it is the foundation of wisdom.

Take time to pray, it is the greatest power on earth.

Take time to love and be loved, it is a God given privilege.

Take time to be friendly, it is the road to happiness.

Take time to give, it is too short a day to be selfish.

Take time to work, it is the price of success.

Take time for God, it is the way of life.

So that's three of the four pastoral lessons that Jesus taught us. The first involved the Apostles Jesus sent out to teach. The second is that they answered to Jesus and were accountable to him, third, take time to rest.

In *the fourth pastoral*, Jesus showed us his selfless commitment to his ministry. Do you remember when Jesus preached to the huge crowds by the Sea of Galilee and provided them all with food from a few loaves and fishes? He was a little worn out by it all, so He went to the other side of the water for some peace and quiet.

Only more people were there waiting to see Him and hear Him. Jesus put His plans on hold—He had compassion for the people because they were like sheep without a shepherd, and He began to teach them. He didn't resent them or resist them. For us, too, the call to ministry is never silenced. Some great examples of people whose work requires them be selfless are doctors, priests, firemen, and parents.

Jesus was people-conscious. He did more than resign Himself to people's need for His time and attention. He responded to it. He saw them as sheep without a shepherd. He saw them as scattered on a hillside, hungry, hurt and cold.

If we see ourselves as a lost sheep in need of our shepherd, how do we go about looking for Him? How do we find the sanctuary He offers us?

I think we need to spend some quiet time to get in touch with the core of our own being. Some people find it with a cup of coffee in the morning before others get up. Some find it in a quiet room after all are in bed. Some light a candle to let that sense of serenity come over them. Some have other creative ways of finding the sanctuary.

The important thing is to get in touch with the inner core of our being and with God, who lives there. We need to nourish our spirit in God's presence so that we can continue to do God's work in the hectic rat race of daily life. Spend five or ten minutes of each day in quiet communion with God, who wants to speak to our soul and renew our spirit.

There's a beautiful prayer called "Slow Me Down, Lord" by Wilferd A. Peterson. It expresses the same point that Jesus makes in today's gospel. It makes a fitting prayer with which to close.

Slow Me Down, Lord

Slow me down, Lord. Slow me down!
Ease the pounding of my heart by the quieting of my mind...
Give me amid the confusion of my day,
the calmness of the everlasting hills.
Break the tensions of my nerves and muscles
with the soothing music
of the singing streams that live in my memory.
Help me to know the magical,
restoring power of sleep.
Teach me the art of taking minute vacations,
of slowing down to look at a flower,
to chat with a friend, to pat a dog,
to read a few lines from a good book.
Remind me each day of the fable
of the hare and tortoise,
that I may know that the race
is not always to the swift—
that there is more to life
than increasing its speed.
Let me look upward
into the branches of the towering oak
and know that it is great and strong
because it grew slowly and well.
Slow me down, Lord,
and inspire me to send my roots
deep into the soil of life's enduring values
that I may grow toward the stars
of my greater destiny.

— Wilferd A. Peterson

Don't Forget How to Play

Excerpt from a commencement address

You will not do yourself a favor or anyone else if you get so bogged down with problems and work that you lose the fun of living.

When we were kids we enjoyed play. Never forget to play. If you do, lots of beauty is gone. All that is left is hard work, the doing of duty.

Duty is a great word—we can't get by without it, but the finest things of life happen when people go beyond duty and move into priorities.

Quit working and play a little.

The finest and happiest homes I visit are where people have remembered how to play. They have problems too, but have fun.

Jesus said, "I come that they might have life and have it to the full."

Look at Jesus: He loved children, they loved him.

He loved Nature.

He obviously worked hard.

Don't forget to create fullness in your life.

So, I'll leave you a different message than other speakers might. Save the world. For your own good, for the good of those around you, for the good of the world—*Don't forget to play!*

Feed Them Yourselves

✝

*"Dismiss the crowd so that they can go to
the surrounding villages and farms and
find lodging and provisions; for we are in
a deserted place here." Jesus said to them,
"Give them some food yourselves."
They replied, "Five loaves and two fishes
are all we have, unless we ourselves go and
buy food for all these people . . ."
Then taking the five loaves and the two
fish, and looking up to heaven, he said the
blessing over them, broke them, and gave
them to the disciples to set before the crowd.*

(Luke 9:12-13, 16)

*F*riends, today we celebrate the Feast Day of the Body and Blood of Jesus Christ. There are different Gospel readings for each of our three liturgical cycles for this celebration, and I think it's helpful to look at all of them. Don't worry, they're short!

The reading for Cycle A, "My Flesh is True Food" is from chapter six of St. John's Gospel. There Jesus says, "I am the living bread that came down from heaven… my flesh is true food, and my blood is true drink."

For Cycle B, we have "This is My Body," which comes from the Last Supper scene in St. Mark's Gospel. There Jesus takes bread, blesses it, breaks it and gives it to his disciples saying, "Take this; this is my body." Then He takes a cup (of wine), gives thanks and passes the cup to them, and they all drink from it. And Jesus says, "This is my blood of the covenant which will be shed for many."

And Cycle C gives us our reading for today, "Give Them Some Food Yourselves." This comes from St. Luke's story of feeding the crowd of 5,000 with only five loaves and two fish. In this Gospel, there is no explicit reference to the Eucharist, to Holy Communion. The focus is on Jesus' response to human hunger. To His disciples, Jesus says, "Give them some food yourselves."

This command of Jesus challenges us to extend our celebration of his Body and Blood beyond this altar table and beyond these church walls.

In his book *Who Speaks For God?* (Delacorte Press, New York: 1996), Jim Wallis includes the following true story. This story illustrates the solidarity we are celebrating today, as members of the Body of Christ who are privileged to be nourished with the Body and Blood of Christ.

The story is an account by a reporter who was covering the conflict in Sarajevo several years ago. The reporter witnessed the shooting of a young girl by a sniper. Shocked by what he'd just seen, the young man flung off his responsibility as a reporter. He threw down his writing materials, and rushed to the aid of a man who had picked up the child and hurriedly helped both of them into his car. As the reporter floored the accelerator and raced to the hospital, the man cradled the bleeding child in his arms. "Hurry," he pleaded, "my child is still alive!" A moment later, he said, "Hurry, my friend, my child is still breathing" and, after a few more minutes, "Hurry, friend, my child is still warm." Finally he moaned, "Hurry, Oh God, my child is getting cold."

When they finally arrived at the hospital, the little girl was dead. As the two men were in the lavatory, washing the child's blood from their hands, the man turned to the reporter and said, "This is a terrible task for me. Now I must go and tell her father that his daughter is dead. He will be heartbroken."

Stunned, the reporter stared in silence at the grieving man. Then he said, "I thought she was your child." "No," the man replied, "but aren't they all our children?"

Today's feast of the Body and Blood of Christ encourages us to ask similar questions. Aren't all the members of Christ's body our children, our brothers and sisters, with whom we share a bond that is deeper and more binding than blood?

There are two aspects to today's feast:

We are celebrating the sacramental Body and Blood that Jesus offers as food.

Through the Eucharist, Jesus gives Himself as food. Jesus has a great desire to feed and nourish us. And He wants us to be fed with the best kind of nourishment there is. And so He gives His very self to us in Holy Communion. The Eucharist is a symbol of the heavenly banquet to which we are called. But we are also called to partake of the best there is on earth in order to nourish our spirits while we are on the way to this heavenly banquet.

We are celebrating the fact that we are the Body of Christ in the world.

Through the centuries many have marked this day and expressed their gratitude for this great gift with elaborate liturgical processions, during which the Real Presence of Christ in the Eucharist is carried through the streets of our cities and villages. In receiving this gift, we are fed with the very life of Jesus Christ. We who eat the sacramental Body and Blood of Christ then become the living, breathing, visible, palpable Body of Christ in the world. When we live in the realization that we are the Body of Christ, our very lives become a "procession" that brings the Real Presence into every aspect of the human experience. This is what the reporter discovered in war-torn Sarajevo with the man who tried so desperately to save "his" child.

We each have an individual relationship to Jesus and that is very important. In fact, it's the basis of our spiritual life. But we must not forget the wider meaning of taking the Eucharist. When you and I receive the Eucharist, we are not only united to Christ, we are also, in a wonderful and mysterious way, united to one another since we all partake of the same Jesus Christ. This union with others must be lived out in our day to day lives.

Just as we must nourish our relationship with Christ, so we must also nourish our relationships with each other. When we say "Amen" to the Body of Christ, we are saying "Amen" to the mystical Body of Christ. That includes all the other people who are united to Jesus. Anytime we reach out to each other in love, we are living out the commitment that we made when we received the Eucharist; and at the same time we are preparing ourselves for our next taking of the Eucharist. This is what the Vatican Council meant when it said that the Eucharist was the source and the summit of our Christian lives.

Starvation and Hunger

Jesus knew that we live in a world where hunger and starvation exist in massive areas. A few facts will help you get the picture. In

Kenya, Africa, drought and crop failure left an estimated 3.5 million people at risk of starvation. In Ethiopia, an estimated 10 million people confront severe hunger and starvation. In Sudan, the number approaches 2.5 million. Then we also have 1.2 million in Somalia; 750,000 in Uganda; and 550,000 in Eritrea. That's a staggering number of people and all on one continent.

Jesus also knew that many people in our world experience other types of 'hunger' besides starvation, such as loneliness, depression, and spiritual emptiness.

Therefore, we who eat Jesus' flesh and drink his blood must keep His command, "Give them some food yourselves," as he said in Luke's Gospel.

What can we do, then, to carry the Body and Blood of Jesus to others? Well, here are some suggestions:

- If you have a computer, once each day you could use the website, "The Hunger Site at the U.N." to have food donated free. This is how it works: Go to http//www.thehungersite.com. All you do is click on "Donate Free Food," and a free donation of a cup or two of food is made by designated sponsors. Those without computers have a variety of relief agencies to choose from.

- Here in our own community, there are many families who depend on food shelf donations to get them by until their next paycheck. And others who, without a little help, would find themselves homeless, even though employed.

There are many needs in our world, close to home and far away. We each need to reach out to help. Find a way that works for you and do it. "Feed them yourselves."

May we all come to love one another and Jesus more as we celebrate this most profound mystery of the Body and Blood of Jesus Christ.

Like so many in our parish community, I also have memories of Fr. Arnold and many of them are one-on-one encounters that have stuck with me.

Two favorites of mine include the time we used to hang arches between the columns on the Southern Worship Space wall during the Passion Play. They were painted the same color as the walls of the church and really looked like they had been constructed that way. After the show one year, Fr. Arnold asked me to leave them up because he liked the look of it and thought it was pretty cool. That was neat. When the plans for the last parish expansion came out, I was wondering if he would insist those arches actually be built and put in there, but they weren't.

My other favorite is the fact that every year, right after auditions and call-backs were done, Fr. Arnold would seek me out, wanting to know the name of the young man I had chosen to play Jesus. Without fail, he knew the kid, the family, and was always very enthusiastic about our selection. "Great kid" he would say. "Great family" and usually he could rifle off their names, where they lived, etc. Of course I always made him promise not to say anything to anyone until we announced the cast in November. It was something he did but didn't particularly like to do because his natural reaction was to congratulate the family and really make a big deal out of it. Having to wait was hard for him, I think, but to his credit, he did it.

Mark Best, Director of 9th Grade Passion Play, Holy Name of Jesus

Live as a Community of Salt and Light

✝

You are the salt of the earth . . .
You are the light of the world.

(Matthew 5:13, 16)

riends, Jesus uses two metaphors several times in today's teachings: salt and light. First let's look at salt. To understand the significance of this metaphor, you need to realize the importance of salt in the daily lives of the people of Israel 2,000 years ago. To them, salt was an irreplaceable item. It wasn't used yet for Margaritas, but it was used to improve the taste of meat and fish, as we use it today. Most importantly, it was used to preserve meat and fish. Just a small bit of salt was needed to prepare and preserve meat and fish, yet that little bit of salt was incomparably important because it changed what it touched. It kept the food from spoiling, from rotting. That's why in Old Testament times, salt was used to season every sacrifice. It was a sign of the permanent covenant between the Lord and his people, a covenant meant to last forever.

What about Jesus' other metaphor, light? Picture a one room dwelling lit by a few small dish-like oil lamps. These lamps did not emit a very bright light, certainly not like that of a three-way Sylvania!* Yet they were indispensable. Without them life would have been dark indeed, especially once the sun set. People wouldn't have been able to see each other in the room. It would have been very difficult, if not impossible, to do any work, read the Torah, or move about.

With these two metaphors, "You are the salt of the earth… You are the light of the world." Jesus identifies all of our tasks as Christians. In fact some years ago, there was a diocesan effort to become a "Becoming a Community of Salt and Light", which came directly from today's Gospel reading from Matthew. So how does that touch us as a parish, as Catholic ministers to each other and our community?

The diocesan explanation for the effort to become a community of salt and light said "The parish is where the church lives." Think about that for a minute. It doesn't say the church is where the parish goes to Mass, or where the annual rummage sale is held, or the place to meet for doughnuts and coffee.

It says the parish is where the church lives. We are the church, and although many of us spend quite a bit of time at Holy Name, none of us actually lives here. So that means the parish is where we live—in our homes, our places of work, and our schools.

The diocesan document went on to say: "The local parish is the most important ecclesial setting for sharing and acting on our Catholic social heritage. We see the parish dimensions in social ministry, not as an added burden, but as a part of what keeps the parish alive and makes it truly Catholic. Effective social ministry helps the parish not only do more, but be more—more of a reflection of the Gospel, more of a worshipping and evangelizing people, more of a faithful community. Work in social ministry is an essential part of parish life."

There are two additional passages in Scripture that are pertinent here. One is from Luke 4:18, which is a summary of Luke's own mission: "The spirit of the Lord is upon me, for He has anointed me, He has sent me to preach good news to the poor. He has sent me to proclaim liberty to captives and recovery of sight to the blind, to let the oppressed go free."

The other is from Matthew 25:24-39, which speaks of how we will be ultimately judged: "Come, inherit the kingdom prepared for you... for I was hungry and you gave me food, I was thirsty and you gave me drink, I was a stranger and you welcomed me, I was naked and you clothed me, I was sick and you visited me, I was in prison and you came to me... as you did it to one of the least of these my brethren, you did it to me."

Living as light and salt means more than just listening to and reflecting on the Gospel. It means becoming more of a worshipping community. And our community worship should not only be done in God's presence in the church, but also in his presence in the world. We must burst forth from church to the world, to all God's people. We must bring Christ-crucified-in-Jerusalem to Christ-crucified-in-the-crossroads-of-our-cities.

We need to work harder at evangelizing. Pope Paul VI explained what that really means in this way: "Evangelization cannot be complete unless account is taken of the links between the Gospel and the concrete personal and social life of men and women. In proclaiming liberations and arranging herself with those who suffer, the church cannot allow itself a whole mission to be limited to the purity of the religious sphere. The church considers it highly important to establish structures which are more human, more just, more respectful of the rights of the person, less oppressive and concise."

To evangelize means to live out our faith so others can see the results of living as a faithful community in Christ. We show how we love God by loving others. We love each human person like we love ourselves. It is the task of Christians to improve the quality of human living, change what we touch, and in doing so preserve our sin-scarred, tear-stained heart from corruption.

You know, time and again, missionaries have found that the most effective form of evangelizing is to provide people with basic human needs. That was really brought home to me not long ago when I got a call in the middle of the night from a single woman on the verge of being evicted from her apartment. I was trying to teach her about Christ's love for her, what a good shepherd He is to us, the salvation He offers us, when she interrupted me. "Are you going to preach to me or are you going to help me?" she asked.

I decided to help her. I had been a priest for 30 some years, and what a lesson she taught me!

Poverty has been an enduring problem for our world. Two thousand years ago, Christ prophesied that the poor would be with us always, and how right he was Today in our land of plenty, one out of every four children grows up below the poverty line.

The Catholic church claims that every human being has a moral right to food, to home, to an education, to a job, and to health care. Friends, these are not mere words. More than any other single organization, the Catholic church feeds the hungry, shelters the homeless, visits the sick, and counsels those who need it. We can be proud of these efforts, but the need for help continues to grow.

Even before it became a country, the United States has welcomed immigrants. We have those marvelous words on the pedestal of the Statue of Liberty: "Give me your tired, your poor, your huddled masses yearning to breathe free. Send these, the homeless, tempest tossed to me." I think I'm safe in saying that nearly all of us at Holy Name are here because of the immigration of previous generations, if not the present. Remember, Jesus instructs us to welcome strangers.

We are commanded to be a light to the world. In a culture imperiled by selfish individualism, where the prize goes to the swift, the shrewd, and the ruthless, we must proclaim a philosophy of promoting the common good. No one lives alone as an island. No one can say to another, "I have no need for you." We proclaim Christ crucified, the foolishness of God that is wiser than human wisdom, stronger than human strength.

How does all this relate to your ministry and mine, specifically with regard to our teaching and preaching? Our whole parish is called to be a community of salt and light, not just a select group of volunteers. As Catholics, we are called to believe, to worship, to love and to reach out to others in love. Love is shown by our actions... the actions that Jesus linked to our salvation: Feed the hungry, clothe the naked, house the homeless, comfort the sick, encourage the Catholic. Remember friends, evangelize with your actions. Simply put, be the salt of the earth. Be a light in this world.

I remember a lot about Fr. Arnold. He always had a smile on his face and was always glad to talk to someone. He enjoyed it when little kids served with him during mass and always thanked the people who helped. He would be in the hallways during school in the morning and would come into our classrooms to talk to us. He would tell us jokes and teach us about God. Fr. Arnold was always fun to be around, and I miss him a lot.

Matt Best, 14, 8th grader BSM,
Holy Name School graduate

Time, Talent, and Treasure

✝

Where your treasure is,
there your heart is also.

(Luke 12:34)

Friends, many people think that stewardship means parish fund-raising. Truthfully, it means so much more than the Church's need for money. Stewardship means being caretakers of everything God has given us through His grace and generosity. This is a large part of our Christian vocation. It's a lifestyle of awareness, accountability, and responsibility for God's gifts. When we truly understand that everything we have comes from God, we feel a strong desire to express our gratitude to Him. We do this through prayer and worship and by sharing our gifts with God and one another. So stewardship, you see, is based more on our need to give, than on the need of God or the Church to receive.

To understand stewardship is to understand the wonderful things of God—creation, redemption, and sanctification. It is understanding that God created us and has given us the world. That He sent his Son to us and saved us, and that He works in us today.

Knowing this is so overwhelming that we want to—no, we need to—take care of and enrich the world. We need to use our gifts—our time, talent, and treasure—to help expand God's kingdom of justice, truth, and goodness on earth.

As Christians, we acknowledge our dependence on God for everything that we have in this life. The Holy Spirit, working in us, causes us to become holy people. When we accept our vocation, we affirm our calling to serve as God's loving stewards. One way that will show itself is in the outreach that we do as a parish. There are many needs in the world, but if we act as stewards, we have the means to meet these needs. All contributions are needed, large and small. Stewardship is the work of the people of God.

When people say they have a good church or parish, they aren't usually referring to the building. What they generally mean is the community. Parish means people. A good parish like ours does many things well. We worship well, we work together well, and we do a good job of contributing time, talent, and treasure for the good of the community.

We all have our functions. My main role as a priest is ministerial. I say Mass, administer the sacraments, preach the Word, give religious instruction, and work to inspire you to love God and your neighbor and live a Christian life. Through baptism you became a part of the lay priesthood. Your job is to assist me with the work of the church—to help with the parochial school, religious education, parish organization, grounds maintenance, parish programs and activities, and so on. I have an obligation to inspire and motivate you to be generous in your support of these things and more. You have an obligation to share your gifts.

Think about your own gifts now. Do you use your time and talent in some way to help further God's kingdom? Do you give a portion of your treasure? These three—time, talent, and treasure— usually go together. People who use their time and talent often become better givers of their treasure. People who give their

110

treasure often feel like better givers when they also donate their time and talent.

Time and talent are important, but special attention, I think, needs to be paid to treasure. Do you realize how interested in money Jesus was? No, He didn't want money for himself, but He paid close attention to how the people around Him got and used money. In fact some Scripture scholars insist that Jesus had more to say about people's relationships to material things than any other single subject.

In truth almost half the parables do address attitudes of possessiveness. Therefore, Jesus' declaration that our hearts are linked to our treasure shouldn't surprise us. It should make us ask ourselves: What rules my life? Who is the king of my heart? It should help us to realize that everything we possess is ultimately God's gift. No matter what our own specific gifts are—great wealth or a widow's mite, intelligence or power, beauty or wisdom, faith or hope, gentleness or compassion, the important thing to realize is that God has gifted each of us somehow. And whatever our gifts are, they are not meant to be held onto, but to be shared with others. We are to use the splendid charisms that we've received, and therein lies the glory of those gifts.

Now that I've probably persuaded you of the need to share, here's the question: How do we know how much we're to give? Well, we get some advice on this from Luke. No other New Testament writer (except James) spoke so bluntly about material possessions. Many of his followers left less than ecstatic because of his emphasis on this subject.

What Luke has to say about how we handle material wealth, though, is somewhat puzzling. We might even ask ourselves: Which, according to Luke, is the real Jesus?

First, Luke describes the radical Jesus, who says:

"Give it all up. Unless you say goodbye to all, you cannot be my disciple."

"You cannot serve both God and money."

"It's easier for a camel to go through the eye of a needle than a rich man to enter the kingdom of God. It is to the poor that the kingdom of God belongs."

Luke also describes the moderate Jesus:

"One may give alms."

To Zaccheus when he promised to give half of what he owned to the poor, "Today salvation has come to this house."

To the crowds He baptized, "If you have two coats, give one to the poor." (Notice, He said, "Just one.")

Will the real Jesus please stand up? Which is it? Give all your wealth away or share just some of it?

Friends, here's the answer. Some of you may need to give it all and follow Him completely. Others may need to share just some of their gifts. You won't know which unless you listen to Jesus. To be able to hear Him on this, you must let absolutely nothing take precedence over Christ in your life. Not million dollar homes nor electronic gadgets, not the presidency nor pastoral life, not profound knowledge nor power, not law firms nor ad agencies, not your book nor stamp collections, not your health nor exercise programs, not even your spouses nor your children. There is danger in any person, possession, goal, career, hobby, or ideal if it, rather than the Lord, becomes the center of your existence. If anything causes Jesus to move lower than the highest place in your heart, then you will not hear His commands on whether to give all or part of what you have.

When you're trying to discern what you're called to give, remember that your spirituality is linked closely to your stewardship. This rephrasing of the beatitudes of Luke might help with your decision:

"Blessed, fortunate, and happy are you who are rich in money and power, time and talent, because you can do much for the poor.

You can lift the yoke of the oppressed but only if you have the mind of the poor, the mind of Christ. Only if you recognize that you may not do whatever you want with what you have. Only if you realize that you are stewards, and whatever you own, you hold in trust. Only if you employ your power for peace, your wisdom for reconciliation, your knowledge to open horizons, your compassion to heal, and your hope to destroy despair."

The bottom line is that everyone must give according to what they have inwardly determined as right. Whether you give all or give some of your gifts, be sure to do it lavishly, not sadly or grudgingly, for God loves a cheerful giver. He does not want to get. He wants you to give, because giving leads to peace, joy, contentment, and growth.

I've learned there are basically three types of givers:

1. The grudge givers who say, "I hate to give."
2. The duty givers who say, "I have to give."
3. The thanks-givers who say, "I want to give."

Which type are you? Which type ought you to be? Friends, figure out where you are when it comes to the beatitudes. All you have to do is look over the last couple of months in your checkbook and your calendar.

Make your giving an act of worship. Don't give because the parish has debt, the roof leaks, or the school needs money. Don't give to have a big number after your name on a published list of donations. If we need to publish names to get the collections up, we have a spiritual problem, not a financial one. When you give, start with God, then take care of everything else. God shouldn't be shortchanged because of inflation. Some people might say to give until it hurts. But, friends, I say, give until it feels good!

A clergyman once went to wealthy businessman to ask for a donation. The businessman, a selfish type, said to him, "As far as I can tell, this Christian stuff is just one continuous give, give, give!"

The clergyman answered with a smile, "Why, thank you, sir, for the best definition I've ever heard for Christianity."

Friends, give, give, give your time, talent, and treasure. And when you do, put your heart into it.

○

teacher: n. a person who teaches, especially as a profession; instructor

Whether Fr. Arnold was giving a "second or third" homily, leading a group of parishioners on a tour of Italy or listening attentively to a Holy Name of Jesus School second grader, he was first and foremost a teaching priest. He taught us about love, forgiveness, lifetime learning, Jesus' love for us and God's infinite wisdom. He taught through example, through his homilies, through his lifetime experience and stories about his beloved parents and siblings.

His description of the elder son in the parable of the Prodigal Son as a "sorehead" helped us identify and root out any overly righteous attitudes we might hold. Homilies given at weddings encouraged young couples to begin their life together by caring for the poor and less fortunate. He told us once that he wanted to be fully aware when he left this earth; he wanted to surrender to God fully—he gave us much to think about and emulate.

Fr. Arnold shared what he learned when a young mother was about to be evicted from her home and sought help from him. He began to lecture her and her retort was: "are you going to lecture me or help me?" Then, the teaching Fr. Arnold shared with the Holy Name parishioners what he learned and exhorted us to welcome and help the poor, not to lecture them. His humility in sharing that experience changed us all.

While Jesus used parables to teach his followers, Fr. Arnold used stories and jokes; he knew hundreds of them. As the Mass was concluding, he always wanted to help us understand one more point, one more example of God's love, one more opportunity to grow and learn. It seemed as though there was not enough time to teach all he wanted us to know.

Our rabbi and teacher, Fr. Arnold Weber, fulfills his vocation with joy, delight and great love for God.

Marcia Copeland, Parishioner of Holy Name of Jesus

Recognize
the Value of Life

✝

Before I formed you in the womb
I knew you, and before you were born
I dedicated you, a prophet to the nations
I appointed you.

(Jerimiah 1:5)

This weekend we are celebrating Pro-life Week. Often the whole month of October is referred to as Pro-life Month. This is a very special time when we rededicate ourselves to the dignity of the human person.

We are blessed at this time to have a pope (Pope John Paul II) who is very outspoken on the issue of having a respect for life. I know of no religious leader—ever—who has been more outspoken on every pro-life issue. This year his focus is on the poor. He always speaks about the unborn.

In a culture like ours I notice some peculiar statistics. A study I read yesterday in the paper said that 85-90% have a very strong devotion to the pope. Yet, only about 45% pay any attention to him. That shows you how tough it is to speak out about the importance of pro-life issues because of this culture.

The behavior of many young people is formed by the culture. That's why it is so important to have someone who has a strong connection with the youth, as Pope John Paul II does, to speak up about pro-life. It also tells us that it is time for you parents to pick it up. Hopefully, the generation of parents now will not let this culture influence our youth so much. I know of no other way to develop a respect for life within our children than by discussing this issue with them. Follow the example of our Pontiff, especially in the area of the unborn.

The issue of pro-life encompasses all areas of life—the unborn, the elderly, the poor, etc. For me, abortion is the most important issue. It makes me weep to think that a country having Christian roots could end up making abortion legal. I can only wonder what our Lord would say to us about legalizing the murder of the unborn. In my opinion, any country that allows over a million abortions each year is bound to become weak.

Having said that, we must be careful not to get stuck on just that one issue. Having respect for life means that we recognize the value and dignity of every living person, from the moment of conception until the moment of their natural death. This includes the most vulnerable people in our society such as the physically handicapped, the mentally handicapped, the elderly, the unborn, and the poor.

In the past I have asked parishioners to take a look at their notion of who God is, what love is, what the sacrament of marriage means, who a child is, and for what purpose we are created. All of these interconnected concepts have to be understood. Once we realize that all comes from God, our Creator, (and that we were created to love and serve God) we can see why there has to be great reverence for the dignity of every single individual from conception until death.

Today, I want to look at the respect for life issue as it relates to life, to love, and to the law.

Life

First, we'll take a look at the issue of life and how we define a life as value. In the United States I see a paradox. On the one hand we are constantly striving to improve the quality of life. We try to improve our healthcare services. We try to increase our educational efforts. We try to build bigger and better entertainment facilities. We have protests to end war and campaigns to improve the environment.

And yet on the other hand, the threat to the existence of the most vulnerable people in our society has increased. In our country it seems that we want to improve the quality of life for those who appear to be "useful." Somehow, we have linked quality of life to our perceived usefulness in life. This view reflects the totalitarian ethic of "Only what is useful is good." This mentality completely ignores the innate dignity of the person as they are created in the image and likeness of God. A bishop once said that one of the dangers of the technological society is the tendency to adopt a limited view of man; they see man only for what he does. Such a tendency overlooks the source of man's dignity and value—that he is made in the image of God.

Friends, we need to ask ourselves, "How do we see life?" Do we value every life knowing that God has created each and everyone of us out of love? Do we value life even if a pregnancy comes at a time that may not be convenient for us? Do we only place a value on the lives of those we deem useful? These are questions each of us needs to answer in our hearts.

There's a story that you've heard before about the auction sale at the music store. One item was to be auctioned off. It was an old,

117

broken violin. They priced the violin at $5.00. Bidding only brought the price up to $10.00. Then a man stepped up and took the violin out of the case. He tightened the strings and began to play. While he played, the crowd grew quiet. When he had finished, the bidding started again. Guess what. The violin sold for $3,000.00.

Anyone whose life has been influenced by Jesus understands this parable. When the master's hands have been laid upon us, our value goes way up. God is our master, and He has laid His hands on us. In fact God has laid His hands upon every single human being. Because of the Master's touch, we all have possibilities yet to be fulfilled. I wonder, if we truly believed this, if we would have so many problems with pro-life in our culture today.

Love

The next issue I want to talk about today is love. I want us to consider whether or not we can truly say that we love all of God's children.

I read a story the other day about a boy named Joseph. Joseph was the older of two siblings, yet he was born mentally retarded. Joseph had a younger brother named Zack. When comparing the two boys, it was very clear to see the limitations that Joseph had because of his mental capabilities. The father of the boys often noticed the difference between his sons and would ask himself, "What have I done to deserve this slow, retarded child?" Many times, the father commented out loud about Joseph's lack of value, his low place in the family, his meaningless place in society. One evening, the father was sitting at the table. He was asking himself over and over again, "What can that boy do? What will Joseph ever be able to do?" Suddenly, he saw the door burst open. Joseph came in scratched, bruised and bleeding. "What happened?" his father asked. The younger brother responded, "Some big bullies were throwing rocks at me down the street. Joseph saw them and came running to help me. He stood in front of me and protected me from the stones.

I'm so happy I have such a loving brother." The mother turned to the father, "Now do you see?" she asked. "Now you know what Joseph can do. He can love."

Love gives an indefinable quality to life. Love enables a person to live life fully. Love gives value to every life. Let us ask ourselves whether or not we recognize the value in our neighbor and love them as Christ has asked us to.

Law

Finally, I want to say a few words about the respect for life issue as it relates to the laws of our country. Friends, in legalizing abortion, the United States Supreme Court was wrong. This decision goes against the very teaching of natural law and the common law. We as Catholics must reject this decision.

I think it might be helpful for us to understand what the Church teaches us about natural law and common law, and the basic rights we have as children of God. The Catechism of the Catholic Church tells us that natural law extends to all men and expresses the dignity of the person. Likewise, the Catechism explains that the "common good" is "the sum total of social conditions which allow people, either as groups or individuals, to reach their fulfillment more fully and more easily." It goes on to say, in the very next sentence, that "The common good concerns the life of all." (CCC 1955, 1906)

From the very birth of our country, American Catholics did not have to fear that its government would do anything to oppose the common good or the natural law. In the early years of our country, our churches could stand with conviction knowing that, in the USA, God and country would stand together. Faith and patriotic obedience were complimentary virtues.

Two hundred years later we know that this is no longer the case. We recognize that the American government is able to oppose itself to the natural law and to defending the common good. Today we can understand why the bishops would state that "Whenever a conflict arises between the law of God and the human law, we are held to follow God's law."

And that brings us here today. How does all of this affect us? If we open the newspaper on any given day of the week, we can see how the most basic of all human rights, the right to live, is being threatened at nearly every stage of the life cycle. Abortion and embryonic stem cell research threaten the life of the child from the moment of conception. Euthanasia threatens life, and the dignity of life, at the end of the life cycle. So called "mercy killing" threatens those people, (of any age and any physical condition) who society deems to be living a life of little or no value. Friends, each one of us should be advocates of life, love and law. Is this totalitarian ethic of "life is only of value if we can observe its usefulness" part of our beliefs? Is the concept of loving a person because of what he does infringing upon our understanding that we all have value because we are children of God? Do we work to change laws that legalize the killing of the most innocent and vulnerable of God's people in our society—those who have no voice?

We, in this parish, must look within ourselves to see how we respect life—all life. Do we respect children? Do we respect people with handicaps, illnesses and deformities? It is the duty of every single person in this parish to fight for pro-life in all aspects. Pray for our leaders. Pray that the hearts of our people will be turned toward having a respect for all life. And to you parents, talk to your children. Begin the discussions at a young age. It's up to us to influence the culture—rather than letting the culture influence us and our children.

Role Models for the Active Christian

✝

Jesus

Mary

Ourselves

Our Mothers

Our Fathers

Who do you say that I am?

✝

When Jesus went into the region of Caesarea Philippi He asked His disciples, "Who do people say that the Son of Man is?" They replied, "Some say John the Baptist, others Elijah, still others Jeremiah or one of the prophets." He said to them, "But who do you say that I am?"

(Matthew 16:13–15)

The noted English writer, G.K. Chesterton, was once playing a quiz game with some friends. One of the game questions was, "If you were shipwrecked and alone on a deserted island, what one book, above all, would you wish to have with you?" One of the players immediately said, "The Bible." He then gave a very pious reason for his selection. Another answered, "A volume of Shakespeare," and gave

122

a very learned reason for wanting Shakespeare. Chesterton said, "Well, if I were allowed just one book on that deserted island, I would choose a one volume manual of instruction for amateur boat builders." Chesterton was a very practical person.

Our relationship with Jesus needs to be practical as well. We need to make certain that we are doing the right things, not just saying the right things. The more we get to know Jesus, the more we will understand what the "right things" are for us to be doing. Then we will be able to put our faith into practice.

So who is this Jesus that we are meant to follow? In the early 1900's, theologians and catechists studied the Bible in an effort to answer this question. Then, in 1971, Jesus Christ appeared on the cover of Time magazine—twice (June 21 and October 25). He was Jesus Christ the Superstar. We've seen bumper stickers that read "Jesus is Lord" and "Honk if you love Jesus". This all became part of what was known as the "Jesus Movement."

Today we find ourselves still asking, "Who is this Jesus? Is He a mystery? Is He a superstar? Is He the leader of a movement?" This man whose birth affected the calendar system of the entire world; this man who was the answer to the greatest love story ever written; this man who is our Savior: Who is He?

There's a story about a little boy who was getting a dog for his birthday. His parents brought him to the pet store and said he could pick out the puppy he wanted. There were a lot of puppies, but one in particular caught his eye. This puppy was wagging its tail very enthusiastically. When asked why he chose that puppy to be his own, the boy answered, "Because I wanted the one with the happy ending."

If we, too, want to have a happy ending, we have no choice but to accept the truth that Jesus is our Lord and Savior. Beyond that, to get a better understanding of who our Lord is, I'd like to share some thoughts with you on who He is to me.

Jesus As Teacher

I'd like to tell you a story, about a young man. He was rather shy but liked a girl at work. He wanted to ask her out on a date. He finally mustered up the nerve to ask her, and to his surprise she said, "yes."

Well as the day of the date approached, the young man became nervous and wondered what he could do to make certain their conversation would flow smoothly. He decided to ask one of his high school teachers for some help. The teacher said to the young man, "When you can't think of anything interesting to say, try one of these three topics: food, family and philosophy. If you can't find any common ground in the subject of food, then move on to the subject of family. If that one doesn't work, then move on to philosophy."

Well on the night of the date, the young man went to her house to pick her up. When she got into his car, he immediately became tongue-tied. Then he remembered: food. "Do you like eggs for breakfast?" the young man asked. "I hate eggs," she replied. "Okay," he thought, "I'd better move on to family."

"How's your brother?" he asked.

"I don't have a brother."

Well, now he was down to his last subject area, and they had barely gotten out of her driveway. Philosophy.

"If you had a brother, do you think he'd like eggs?"

"Take me home," she replied.

Well the young man in this story could have benefited from some more coaching. Maybe a different teaching technique. Without question, Jesus was a teacher. But, He was different kind of teacher. Jesus understood and proclaimed the spirit of the law that went far beyond the Pharisees' teachings that focused on the letter of the law. This created a great deal of controversy. Jesus was not a "go with the flow" kind of teacher. He knew how to take a stand, and He did. He also knew how to teach. He used sermons (the Sermon on the Mount), parables, miracles, questions and challenges to teach to those who would listen. Jesus was the Bread of Life; the Light of the World, the Good Shepherd, the Way, the Truth, and the Life; and He was a good human being.

Jesus As King

Jesus was a different kind of ruler and judge as well. His kingdom was not of this earth, and He judged with mercy. Jesus ruled with love, truth and justice. He wanted to build His kingdom, but I believe He wants us, too, to help Him build it.

Jesus As A Holy Man of God

As a Holy man of God, Jesus lived as He preached. Jesus was real. He observed the Jewish traditions, He fasted, and he even went on spiritual retreats: to the desert, in the garden, and on the mountain. Above all, though, Jesus prayed. And He did all of this with a spirit of love and commitment to God.

Jesus As Liberator

Jesus brought with him a new theology. He came with the new law and a New Kingdom. Jesus taught us to love God and our neighbor. This was a radical idea back then. Jesus came for the sinners and the poor. Jesus came to set us all free from the bonds of sin. The prodigal son, the adulteress, and the good Samaritan: In every case, Jesus was the champion of love. He had a love for all people, especially the poor and the sinners. If we want to deepen our love for the poor, we must first begin by having a stronger love for Jesus.

Jesus As Our Brother

One hundred-sixty times in the New Testament, Christians are referred to as brothers. Jesus was our brother. He was human. And it is through His humanness that He came to understand our suffering, our temptations, and our struggles. As a man Jesus suffered, Jesus was tempted, and Jesus struggled. Jesus is our brother, and He asks us to love each other as He has loved us.

Friends, the Jesus we prepare for and become one with was a teacher, a ruler, a holy man. Jesus was a liberator and a brother. And practically speaking, Jesus is our Lord. I would also like to add that Jesus is our friend. And, as with any friendship, you need to spend time with Him to cultivate the relationship. This week, my challenge for all of us is to spend time with Christ every day. Ten minutes a day. Pray and get to know Jesus. Get to know Him as teacher, ruler and liberator. Become acquainted with Him as brother and friend. Accept Him as your Lord and Savior.

○

I developed a close relationship with Fr. Arnold during the 12+ years I was the sole deacon at Holy Name of Jesus. During that time I was equally touched by his homilies as well as his pastoral dedication to the people he served both inside and outside the parish—in particular, his concern for the poor and oppressed as Jesus notes in Scripture. (Mt. 25:31, 46)

I knew him to be always available to reach out to people's needs on a 24/7 basis. He even had an extension phone next to his bed so he could keep this 24/7 commitment.

One memory I have of Fr. Arnold is visiting him in the emergency room after he had suffered a recurrence of an intestinal problem. My initial thought upon seeing him was that he was sure to be in the hospital for the weekend. But not Arnold! He said, "Joe, go and get my appointment book so we can take care of the weekend activities." It's hard to believe, but he talked the doctors into releasing him so he could preside at two weddings and all of the weekend masses!

I can also remember him saying, "Joe, I've been asked to do a talk on burnout. Joe, there is no way for me to talk about burnout. For me, there is no such thing as burnout when you're doing the Lord's work."

Arnold's homilies had a unique, heart touching method that led people to want to become active, practicing Christians dedicated to Christ. And he walked his talk by personally living out the faith, love and personal service he preached. Former Archbishop Roach summarized it well when he told a group of us that if he had a few more like Arnold Weber, his job would be much, much easier!

Deacon Joe Wierschem

How Jesus Looked at People

✝

"When He disembarked and saw
the vast crowd, His heart was moved
with pity for them, for they were
like sheep without a shepherd; and
He began to teach them many things."

(Mark 6:34)

I t is impossible to understand the life and work of Jesus without taking serious account of His attitude toward people. This is one of the most distinctive things about Him. Every time I read the Gospel stories, I cannot escape the impression of His high regard and deep reverence for human personality.

Those of us who think of ourselves as His followers usually describe His attitude toward people by simply saying He loved them. That is a true statement but doesn't really tell us much. Love is a very broad word and can be expressed in many different ways. Anger, for example, can be just as real an expression of love as affection. Today I want to consider some specific ways in which Jesus related to people. My reason for doing this is two-fold: first, it will give us some insight into what He thinks about us. Second, it will give us guidance as we try to relate to one another.

Today's Gospel reading tells of a time when Jesus organized His 12 Apostles into teams of two and sent them on a mission of preaching and healing. The details of this story are sketchy, to say the least. Mark doesn't tell us very much, but enough that we can gain some understanding of how Jesus looked upon people.

People Are Co-workers

The first and most obvious truth is that Jesus saw His disciples as co-workers. Jesus believed with total commitment that He was born to do the work of God. Being convinced of this, His first order of business was to recruit some helpers. The ones He recruited were people—nothing more, nothing less.

Many of us think of the Apostles in images that are bigger than life. We call them "Saint Peter, Saint Andrew, Saint John," and so on through the entire list. But that is not how their contemporaries saw them, and that is not how they saw themselves. They were just men. They were not even polished men. Not a single one of them had a halo around his head. Nevertheless, Jesus looked upon them as helpers in doing the work of God.

The idea of people as co-workers with God has a long and rich Biblical history. It goes all the way back to the story of creation. In the book of Genesis, we are told that God planted a garden and entrusted Adam and Eve to care for it. It was a partnership, a joint venture. God planted the garden, the man and woman took care of it. They were co-workers.

I also want to point out that Jesus called women as well as men to be co-workers. This was a radical idea back then. Jewish men at the time were very concerned about their reputations and made sure not to be too friendly with women. Jesus demonstrated no such caution or fear. It wasn't that He was indifferent to His reputation, but that it was not His chief concern.

For example, in one Gospel story, Jesus is seated at dinner in the home of a prominent Pharisee, when a woman comes in and begins washing His feet. This was a potentially scandalous situation, as everyone knew she was a sinner. Jesus accepted the woman's touch, despite the risks, because when He looked at her, He didn't see a sex object or a second-class citizen. He saw a full-fledged person with all her needs and possibilities. He treated her openly and honestly and with respect. That's the key word—respect.

The Scriptures tell us that many women—Mary Magdalene, Joanna, Susanna, and many others—accompanied Him as He moved from place to place. The women were with Him at the end also. In fact, the first person to exclaim that Jesus was gone from the tomb was a woman.

Both men and women are called to be co-workers, and today, it is our turn to be the co-workers—yours and mine. We have both the privilege and the responsibility to see ourselves in that same light. Christ has chosen us just as surely as He chose the original twelve. He has sent us out just as He sent them out. Our mission in life is to share His love with our generation. Like Abraham, Moses and the prophets, Mary, Jesus and the Apostles, we are co-workers with God. Knowing that we are co-workers for Christ's Kingdom should fill us with a zeal to dive into the Gospels and begin sharing the Good News with others. It should, as they say, "put a fire in our belly."

And yet there are people who do not do this. They don't have the drive or the energy to go into the Gospel and make Jesus known to others. Do you know who does have this drive, however? The children. When I walk into a classroom of the faith formation students or spend some time with the Holy Name School children, I see such a love and hunger for our Lord. It's beautiful. We adults need to have that same desire. After all, we're co-workers for Christ.

People Are Both Good and Evil

Jesus had another view of people, which we also need to keep in mind. He saw them as a strange mixture of good and evil. Before sending His Apostles out, He gave them a sermon to preach. The name of that sermon was "The Need for Repentance." The Apostles were instructed to preach that sermon wherever they went, because everyone needed to repent.

Jesus warned the Apostles that some people would receive their message, while others would refuse it. That's to be expected when your audience is a mixture of good and evil. But the real irony was the Apostles themselves. They, too, were a part of that same good and evil mixture. If they had ever forgotten that, their usefulness as co-workers with God would have come to an end. You and I need to remember the same thing about ourselves. We are all a mixed bag.

There's a book that most of us studied during junior high English. It's one of the most powerful novels Charles Dickens ever wrote and is called *The Tale of Two Cities*. The story begins with these well known words: "It was the best of times, it was the worst of times. It was the age of wisdom, it was the age of foolishness. It was the epoch of belief, it was the epoch of unbelief. It was the season of light, it was the season of darkness. It was the spring of hope, it was the winter of despair."

These beautiful words not only describe that period of history that we call the French Revolution, they are also a good description of the condition of our hearts: the best and the worst, wisdom and foolishness, belief and unbelief, light and darkness, hope and despair all wrapped up together in one life.

Jesus sees all people, including you and me, as sinners in need of repentance. But He also sees us as savable sinners, otherwise He would not call us to repentance. The Prodigal Son was a sinner, a selfish young man who cared for no one but himself. But he was a savable sinner.

That is how Jesus saw people—a strange mixture of good and evil, but each with the potential of becoming a co-worker with God. He looked at everyone through eyes of love. I'd also like to add that, not only did Jesus love people, He liked people. Jesus was not a lonely and isolated person who needed no one but Himself and God. He could live that way when it was necessary, but He also needed people. Jesus was a people person. He enjoyed sharing meals with them. Barbara Streisand used to sing a song that said, "People who need people are the luckiest people in the world." Jesus was one of those people.

People Are Lost and Need Someone to Guide Them

A third truth is that Jesus looked at people with sympathy. Do you remember in Matthew's Gospel when Jesus preached to the crowd of 5,000? Afterward, Jesus was really tired so He and His disciples took a boat to the other side of the Sea of Galilee to get away from the crowds. But when their boat arrived on the other side of the lake, a crowd of people was already there. Most of them were the same people He had left behind on the other side. Jesus could have been irritated, but He was not. Mark's gospel tells us that "He pitied them, for they were like sheep without a shepherd."

Jesus taught His disciples to live by the Golden Rule: "Do unto others as you would have them do unto you." To follow this principle, we need to have a little imagination. We must place ourselves in the position of the other person and try to understand what is going on in their heart and mind.

If you and I could go home with people for a few days and see where they live, how they live and what is taking place in their lives, we would probably be more understanding than we are now. I don't remember who said it, but it is sound advice, "Be kind, be gentle because everyone you meet is having a hard time." Even everyday life can be challenging. Jesus looked upon people sympathetically.

Everyone Has Possibilities

Finally, Jesus looked upon people positively. He saw possibilities in people that others did not see. This was the genius of Jesus as He dealt with people. He saw possibilities in everyone. A Prodigal Son had the possibility of coming home. A despised Samaritan had the possibility of being a good neighbor. An unstable Simon Peter had the possibility of becoming a rock. Jesus saw the ultimate potential in everyone.

Friends, we have been talking about how Jesus looked at people. What we need to keep in mind, though, is how He looks at us and how we should look at one another. Jesus looks at us through the eyes of love. He considers us co-workers in the Kingdom of God. Jesus is sympathetic and can see the potential in all of us. This, my friends, is how we are to look at one another. We must look at our neighbor through the eyes of love. We must be sympathetic with one another. And, we must recognize that we all have potential, because we are all called to be co-workers in the Kingdom of God.

○

I remember how Fr. Arnold used to hand out the spark plug to people in the community. He would hand it out to people that helped the community run, like a spark plug helps a car run. I also remember how he included the little kids in all of his homilies. He would have the kids come up and sit on the altar steps, while he gave his homilies. Then a couple of years later I started to be an altar server, and it was fun to serve with Fr. Arnold because he would help you if you forgot something and was nice to serve with. I miss Fr. Arnold not being at Holy Name, and I hope that he comes back to visit soon.

Nick Best, 7th grader at Benilde-St. Margaret's,
Holy Name School graduate

Tell It Like It Is

†

For God so loved the world
that He gave His only Son, so that
everyone who believes in Him might not
perish but might have eternal life.

(John 3:16)

The words that we have heard today have been quoted more often, preached about more often and prayed over more often than almost any other words in history. Friends, the words in the Gospel today, John 3:16, tell it like it is.

Yes, "God so loved the world that He gave His only Son, that whoever believes in Him may not die, but may have eternal life." God did not send the Son into the world to condemn the world, but that the world might be saved through Him.

These are beautiful words to be heard in our hearts. They are the center of the Good News.

And it is from these words that we know that God loves us. Indeed, He loves us so much that He gave His son—and the Son has orders to save the world.

If there is anything like Irish pride, Polish pride, German pride, Spanish pride, etc., today that pride is humbled before God. God loves us not because we are Irish, Polish, German, Spanish, Italian or sixth generation American. He loves us because God is Love. And He has enough love for all. His love is not a bonus for being "good". God's love is freely given.

The central theme in our religion, pictured both in the Old Testament and the New Testament, is that God is love. That message is stated clearly and concisely in today's Gospel. However, God's love is hard to comprehend. How do we explain God's love? Let's start by taking a closer look at God's love.

Universal love

First, God's love is universal. This was a difficult concept for Nicodemus to understand. He couldn't imagine that God could love anyone outside of the Jewish faith and nationality. Friends, we shouldn't be too critical of Nicodemus until we understand where we are at. We can sing "God Bless America" with great gusto. Could we also sing "God Bless the World" with that same enthusiasm?

There is a children's Bible song that addresses this point beautifully:

> *"Jesus loves the little children*
> *All the children of the world.*
> *Red and yellow, black and white,*
> *They are precious in His sight.*
> *Jesus loves the little children of the world."*

Personal love

A second important characteristic of God's love is that it is personal. God loves each of us personally. He loves you and He loves me. In John 3:16, John spoke of God's love for the world, and then he switched to the singular pronoun.

…That whoever believes in Him may not die…

God loves the whole world, and He loves the individual. Similarly, a parent loves the whole family, as well as each member of the family as an individual.

Some of Jesus' parables emphasize the personal quality of God's love. The shepherd looked for the *one lost* sheep. The father lost *one prodigal son.*

God's love is so inclusive that it embraces the entire world. At the same time, it is so specific that He cares about just one person—you.

Redemptive love

Finally, God's love is not a sentimental affection. His is a strong, saving and redemptive love.

"For God did not send His Son into the world to condemn the world, but that the world might be saved through Him." John 3:17

He came to save the world. But, He specifically states, "whoever believes in Him avoids condemnation." If we believe in Christ, we are saved.

Three points to remember: God's love is universal. It is personal. And it offers salvation.

It may help to remember that Jesus referred to God as "Father." There are all kinds of fathers: good, bad, and indifferent. Good fathers can be demanding at times. Likewise, we can't share in His fellowship on loose, easy terms. God isn't "somebody up there who likes me." Rather God wants the best for you and expects the best from you. And that is a Father who cares.

Our Love for Christ

Before I close today, I'd like us to take a look at our love for Jesus. One of the greatest privileges for me as a priest is to preside over the First Communion for the young people of our parish. In the young people, I see such a hunger for our Lord. They have such a a desire to have a stronger faith and to get to know the Lord Jesus Christ. Hopefully, the adults won't kill that hunger. I'm serious about this. That is why I encourage you to bring your children to church every week. Let the children learn about Jesus. Let the children receive Jesus. Let the children become strong in the Lord.

What a joy it is for me to have more than 3,000 children who are under the age of 18 years in this parish that I can help to find the Lord Jesus. Of course, this ultimately falls to the responsibility of the family. I hope that you will help your children to make a commitment to Jesus in a culture that's tough to handle.

Friends, God loves you. He loves you so much that He gave you His only Son so that you would be freed from sin. Let us never forget this love that God has for each of us. And, let us never forget to love the Lord.

I'd like to close this homily by having all of you recite together with me John 3:16.

"For God so loved the world that He gave His only Son, so that everyone who believes in Him might not perish but might have eternal life."

Mary our Mother

✝

*Behold, I am the handmaid
of the Lord. May it be done to me
according to your word.*

(Luke 1:38)

*F*riends in Christ, one of our chief needs as people of God
is not necessarily to find somebody who tells us what we
ought to do. We usually know what to do. Rather, what we need is
someone who inspires us to do what we know we should. Someone
who helps us make the journey from our head to our heart. It's a
distance of only about nine inches, but it is a journey that some
never make.

Sometimes a friend can play this inspirational role for us.
Sometimes a spouse, a parent, a priest or a counselor is the
inspiration. As Christians today our rich Catholic tradition offers us
a person of great inspiration as we make our faith journey, Mary, the
Mother of God, Queen of Peace. Mary is a beautiful role model of
making the journey from head to heart particularly well.

As we take a look at Mary's life, we can see three areas where
Mary offers us an example to follow when trying to make this
journey in our own lives.

Faith When Suffering

In the face of suffering, Mary is a beautiful example of how to carry our crosses with faith and grace. Mary's life contained a great deal of suffering. Let's take a look at her circumstances.

First, she gave birth away from home. Most mothers would understand this trial. Then, she delivered her baby in a barn. After the birth, she could not return home because of King Herod's threat to have the baby killed. All of this was just the beginning. When Mary and Joseph brought Jesus to the temple after His birth, as was the Jewish law, Simeon said,

"Behold, this child is destined for the rise and fall of many in Israel, and to be a sign that will be contested. And sorrow, like a sharp sword will break your own heart." (Luke 2:35)

Later in life Mary began to see the words of Simeon come true. When Jesus was just 12 years old, they lost Him for three days— only to find Him teaching in the temple. Of course, the greatest suffering came when Mary watched as her son was crucified.

When we find ourselves suffering, we need to look at Mary. When there's a death in the family, illness, or injustice, we need to try to imitate Mary. The most important lesson Mary teaches us about suffering is how to remain strong in faith. When Mary was faced with suffering, when she herself was given crosses to carry, Mary responded with the beautiful words, "Let it be." Mary said, "Behold, I am the handmaid of the Lord. May it be done to me according to your word."

This act of faith shows us the choice Mary made in the face of incredible suffering. Mary made the choice to become better in life, not bitter in life. When we are given crosses to carry, we too are offered this same choice. We can turn away from God, our friends and our family and turn bitter. Or we can cling to our faith and become a better person through our suffering.

So much suffering today goes wasted. By choosing to carry our crosses with faith and grace, as Mary did, we can turn our suffering into something positive. We can choose to become better. For many years I had been preaching this advice. But, I'll tell you, it's one thing to say it and another thing to do it. This became a reality to me when my brother Otto died. Many of you know that my brother Otto was a priest and teacher at St. John's in Collegeville, MN. He was also my best friend. One night, while out jogging, Otto died suddenly of a heart attack. He was just 52 years old. I can't begin to tell you the loss I felt, still feel today, at not having my brother. It was at this time in my life that I, too, had to make a decision. I could remain angry at God for having taken someone so young, who offered so much to so many. Or, like Mary, I could cling to my faith and carry the cross. I chose to become better rather than bitter.

Spirit of Service

The second area of Mary's life that offers us an example of how to make the journey from our head to our heart is her spirit of joyful service. In the beginning of Luke's gospel, the angel Gabriel appears to her to let her know that she has been chosen by God to bear God's son. This came as quite a shock to Mary. She probably wasn't expecting her life to take this turn. She asked the angel only one question, "How can this be for I do not yet know man?" After that, her next comment was a joyful "yes." As I said earlier, Mary responded with, "I am the handmaid of the Lord," and followed this with her beautiful magnificat praising God.

When we are asked to do the work of God in our lives, do we answer with the same joyful spirit as Mary? Do we find excuses to say "No"? Do we serve God with joy in our hearts, or do we serve Him grudgingly or self-righteously?

Someone once said,

"My life turned around when I stopped asking God to do things for me and asked God what I could do for Him."

That was Mary's spirit. She inspires us to try to serve God joyfully.

Spirit of Prayer

This brings me to my third point about Mary. Mary possessed a spirit of profound prayer. When the shepherds appeared and rejoiced at the birth of her Son, Scripture says that "Mary pondered these things in her heart." Mary had an intimacy in her prayer. She devoted herself to prayer—prayer alone and prayer with the apostles in preparation for the coming of the Holy Spirit.

For Mary, prayer reinforced her faith, and her faith reinforced her prayer. Mary understood that the only way to have true happiness is to give your life over to God. Only when you can say, "Let it be," and believe it in your heart, can you find peace. You might pray, "God, please don't let this happen to me." Or, "Lord, help my 15 year old daughter." Or, "Lord, give faith back to my husband." However, after you've said these prayers can you truly add, from your heart, "Let it be"?

Mother Teresa once said, "Prayer enlarges the heart until it is capable of containing God's gift of Himself." Mary made this happen in the truest sense. In difficult situations we need to look to Mary. Through her faith, her willingness to serve, and her profound prayer, she was able to say "yes" to God again and again.

She said "yes" to the incarnation. She said "yes" to the presentation of Jesus and Simeon's prophesy. Mary said "yes" to finding Jesus in the temple doing His Father's work. She said "yes" to the crucifixion, to the resurrection, and to Pentecost. Through faith, service and prayer, Mary found the strength and trust to say, "yes."

Today, let us ask God to give us the courage, the positive zeal, the love and the peace to imitate Mary in these three ways. Mary will then inspire us to carry our crosses patiently, to serve joyfully, and to pray unceasingly.

To close, I'd like us to say the Hail Mary, together.

Hail Mary, full of grace
the Lord is with thee.
Blessed art thou among women
and blessed is the fruit of thy womb, Jesus.
Holy Mary, Mother of God,
pray for us sinners
now and at the hour of our death.
Amen.

The Value of the
Individual

✝

*"There is a lad here who has
five barley loaves and two fish"*

(John 6:9)

I have always been fascinated by that boy in our reading
today. We really don't know much about him. Most likely he
was a peasant boy, and not too little, or he wouldn't have been too
far from his mother. What we do know is that he happened to have
his lunch with him. It consisted of five barley loaves and two fish.
And he just glides into the Gospel and then he glides right out again.

He reminds us of something we often forget: the importance of
one person.

In many homilies we talk about the Christian ideal of
community. A Christian community should be united in our efforts
to live out our beliefs, but we can't lose sight of the importance of
one single individual.

Think back to that day in John's Gospel. There was a huge crowd
that day, 5,000 men, not counting women and children. One boy

would easily have been forgotten, but the Gospel mentions him. He was important—just as each one of us, you and I, are important.

This boy reminds us of the uniqueness of the individual. Externally he was probably like the rest of the kids there that day. Picture him with his dusty feet, hair uncombed. But he had something the others didn't. He had lunch. And it seemed he was the only one in that huge crowd who did.

He was unique. We need to see that there is something distinctive about every person. In some way each of us is unique. We have an expression in the Western World: "When God made him or her, He threw away the mold." The only thing wrong with it is that it's usually only applied to someone great. Abe Lincoln, John Paul XXIII, Shakespeare, Florence Nightingale, Dorothy Day, Albert Einstein, Mother Theresa. But it's no truer of those famous people than it is of us.

When God made you and me, He threw away the mold, the pattern. You can make a contribution that no one else in the world can and if you don't do it, it won't be done. Think of it, there is no one in all of the world quite like you.

There never has been
There never will be
You are an original
You are unique
You are not a carbon copy
The mold is gone

No one can make the same contribution to this world that you can. That's important in many ways. It's even important in developing community. If you don't use your gifts, you rob the community, you rob yourself, and you even rob Christ. Your gifts are blessings given by God, and you can't afford not use those gifts.

We need to have confidence that we all have something to offer. Never give up on people, and don't judge people easily. We can't tell by looking at a person what's in his or her mind or heart. We don't want to be like the sign I saw in a restaurant in Minneapolis that says, "In God we trust; everybody else pays cash."

I always begin by looking at the good in people and knowing that each one has gifts, and deep down, a good heart.

So we have the uniqueness of each individual. Second, we have usefulness of the individual.

Remember our boy with the loves and fishes? This boy—he saved the day! He had very little, but what he had, he gave. It wasn't easy. Lunch must have been pretty important for him to have come prepared with it. Just think, to get to where this big crowd gathered, he'd have walked halfway around the Sea of Galilee. And I don't think he found a McDonald's along the way. And being the forward thinking kind of kid he seemed to be, he knew he'd have to walk back too. Inside his head that boy must have said: "This is mine," when these men started looking to see who had food. But the boy gave it up.

I don't know why this boy gave up his lunch, unless he had the sensitivity to see that the one asking was the one who gave it in the first place. God asks us the same thing. He asks us to use our talents and to give our possessions. That's not an unreasonable request is it? He gave us those talents and possessions to begin with. If you are a good lawyer, or businessman, or carpenter, or teacher, that comes from the Lord. If you're a good worker, physically strong and mentally alert, God gave you that. If you're a math genius, or an Olympic athlete, God gave you that. An astute woman named Joyce Kilmer once said, "Poems are made by fools like me, but only God can make a tree."

Once we fully get this concept of how great we are, how unique we are, how beautiful we are, we need to move on to another concept: that all of it comes from God. When we understand that, then we know that giving to the cause of Christ is no longer a sacrifice to work for Jesus, it's a privilege. And once we catch the idea of sharing these gifts and talents from God, we will be amazed what God can do with "the little" we have.

The boy, after all, had only a few loaves—and look what Jesus did with that! With one small bucket of lunch, Jesus fed a whole crowd! And even had leftovers!

I have another bread story for you. A man whose wife was out of commission for a while with a badly broken leg decided he would do the cooking while she recuperated. He actually did pretty well at it until one day when he became a little too ambitious. He thought he would bake some bread. As often happens the first time around, he misread the recipe and he put two pounds of yeast into the dough rather than two ounces. After carefully following all the other instructions, he put the dough to rise near the heat and waited. Some time later his wife called from her upstairs bedroom: "Have you put the dough in the oven yet, honey? He replied frantically, "Put it in the oven? I can't even keep it in the kitchen!"

Isn't that just like the New Testament? The New Testament is the leaven of the Word of God, you "can't even keep it in the kitchen." You can't even keep it in the church. It just expands into the world. And isn't that like the multiplication of the loaves? And sometimes that happens when we use our talents too.

Many people hold back because they feel inadequate. They say they have no talent. "What can I do with the little I have?" they ask. Maybe instead they should ask, "What will Jesus do with me?" We give our share, our talents, our abilities, big and small, and the results we leave to God.

I heard a story about a little boy playing in the sand box on a hot day. His father was cutting the grass and called for his wife to bring him a drink of water. She wasn't able to hear over the noise of the lawnmower. The little boy ran into the house, pushed a chair to sink and filled a glass with water. Being a little boy he gets his fingers down inside the glass somehow in the process. He didn't think to wash his hands first, of course, so you can imagine that the dirt washed off into the glass of water. He ran outside and offered the water to his dad. The dad took that glass of water, being very careful not to look too closely at it after noticing the grimy handprints all over it. He drank every drop. Then he looked at the big beaming smile on the boy's face and beamed right back at him. I guess if a man can feel that way about an imperfect gift of a kid, imagine how God feels about our efforts.

You are important to God, friends, and don't ever forget it.

●

Father Arnold still continues to inspire us long after he's been gone from Holy Name of Jesus. He set an example of enthusiasm and love of Jesus and people. Always welcoming and never tired of enjoying life and everyone and everything around him-young and old.

His words to live our life by also stay with us, keeping our priorities in line, God first, spouse, family and then everything else. It's easy to be distracted with daily routines; and so these words can put everything back on track.

We especially liked the cards he had made for Father's Day that said, "If you want to show your children how much you care about them-love their mother!" We shared this with all our friends and family along with many of his little quotable quotes and amusing little stories.

His example, energy, and love of Jesus and those in need still lives on at Holy Name.

Rev. Mr. Dennis & Marilyn Hanson, Holy Name of Jesus

Behold Your Mother

When Jesus saw His mother and the disciple whom He loved standing beside her, He said to His mother, "Woman, here is your son." Then He said to the disciple, "Here is your mother." And from that hour the disciple took her into his own home.

(John 19:26, 27)

Today is Mother's Day. Now it would be a big mistake if this were the only day of the year that we give any consideration to our mothers. It probably is a good idea, though, that one Sunday is set aside to remind us to acknowledge how great our mothers are.

Mother's Day in the U.S. first began in 1872, when Julia Howe—the one who composed the Battle Hymn of the Republic—advocated for a Mother's Day for peace. In 1914, Mother's Day was declared a national holiday. But the tradition of honoring our mothers really goes back a lot farther than the time Mother's Day was put on the U.S. calendar. It actually started back when Moses brought the Ten Commandments down the mountain. Remember, Commandment #4: Honor your father and your mother.

Joseph Cardinal Mindszenty once stated that the most important person on earth is a mother. She doesn't build cathedrals, but she provides a dwelling for an immortal soul. No one can be closer to God than the one who participates so intimately with God in the creation of new life.

Once the children are born, the mother's work really begins. She's usually the one who tends the children and squares things away, especially if there's trouble or bother involved. I see this scene often: The family's in the pew, Dad's holding one of the small kids. After a while, the kid gets restless, and finally begins to cry. Automatically, Dad holds the child out for mother. "Here, you take him!" And she does. Before the kid has actually begun to fuss, her arms are open and ready.

A mother is never on an eight-hour per day or 40 hour per week work shift. She is usually the first one to get in gear in the morning and the last one to fall asleep at night. She's least likely to be the one in the easy chair at home and most likely to be the one pushing a cart in the supermarket any time of the day or night. I don't think most people really ever know all that a mother goes through day after day in the rearing of children.

Here's another example. After a day out in the world, the people in a family often come back home wounded and needy. The husband's boss raked him over the coals, and he sat in a traffic jam for an hour and a half. One kid's teacher blamed him for something he didn't do. Another one lost her homework and had her lunch stolen. The third needs help right now with a project due tomorrow.

Who becomes a one-person intensive care unit for these suffering family members? Yes, it's usually the mother, though she herself might have just gotten home from her job or from the carpool or errand-running two minutes earlier. And she does this at the same time that she makes dinner for the family! Sometimes women are called the weaker sex, but I have my doubts about that.

When there's dissension, Mother is the peacemaker. She defends the weak and guides the strong. She knows how to cook, make costumes, and find lost things. She helps with homework and listens to kids' prayers. And often much of her work goes unnoticed by her family. Or if they do notice, they figure she owes it to them. What really hurts a mother is this lack of appreciation and affection.

Sometimes the children might be assigned a few chores. Usually they don't like this. Once a young boy in a busy family was given a list of tasks to do by his mother. He did the tasks, but when he was done, he left a note by his mother's plate at the table. Here's what it said:

You owe me:

$1.00 for doing dishes

$1.00 for practicing piano

$0.50 for doing my math

Your son

His mom read his note, and put $2.50 in an envelope along with this note:

You owe me:

Nothing for feeding, clothing, and sheltering you for 10 years

Nothing for staying up all night with you when you're sick

Nothing for 10 years' worth of birthday and Christmas gifts

Nothing for being your mother all of your life

Your mom

After the boy read his mother's note, he gave the money back to her. "I never thought of it that way," he told her. Well, he should have thought of it that way. We all should.

Jesus appreciated His mother. One of the very last things that He did on earth was make sure that she would be taken care of when He was gone. He said to John, "Behold your mother." So today, right now, I want you to behold your mother.

Just think, much of what you have in life is there because of this woman: your mother. Even more important, much of who you are has come from her. Largely because of your mother, you know what it's like to love, be loved, and feel worthwhile.

Mothers are like other people. They usually don't mind hard work if they know it's appreciated. They don't mind the time, the inconvenience, the difficulty, so long as they know you care. Mothers don't do what they do for merit. All their efforts can only be explained by LOVE.

So husbands, college and high school students, and young children, appreciate the mother in your family. LOVE her. It helps her be even better at her job.

Husbands: The greatest thing you can do for your children is not to love them more, but to love their mother more. You must be concerned about her and share in her work with the household and family. Teach your children to love her and honor her.

High school and college kids: Make a big effort to be good to your mother. Try not to worry her. If you're out later than usual, call and let her know. It will set her mind at ease. She's concerned about you.

Young children: Thank your mom every day for all the things she does for you.

Yours will be a peaceful home if the mother in your family is loved and appreciated.

A Vocation
Second to None

Then Jesus' mother and His brothers came to Him, but they could not reach Him because of the crowd. And He was told, "Your mother and brothers are standing outside, waiting to see you." But He said to them, "My mother and brothers are those who hear the word of God and do it."

(Luke 8:19-21)

It's Mother's Day, so let's take a close look at the mother of today. She's in trouble. After I get finished with my remarks, I might be, too. All I ask is that you listen to and pray about what I say.

When we think about God, we usually emphasize His image as a father. Rarely do we think about God as a mother or recognize that He possesses both male and female characteristics. But this is so. Most certainly we would agree that we see His reflection in the face of Mary, the mother of Jesus, who became the mother of us all when Jesus presented her to His disciple John, saying, "Behold your mother." My question is this: Don't we also see God's reflection in the faces of many of the busy modern women around us?

Nowadays in our U.S. culture, both the husband and the wife in many families are breadwinners. That is, they both have jobs outside the household. Women who have the sole vocation of wife and mother are all too often seen as relics of the past. People ask: How can a stay-at-home mother be a good role model? What does she achieve? Who is she in her own right? Why doesn't she get a job and work?

Please don't misunderstand me. I'm not here to argue motherhood vs. career. In that complex realm, much depends upon a family's concrete circumstances rather than on abstract principles.

I am not downgrading women with challenging work outside the home – administrative assistants, women CEOs, teachers, Congresswomen, healthcare workers, female heads of state, or women with Wall Street careers. I am certainly not insinuating that motherhood and a career are incompatible. I am, however, stating that there is a need and a call for some women to be 'just' wives and mothers, and the refusal of many people to acknowledge that these women contribute something of great value to society is deplorable.

After all, both women with careers outside the home and those whose careers are inside the home, have been called to the vocation of motherhood. The image of God can be seen in all of their faces.

Today there is much dialogue about the freedom or liberation of women. This is good if it refers to increasing their dignity. It's bad if it means diminishing their dignity or treating them exactly the same as men. Women's liberation should make it possible for all women to grow in confidence and self-acceptance. It should allow them to appreciate and develop their unique and outstanding feminine qualities. It should help them to better and more easily manage their homes and raise their children. It should not dictate that, to be counted, they must work outside the home. It should not mean that they must rearrange these priorities: 1) God; 2) Husband; 3) Children; 4) Work—inside or outside of the home.

No doubt, many injustices existed in the past. Less than a hundred years ago, women couldn't vote or easily get an education or hold property in this country. They couldn't run for public office or serve on a jury.

Today, although it's much better, many double standards and inequities remain, even in our Catholic Church and in the law-making bodies of the government. For example, most laws that directly affect the family unit are still made mostly by men. Certainly issues related to health, education, and welfare could benefit from the input of women, who have a delicate sensitivity to the needs of others.

Women add a special dimension to many places of work. Yet they are often not paid the same as men of equivalent skills. They aren't promoted as often and don't accrue the same benefits and pensions as men because they are usually the ones who must take off work to deal with the needs of the family. The flexible hours and part time work opportunities that many women would prefer are rare and hard to find.

These are the difficulties that relatively affluent well-educated women deal with. What about mothers who are young, poor, and uneducated? Along with bitterness, anger, apathy, and despair, do we see God's reflection in their faces? For they, too, have been called to the vocation of motherhood.

On this day dedicated to mothers, I suggest we recognize the female face of God and celebrate the unique vocation of motherhood by praying. Let's do that now using the four types of prayer that we older Catholics were taught:

Praise

Glory to God for our mothers, those life-givers who let us be born, despite pain and peril to themselves. Glory to God, who has shared with women the divine power of creation. Glory to God for shaping in His image those women who reveal to us the female face of God.

Thanksgiving

Thank you, Lord, for the vocation of motherhood, which is second to none—not to the priesthood nor the presidency, to being a CPA or a CEO. Thank you, Lord, for my own dear 90-year old mother and for all of our mothers. Not only for our existence, but for all that went into mothering us: for taking care of us as infants and children; for tolerating our adolescent antics and moods; for going without so we could have things; for supporting our growth, freedom, and independence; and especially for helping us to become more like Jesus in age, wisdom, and favor with God.

Petition

We pray today for all mothers, but especially for those mothers in the world who are raising their children in poverty, acting as both mother and father, too young to be parents, or living with crime and violence.

Contrition

Forgive us, God, for all that we do individually and as a society that makes it difficult for mothers to raise their children properly. Forgive us for the feminization of poverty in the U.S.: for unequal wages and inadequate training; for unfair divorce settlements and unpaid child support; for the lack of affordable housing and daycare; for domestic violence; and for hateful and condescending attitudes.

Friends in Christ, I suspect that this is a different sort of Mother's Day homily than you usually hear, but I would be less than honest with such an intelligent congregation if I did not reveal to you the image of God as both male and female, father and mother; my own deep delight in the mother I've had for 68 years; and my distress at the misery of millions of women across the world.

I offer this Mass today with deep devotion to all mothers, beginning with my own and reaching down through the decades to so many of you women in this congregation today. For like Mary, the mother of Jesus, you reveal to me the female face of God, and for this, I am eternally grateful.

●

I remember when Father Arnold would come up to the school and say hi to everybody. He would say good morning to the kids as we came upstairs, and then he would come into our classrooms and talk to us. He was always funny and made us laugh. I also remember when he would have the kids come up and sit on the steps to the altar when he gave his homilies. After Mass he would go into the Good Samaritan Center and always eat a donut or get a cookie and say hi to me. He always remembered my name, and he baptized me (although I don't remember that, but I have pictures!).

When the school had a marathon, he would always be there and talk to everybody. He really helped the school with fundraisers and special events. He would always be at church even if he wasn't doing the Mass; he would just walk around and say hi to everybody. At Vacation Bible School, he would always ride around in his "Pope Mobile" and see what we were doing. And he was always happy. These are the things I remember about Father Arnold.

Peter Best, 5th grade, Holy Name of Jesus School

Things Dads
Understand

✝

For all who are led by the Spirit of God are
children of God. For you did not receive
a spirit of slavery to fall back into fear,
but you have received a spirit of adoption.
When we cry, Abba! Father!, it is that
very spirit bearing witness with our spirit
that we are children of God, and if children,
then heirs, heirs of God and joint heirs with
Christ—if in fact, we suffer with Him so
that we may also be glorified with Him.

(Romans 8:15)

*F*or most of us, our dads have been very special. I remember a friend telling me he once wanted to call his father by his first name. He thought it meant that their relationship would take on a more adult tone. His father didn't really object, but he pointed something out to him. He said, "You can call me by my first name if you like. There are hundreds of people who do, but there are only three people in the world who can call me dad."

Dads are important to us, and believe it or not, there are some things almost all dads understand. I would like to share some thoughts with you about that.

Provide More Than a Paycheck

The first is the importance of providing for their family's physical well being. Most dads are aware of the role to provide. And often these days, the dad isn't the sole provider in the family. In fact, it isn't uncommon for the mother to earn more. Nevertheless, most dads are acutely aware of their need to provide for the physical needs of their families.

But the wise father understands that being a provider has never been the most important role of a dad. If a dad spends time with his kids, if he teaches them positive lessons that will last them a lifetime, they will remember those things far more fondly than what kind of car the family drove or how big the house was. How much healthier most kids would be if dads understood that providing for a family involves much more than a paycheck.

Be Models, Not Critics

The second thing that most dads know is that children need models and not critics. We can be more effective not by nagging, but by modeling love, acceptance, and responsibility. This is the way children grow to understand what responsible Christian living is all about. They watch how we handle anger, frustration, and disappointment. They watch how we treat people who are different than us. We can teach them all kinds of positive values here at church, but they will not have much impact if those values are not reinforced at home.

Children Always Need Love and Support

The third thing most dads know is that their children will always need their love and support. Parenting does not end when children enter school or when they finish school. Parenting is a lifetime commitment to always be there in love and support.

Let me share this story with you about an Olympic runner. Several years ago a young track star from Great Britain, Derrick Redman, competed in the Olympics. Derrick was considered a sure bet to win the gold medal in the 400 meter running competition. He got off to a good start. He moved out well ahead of the other runners. But just short of the finish line, Derrick collapsed, screaming in pain. He had ruptured his Achilles tendon 50 yards before what would have been a certain victory.

But that's not the end of the story. Out of the stands jumped Derrick's father. He lifted his injured son off the ground, put the athlete's arm around his shoulder and took his son to the finish line. Derrick didn't win the gold medal, but he did finish the race, thanks to his dad.

That's what being a dad is about. Most of the dads I know understand that because most of the dads I know go to church, which makes a difference. The dads know they have a commitment to their children that goes beyond putting a roof over their heads. They understand that they have a spiritual commitment to their children and they take it seriously. They try to model Christian values and offer ongoing support and encouragement.

Now, it's not easy being a good father any more than it is to be a good mother or a good son or a good daughter. Family life always has its tensions, even in the best of families. In thinking about how to advise fathers to follow Christ's teachings, I see quite clearly three things that Christian dads ought to do.

Love as God Loves

First of all, Christian fathers ought to love as God loves. The word Jesus used in talking to God was one of intimacy: "Abba", which means 'Daddy.' In doing this, Jesus helps us see God as a loving father who is not somewhere far removed from us, but someone who knows us well and loves us unconditionally. God does not seal Himself away from us. He is not unavailable, unyielding, or uncaring. Rather He is Abba, who sees every sparrow fall from the sky, who counts every hair of our head. Think of that. It is really a radical view of God. It's one of closeness and deep caring.

Unfortunately, in the past, our fathers were not easily able to express the depth of their caring. Therefore, many of today's fathers have had no models for showing affection to their children, affirming their children, or encouraging their children. Perhaps their own fathers were distant and remote, and society hasn't always provided good models. I see this changing somewhat in the younger fathers, but it doesn't happen overnight.

A United States senator had this to say about her father: "My father would come home and say, 'You did well, but could you do better?' I would come home from school with a good grade and he would say, 'Must have been an easy assignment.'"

You could say that her father's conditional expressions of love probably helped make her the over-achiever she is today, but don't you think that it also exacted an emotional price?

I have another story about a father who was scant with praise. Lee Strobel is an immensely gifted man who has had at least four successful careers: as an award-winning journalist for the "Chicago Tribune"; as a teaching pastor at two of the largest churches in the country; as a best selling Christian author; and host of "Faith Under Fire" on PAX television. As a boy growing up, and then as a man pursuing his careers, Lee secretly wished that his father would affirm him more. He longed to hear the words, "Son, I'm proud of you." But he never heard them.

In 1979 Lee's father died. At the funeral many of his father's friends and business associates came up to shake Lee's hand and tell him the same thing: how proud his father was of him. According to these men, Lee's father had bragged about him all the time. What a bittersweet moment it was for Lee to hear those precious words from his father—after the man's death. What a difference it would have made if his father had said them while he was alive. Tell your kids you love them and tell them often.

You know in my wedding homilies I usually talk about how our priorities in life should be. And this is what I say: God comes first. Then your spouse, then the kids, and then work.

And for Father's Day, I'd like to add a quote from Reverend Theodore Hesburgh, former president of University of Notre Dame. He says that "the most important thing a father can do for his children is to love their mother." What your children need is not that you love them more, but that you parents love each other more.

Reflect God's Character

A Christian father ought to reflect God's character. I already mentioned the need for good role models, and this is especially important in helping to build character. An Internet poll asked respondents to answer the question, "Which one family member is best identified as your role model?' The father was listed as the top role model in most families, with mother coming in a close second.

One Minute Can Change a Life is a book by Steve Goodier. In it he tells about tennis great, Arthur Ashe, who was known for leadership on and off the court. Ashe was 17 years old and playing in a tournament in West Virginia when a defining incident in his life occurred. As was often the case at the time, he was the only African-American contestant in the tournament.

One night some of the kids trashed a cabin. They absolutely destroyed it and then decided to say that Arthur was responsible. The newspapers picked up the story, Arthur denied any involvement, but the boys persisted in laying the blame on Arthur. Ashe said that the worst part of it was worrying about how his dad would react. After putting it off as long as possible, Arthur finally called his dad. His father had already heard about the vandalism; and had only one question for Arthur. "Arthur Junior," he asked, "all I want to know is, were you mixed up in that mess?" Arthur replied, "No, Daddy, I wasn't."

His father never asked about it again. Arthur learned that day why he had always been encouraged to tell the truth. There would come a time when he must be believed and this was such a time. Because he had already earned his trust and respect, he knew his father believed him. From that day on he was determined, above all else, to live a life of integrity.

Arthur Ashe learned about character from his father—the way most children learn from their parents about character. Ashe was a great tennis player, one of the best we've ever known. But in his book *Days of Grace*, Ashe says something along the lines of: "My life has been a failure if all I'm remembered for is being a tennis player." No one would consider Arthur Ashe a failure in any sense of the world. He was known for his work in helping to open doors for African Americans in tennis, other sports, and elsewhere in our culture.

Reflect God's Gentleness and Strength

Along with love and character, Christian fathers need two other important qualities: gentleness and strength. They ought to reflect God's gentleness and at the same time God's strength. Obviously, we're not talking about physical strength, but emotional strength and spiritual strength.

Real dads have emotional strength and spiritual strength. They are gentle, yet strong, in the same way that Christ was gentle, yet strong. My guess is that there are some people in this room who grew up somewhat afraid of their dad. Perhaps your dad embodied a style of parenting that confused strength with stoicism. Perhaps your dad was relatively absent except when discipline needed to be meted out—and then it was with an iron hand.

For some of you, this awkward relationship with your dad may have affected your relationship with God. You see God as a harsh, remote God. If that is your experience, listen again to the words of our scripture lesson: "For all who are led by the Spirit of God are children of God. For you did not receive a spirit of slavery to fall back into fear, but you have received a spirit of adoption. When we cry 'Abba!' (Daddy) Father!' it is that very spirit bearing witness with our spirit that we are children of God."

That is the God we worship—and that is the God we should reflect as parents—loving as God loves—living as people who reflect God's character—people of gentleness and strength.

And now, all you children can come forward and get a flower out of one of the vases on the altar and give it to your dad. When you do, remember to tell him you love him. There was a beer commercial that ran on TV a while back that featured the perfect punch line for this occasion: Fathers, for all you are and do, this Bud's for you!

The following are excerpts from other Father's Day homilies.

I saw a bumper sticker a while ago that seems appropriate to mention today. It said, "Any man can be a father. It takes a special man to be a daddy." This is a pretty sweet way of pointing out that it takes more than biology to be a father.

Fathering takes a lot of time, but often not great chunks of time. Let me give you a few examples. How much time does it take to touch a shoulder or give a hug? How long does it take to say, "Way to go!" How long does it take to say, "I noticed that you were nice to your sister."

Kids don't communicate by appointment only. Just being there and showing up counts for a lot with kids.

****

In the Lord's Prayer, Jesus taught his disciples to say "Our Father." Jesus' favorite name for God was "Abba," which means Daddy. Jesus first recorded sentence was, "Did you not know that I had to be in my Father's House?" And the last sentence He spoke came from the cross, "Father, in to your hands I commend my spirit." In between, He used the word over and over, teaching that God is "Daddy."

****

If God is Father, then fathers ought to be God-like. A father is a man who cares about children, whether they are his own or not. They are children who belong to God. Today, all fathers should care about all children, not just their own. A father is a man who is committed to children. To care about someone is nothing but an emotion until it becomes a commitment.

****

I ran across the results of an interesting study some years back. A West German medical magazine reported the results of a life insurance study. This is what the study found:

Husbands who kiss their wives every morning before leaving for work:

1.) Live 5 years longer

2.) Earn 20 to 30 % more

3.) Lose up to 50 % less time due to illness

4.) Are involved in fewer accidents

I'd like to add a fifth—by showing affection, he brings joy to his wife. And actually a sixth—it really isn't that tough on a man.

****

If a father is to love, then he must be loved. He must be appreciated. Tell him often, daily, that you love him and appreciate all he does for you.

Today, especially, tell him. Today, children and wives, do more than give a card or a necktie. Sit down and write a letter to your father or your children's father. Tell him what he means to you, how important he is to you, how great he is. That's a gift he'll always treasure.

Here is one of my favorite recollections of Father Arnold, of which I have many. My name is Jim Sable. My wife Sharon and I went on tours of the Alps and Ireland with Father Arnold. The memory I want to share did not come from either of those tours, however. It came while ushering on an Easter Sunday.

On Christmas and Easter, when the crowds are overflowing at Holy Name, Father Arnold would press his long time friend Monsignor Habiger into service.

Monsignor Habiger is a "robust" man with a beautiful head of wavy white hair. On this occasion the church had filled even earlier than usual. Father Arnold asked Monsignor Habiger if he would check on the chairs in the Good Samaritan Center to see how fast it was filling up.

Monsignor Habiger responded, "Arnie, I'll do anything you want. I'm putty in your hands." Father Arnold sized up Monsignor Habiger and said, "that's too much putty."

Jim Sable, parishioner of Holy Name of Jesus

The Active Christian and Relationships

✝

Marriage

Children

Community

The Best is Yet to Be

On the third day there was a wedding in Cana of Galilee, and the mother of Jesus was there. Jesus and His disciples had also been invited to the wedding. When the wine gave out, the mother of Jesus said to Him, "They have no wine." And Jesus said to her, "Woman, what concern is that to you and to me? My hour has not yet come." His mother said to the servants, "Do whatever He tells you." Now standing there were six stone water jars for the Jewish rites of purification, each holding twenty or thirty gallons. Jesus said to them, "Fill the jars with water." And they filled them up to the brim. He said to them, "Now draw some out, and take it to the chief steward." So they took it. When the steward tasted the *water that had become wine, and did not know where it came from (though the servants who had drawn the water knew), the steward called the bridegroom and said to him, "Everyone serves the good wine first, and then the inferior wine after the guests have become drunk. But you have kept the good wine until now."*

(John 2:1-10)

*I*n 1864 Robert Browning wrote the following lines of poetry, which, in my judgment, are some of the most beautiful and meaningful in the English language:

"Grow old along with me,

The best is yet to be,

The last of our life, for which the first was made;

Our times are in His hand

Who says, 'A whole I planned,

Youth shows but half; trust God, see all, nor be afraid."

Isn't that great? Jesus did not preach a 'pie in the sky' kind of religion, but He certainly proclaimed that the best is yet to be. Today's Gospel reading symbolizes this idea beautifully. Jesus, along with His disciples, went to a wedding celebration in Cana of Galilee. It must have been a festive occasion, because the wine ran out before the celebration was over. Jesus' mother Mary told Him about the problem, and He came up with a marvelous solution. At His instruction six stone jars were filled with water, then some was drawn out and taken to the headwaiter. He tasted it, then said to the groom: "People usually serve the choice wine first, then later a lesser vintage. What you have done is keep the choice wine until now."

It is not my intention to try and explain or explain away the miracle in this story. I'll leave that to your own interpretation. Instead I want to focus on the comment of the headwaiter, which symbolizes the life that Jesus lived and taught. He always served the lesser vintage first and the choice wine later. In other words, His way of living moved upward—from the good to the better to the best.

Unfortunately for many people, life seems to move in the opposite direction. For example, take something as basic as the process of aging. First comes childhood with its joy and wonder. The whole world is filled with mystery and charm. Next follows youth with its ideals and visions. Then young adulthood with plans and promises. The world is still a noble place and the body a powerful instrument, both for work and play. This is followed by the heat and battle of life's middle years, and finally, the weakness and weariness of old age. Leave God out of the aging process, and it's all down hill. That's why, I'm convinced, that our society is so obsessed with youth. Nobody wants to get old, because everybody thinks that life belongs primarily to the young. So they drink the choice wine first, then finish up with the lesser vintage.

For another example, let's look at marriage. I bet there are a few husbands and wives here who have had the same experience. They can remember a time when their lives together were filled with courtesy, kindness, warmth, and affection. They could sit across from each other in a crowded room and make eye contact that spoke volumes. Now most of that is gone. Warmth and kindness have been replaced with irritation and bitterness. Could that cold voice be the same one that was so tender not too many years ago? It's plain to see what's happened in those marriages. They drank the fine wine first and did not replenish the supply, so it ran out. They survive now on a lesser vintage. I call this spousal neglect—one of the greatest problems in marriage. The truly sad thing is that this doesn't have to happen.

We have to get old. Nothing can keep us from this, unless of course, we die young. This reminds me of a story: One day a gray-haired woman said to her husband, "Honey, there are so many places in the world, and so many things I still want to do. I sure hope I don't die young." He thought for a moment, then said, "Don't worry, dear. You didn't."

Yes, we do have to get old, but we don't have to get bitter or sour. Old age with its failing health and financial strain can be difficult. But it can also be good. We don't have to lose our love for life, not if we partake of the wine that gets better and better with the passing of time. Let's be like the 75 year old man I know who told his young grandson, "I've learned two things about life: One, it gets harder and harder and two, it gets better and better."

Jesus' first miracle—the changing of water into wine—took place at a wedding. One cannot help but wonder what kind of marriage this turned out to be. I hope it was like the wine. Marriages change with the passing of time, that's inevitable. But they don't have to change from good to bad. They can change from good to better to best. I once heard a story about an elderly man in Dallas who supplemented his Social Security income by giving golf lessons. He was past 80, and his wife of 60 years was about the same age. As he worked with his students, she sat in the chair nearby so he could keep an eye on her. She had Alzheimer's disease and was like a child again. He bathed her, fed her, and watched her constantly lest she wander away and get lost. To the casual observer, she would seem to be a terrible inconvenience. But not for him, because he loves her. He said, "If I had my life to live over, there are some things I would change. But whatever else might change, one thing would stay the same—I would spend it all over again with the same woman." That couple may have started with a lesser vintage, but it was a choice wine that kept getting better and better with age.

Whatever our role in life happens to be—married, single, old, young, rich, poor,—if we go with Christ and do things His way, we can truthfully say "The best is yet to be, the last of life, for which the first was made."

Love Isn't Love
Until It's Shared

✝

...Love is patient; love is kind;
love is not envious or boastful or arrogant
or rude. It does not insist on its own way;
it is not irritable or resentful; it does not
rejoice in wrongdoing, but rejoices in
the truth. It bears all things, believes all
things, hopes all things, endures all things.
Love never ends...

(1 Corinthian 13:4-8)

*L*ove. It's a word you hear all the time every place you go—
when you listen to songs, read the newspapers, go to movies
or parties or even a tennis match!

170

But what is love? No dictionary can define it, no philosopher can explain it, and no psychiatrist can analyze it fully. The apostle Paul probably does the best job of anyone describing what love is in his letter to the Corinthians.

No matter that we don't understand all about love, we all know how important it is. And we would probably all agree that real love is so powerful and vibrant that it can't be kept to oneself. As the poem goes:

A bell isn't a bell till you ring it,

A song isn't a song till you sing it,

Love isn't love till you share it.

That means that love is something that is given and received. Nowhere is this concept more important than in a marriage relationship.

God loves the sacrament of marriage. To Him, it's certainly more than a friendship, partnership, or sexual liaison. It's a covenant reflecting the relationship of Jesus to His Church. Yes friends, to God marriage is a serious commitment. The "I dos" at the wedding ceremony are not the end of the process for a married couple but the beginning of their commitment to grow together in many ways. It's not a one-time thing but a commitment that needs to be constantly revisited and updated.

Married couples, God wants you to have abundant life together. He wants your relationship to be one where love is continually given and received. To make sure this happens, you husbands and wives both have to work at it. Take your vows seriously to protect and enrich your marriage. What brought you together must stay alive. Keep in mind that people are made up of heart and soul, mind and body. Learn to know and support all of those within your spouse.

A special word to husbands: Give your wife attention and show appreciation more now than when you were engaged or dating.

Use these two phrases often: "Thank you" and "I'm sorry." I say this because these things will go a long way to helping keep the closeness in your marriage. The greatest complaint I hear in marriage counseling concerns the loss of intimacy. That is, the mutual trust, respect, and meeting of needs that make up much of spousal love have gone away.

Jesus knew the importance of intimacy. His prayer was that we may become one with Him in His intimate union with the father. He wanted us not just to know about God but to have a deep personal intimate relationship with Him. In other words, He wanted each of us to move from "I know there is a God" to "I know God." That's spiritual intimacy. Only then can we know the transforming power of God's love that changes darkness to light, sorrow to joy, trouble to peace, alienation to affection, and death to life.

A similar type of intimacy is at the heart of a good marriage. Just the opposite of a Peanuts cartoon I saw that went like this:

Charlie Brown: "My dad said that someday I might be able to run for president."

Lucy: "Really, Charlie Brown? He certainly must think highly of you."

Charlie Brown: "I don't know. He also said that he didn't think he'd vote for me."

More than anything else in life, we need to know that God would vote for us. We need to know that He loves us and is with us. In addition, every husband or wife needs to know that their spouse would vote for them. They need to know that their spouse truly loves them, is there with and for them, and will relate to them in a way that says, "I want to bring out the best in you." This shows true intimacy.

For couples who love each other, a ring is usually used to symbolize their commitment to each other. It's a good symbol because this commitment represents an endless circle of fidelity, love, and intimacy. Also, I always say there are not just one or two, but three rings, in a marriage: the engagement ring, the wedding ring, and suffering. How the couple handles suffering may very well determine whether or not their marriage will make it. Spouses, help each other carry your crosses. Work together to resolve problems that can divide you, such as chemical dependency, troublesome in-laws, or shaky finances. Go to church and take on the "be" attitudes— learn to "be" humble and "be" merciful. "Be" peacemakers, and your spiritual intimacy will help protect your marriage.

There are no perfect marriages. Our culture certainly doesn't help, with its emphasis on individualism and self-centeredness. What we may have instead is something like this: Once there was a man who wasn't feeling too well for a while, so finally he went to the doctor to get things checked out. His wife happened to go along, and at the end of the checkup, the doctor asked to speak to her alone. He said to her, "My dear woman, I'm sorry to tell you that your husband is suffering from a serious amount of stress. In fact, with his weak heart, it could be fatal. You must be very careful not to ever upset him so that his anxiety stays low. Here are some suggestions: Always have healthy meals ready for him promptly at breakfast, lunch, and dinner. Don't ask him to do anything much around the house or with the children, just let him relax and watch TV. And always be cheerful and ready for romance whenever he's interested." On the drive home, the husband asked, "What did the doctor say?" His wife answered, "You're going to die."

Even most well known people in the Bible had problems in their marriages. For example:

Adam and Eve: They were conned by a serpent and lost their home. One of their children murdered another.

Abraham and Sarah: One time when he was frightened, he refused to acknowledge Sarah as his wife, and instead said she was his sister.

Isaac and Rebecca: They made their twin sons into enemies by picking favorites.

Jacob: He married sisters Leah and Rachel, who became competitors. He picked Joseph as his favorite child, so several of his other sons sold Joseph into slavery.

David: One wife, Michal, despised and left him because she didn't like his dancing. Another wife, Bathsheba, lost a child because David arranged the death of her husband so she could marry him.

Mary and Joseph: When Mary told him she was pregnant, Joseph began proceedings to break their engagement (betrothal) for being unfaithful. He went about the proceedings quietly to spare Mary embarrassment, but only changed his mind when an angel came to him in a dream and explained the whole business.

No, there are no perfect marriages. Men and women by nature are very different from one another, and differences can lead to division. The best selling book *Men are from Mars, Women from Venus: The Classic Guide to Understanding the Opposite Sex*, by John Gray, discusses this in detail. In spite of these gender differences, God's plan for men and women who marry is to remain in their covenant relationship until death. His plan is for them to grow together in love and intimacy. By His grace, a good marriage, even a great marriage, is possible.

Not all married couples are able to keep the covenant, however. The breakup of marriages was a problem even back in the time of Moses, who had to create laws for divorce due to marital discord among the Israelites. One time the Pharisees tried to trap Jesus by asking His opinion of divorce. He answered them not by condemning divorced people, but instead the hardness of heart that leads to the destruction of a covenant relationship.

Jesus certainly did not condone the practice of divorce; however, His mission was not to condemn sinners for their brokenness, but to help them mend their broken lives. He understood our human frailty, and focused on the real problems behind divorce: division and hardness of heart.

We should follow Jesus' example when it comes to marriage and divorce. We must look to and try to keep the ideal but not be judgmental of those who cannot. I say a divorced person leading a good life is in better shape spiritually than someone who spends his or her time condemning divorced people. Forgiveness is what's called for, not punishment, such as finger pointing or making people wear big "D"s on their foreheads.

Love. We all need to share in it. The young and the single want to experience it. Engaged couples want to make it grow. Married people want to deepen it, and the divorced want to continue believing in it. Love. It's the only thing that leads to the richness of true intimacy.

I'm Proud of You

It happened in those days that Jesus came from Nazareth of Galilee and was baptized in the Jordan by John. On coming out of the water he saw the heavens being torn open and the Spirit, like a dove, descending upon Him. And a voice came from the heavens, "You are my beloved Son; with You I am well pleased."

(Mark 1:9-11)

Friends, I think that every son or daughter in this world is thrilled by the little declaration of praise from their parent, "I'm proud of you!"

When the baseball great Henry Aaron hit his 715th home run, breaking Babe Ruth's record, he said, "I don't remember the noise or the two kids that ran on the field or my teammates at home plate. I remember my mother out there and she was hugging me. That's what I'll remember more than anything about that home run when I think back on it." Hank Aaron was a veteran ballplayer known and applauded by millions. What he remembered most, when he broke that record, was that his mother was there.

Few of us ever escape the desire to please our parents. For some, that is the primary motivation that drives them onto success. They may not even be fully conscious of this, and their parents may even have been dead for years.

For some, pleasing their parents is a crushing burden to carry. There is that feeling that no matter what they do, they will never measure up to what they perceive as their parents' demands. Most of us, in some way or another, are still trying to please Mom or Dad.

Of course it also works the other way. Don't you, as parents, want your children to be proud of you?

It is said of the late Rufus Jones that he spent a lifetime measuring up to the accolades of his son who died at the age of 11. Writing more than forty years after his son's death, Jones said, "I overheard him once talking to a group of playmates, when each one was telling what he wanted to be when he grew up. When it was Lowell's turn, he said, 'I want to grow up to be a man like my daddy.' Few things in my life have ever touched me as those words did or have given me a greater impulse to dedication. What kind of man was I going to be, if I was a pattern for my boy?"

Rufus Jones became a great man partially because his son was proud of him. What a powerful bond there is between parent and child.

I hope all parents in this church are wise enough to tell your children how proud you are of them. I sometimes wonder, though, if instead of saying, "I'm proud of my child," we ought not say, "I'm thankful for my child." When we say "I'm proud," it may sound like an act of self-congratulations, as though we are pleased with ourselves for being the perfect parents. There are many parents who work just as hard at nurturing their young, but a child is not a robot. Sometimes, no matter how hard people work at parenting, a child will still lose his or her way. Someone once said that youth is a time of rapid changes; between a child's ages of 12 and 17, a parent can age 30 years.

A child who has a good mind and a healthy body and, more important, a loving heart, is a gift of God. Say to that child, "I am thankful for you." You know the power of that self-fulfilling prophecy. If you expect good things from your son or daughter, if you let the child know that he or she is accepted and loved and approved of, if you say frequently, "I'm proud of you," or "I'm glad I'm your parent," or "I thank God you are the kind of person you are," that child will live up to those expectations.

But, if you tell a child that he or she is no good, if you fill that child with a sense of shame and rejection, if you make that child somehow feel unworthy, then watch out. He or she may be truly successful in one area or another, but in some way a price will be paid for that neglect. In that famous phrase of a number of years ago ("I'm okay, you're okay"), we all need to know that we're okay.

All of this is my way of introducing the Gospel for today. John was baptizing people in the Jordan River. Imagine his great pleasure in being the one to baptize Jesus. It must have been an important day in Jesus' life as well. Not only did this experience mark the beginning of His public ministry, not only did he give us an example to follow in submitting to this very meaningful symbol of baptism, but something very beautiful happened to Jesus. As He was coming out of the water, He saw the heavens open and the Spirit descending on Him like a dove. And He heard a voice coming down from heaven saying, "Thou art my beloved Son; with thee I am well pleased."

A father pleased with his son. Nothing unusual about that. But this was no ordinary son, and this was no ordinary father. Can you experience the humanness of Jesus on this unforgettable occasion? Can you feel the warmth and the jubilation within His heart as He publicly receives God's approval? Being confident in His Father's love and acceptance of Him allowed Jesus to be humble. And, by being humble, Jesus was able to begin His teaching ministry.

You see, Jesus never acted like royalty. We would expect the King of Kings and the Lord of Lords to be pampered, spoiled, catered to, to demand all the "perks" that go with His position. We would expect Him to be vain, arrogant and proud. Listen. I've learned that when you find someone like that, you will be looking at a person who never got his father's or mother's approval. Only a very insecure person demands special recognition. A secure person can afford to be humble.

There is a story told of Dr. Charles Mayo who, with his father and brother, founded the world famous Mayo Clinic. Once, a group of European medical experts was visiting the clinic and staying as guests of Dr. Mayo at his home. In their own countries, it was customary for these gentlemen to place their shoes outside the bedroom for the servants to polish.

As Dr. Mayo was retiring to bed, he noticed shoes lined up outside the rooms of his guests, but it was too late to wake any of the servants. With a sigh he picked up all of the shoes, hauled them to the kitchen, and spent half the night polishing them. Dr. Charles Mayo was secure enough to be humble.

Jesus, too, was secure enough in His relationship with His father that He was able to humble himself and wash the feet of His disciples. He had no need to say to the world, "Look at me! I'm somebody great!" He had all the approval He needed.

The approval of His Father helped to make Jesus more humble, more accepting of others. Jesus embarrassed His disciples on more than one occasion by His acceptance of the least and the lowest. "Don't you know what kind of woman she is?" They asked as the woman of the streets washed His feet with her tears and dried them with her hair. "Doesn't the master know what kinds of people have invited Him to dine this evening? Can't He see that He will never win the hearts of the people if He insists on being in the company of sinners and tax collectors?"

Jesus didn't seem to put anybody down—not the woman caught in adultery, nor the despised Samaritans, nor the tax collectors of Rome. Instead, He reserved His wrath for the self-righteous Pharisees who were experts at making people feel unworthy.

Listen again, my friends. The person who puts down other people isn't sure of his or her own acceptance or approval. John 3:17, "The Son came into the world not to condemn the world, but that the world through Him might be saved." I like the way 2 Corinthians 5:17-18 is translated in the Cotton Patch Version of the Epistles:

"God was in Christ hugging the world to Himself. He has bridged the gap between Himself and us and has given us the job of bridging the gaps. He no longer keeps track of our sins and has planted in us His concern for getting together . . . So now in Christ's behalf we urge you to open up to God."

That's good. No wonder Jesus pleased His Father. Humility, acceptance, and commitment. The Father's approval made Jesus more committed. No one ever measured up to a father's dream for a child like Jesus did. Even agonizing in the garden with sweat falling from His brow like drops of blood, He prayed, "Not my will but Thine be done."

There may be some parents who think they are doing their children a favor by withholding their approval. "It will make them work harder," they deduce. If so, it will be at a great emotional cost.

Listen one last time. The chronically under-achieving child is often not that way because he or she has been spoiled by a parent's attentiveness. Rather, that child's apathy is caused by a feeling of unworthiness that has broken his or her spirit. A healthy relationship motivates, energizes, and encourages.

I hope you see that I am really preaching two messages here today. The first message is one of praise for Jesus, and all that He means to us. He has given us the perfect model of humility and love.

The other message is for all of you parents, grandparents, aunts, uncles, Sunday School teachers, religious education teachers and others who work with or are around children. The Father said to Jesus on the day of His baptism, "You are my beloved Son, with you I am well pleased." So, too, we need to help the young ones who are entrusted to our care. We need to help them know that we are pleased—pleased with our responsibility to them and for them, pleased for the kind of young men and young women they are becoming and pleased that God has brought them our way. If we can do this, then, I believe, we will produce a generation of new adults with humility, genuine love for others, and a great commitment for making their lives count.

○

"Be sure to try that Catholic church… I've heard the priest is fantastic."

Those were the words of our realtor as we drove past Holy Name of Jesus church for the first time in 1993. New to the area, we took her advice, attended a Mass and never looked elsewhere. It was evident from the first homily we heard that Father Arnold was an incredibly gifted preacher, scholar, and heartfelt leader. As newlyweds and eventually new parents, we were strongly impacted by his messages for families, especially the call to place God first. His celebrations of the Liturgy, his ability to meet all people where they are spiritually, and his genuine love for Christ have inspired us and many others. He encourages people to make the journey 'from head to heart' and to then be ready for God to work in unexpected ways. Because Father Arnold ministers from the heart, he is a gift to us and to all who know him.

Ken and Karen Richelsen

There is a Lad Here

✝

One of His disciples, Andrew, the brother of Simon Peter, remarked to Him, 'There is a lad here who has five barley loaves and a couple of dried fish, but what good is that for so many?' Jesus said, 'Get the people to recline.' Even though the men numbered about five thousand there was plenty of grass for them to find a place on the ground. Jesus then took the loaves of bread, gave thanks, and passed them around to those reclining there; He did the same for the dried fish, as much as they wanted.

(John 6:8-11)

*J*esus was one of the most loved and most hated men who ever lived. His cross reminds us of how deeply He was hated. Sometimes, we can forget how deeply He was loved, and how truly popular He was. During the height of His ministry, there were days when people flocked to Him by the thousands. Today's Gospel reading from John talks about one such occasion.

Jesus spent most of the day teaching a large crowd. He became concerned about sending the people home without anything to eat.

The disciples wondered, however, how they would ever be able to feed such a large crowd. Their numbers counted in the thousands! Then Andrew came forward and said, "There is a lad here who has five barley loaves and a couple of dried fish." As we know, Jesus took these meager provisions and used them to feed the multitude.

Among all of the miracle stories of Jesus, this is the only one told in all four of the Gospels. Each writer tells essentially the same story. John, however, adds one detail that makes his account my favorite. He alone tells us that the five barley loaves and two fish belonged to a little boy. All of the other Gospels make this strictly an adult story.

Focus On The Child

The first thing I like about John's account is that the spotlight falls on a child. The real hero of this story was that little boy. This fact was overlooked by the other three Gospel writers. However, we should not be too critical of Matthew, Mark and Luke until we examine our own attitudes toward children.

In Rodger's and Hammerstein's musical "South Pacific," a young American lieutenant falls in love with a Tonkenese gal and plans to marry her. As he reflects on racist attitudes, he sings his conclusions:

"You've got to be taught to hate and to fear. You've got to be taught from year to year. It's got to be drummed in your dear little ear.

You've got to be carefully taught.

You've got to be taught before it's too late. Before you are six or seven or eight. To hate all the people your relatives hate.

You've got to be carefully taught."

Across the centuries, we have done a tragically good job of teaching that lesson. How sad it is that we continue doing that to our children. Four hundred years before the birth of Christ, the Greek writer Euripides presented a drama in Athens titled "The Trojan Woman." This drama was a protest against war. As a symbol of war, he placed at center stage, not a soldier with a sword, but a woman holding a dead baby. As far as his religion, Euripides would be considered a pagan; however, he understood the tragedy of war far better than many who call themselves Christian.

Andrew said to Jesus, "We have a boy here." Keep the focus on the child. If adults of this world would recognize that reality, perhaps we would find a way to end war. Perhaps we would find a way to end abortion. Perhaps we would find a way to live in peace. "There is a lad here."

See the Child's Potential

Another thing I like about this story from John's Gospel is that it recognizes the potential of a child. Five barley loaves and a couple of dried fish did not seem very significant when compared to the size of the need. But in the hands of Christ, they were more than enough to save the day. No one except a sensitive soul like Andrew could have guessed that a child could make that kind of difference.

In 1852, the English historian Sir Edward Creasy published a book titled, *Fifteen Decisive Battles of the World*. After reading this book, a man of great insight suggested that it would be more to the point to write a book about the decisive babies of the world. This is not sentimentality. It is a fact of history.

When the Hebrew people were in bondage down in Egypt, a baby boy was born to a young couple named Amram and Jochebed. His foster mother, the daughter of Pharaoh, named him Moses.

Because of that baby, a band of slaves threw off their chains and became the nation of Israel.

When Caesar Augustus was ruler of the Roman Empire, in the little village of Bethlehem, a baby boy was born to a young virgin woman named Mary. Under prior instructions from the angel of God, the baby was given the name Jesus. There is no way to measure the impact of that baby upon the history of the world.

In the year 1820, in the ancient and beautiful city of Florence, Italy, a baby girl was born to wealthy English parents. They named the child after the city of her birth. That baby, Florence Nightingale, became the mother of modern nursing and literally transformed hospital practices and procedures in most of the Western World.

There are young boys and girls in our church today. We may see them as nothing more than little bundles of energy. But we have no idea who or what they may become. There is no way of knowing what God will do with their "five barley loaves and a couple of dried fish." We should never make the mistake of underestimating the potential of a child. And above all, we should never allow any child to be killed. We need to have a respect for all life, because only God knows the true potential found within each person.

Follow the Child's Lead

Finally, in John's loaves and fishes miracle story, I see a pattern for us all to follow. It was set for us by the boy who gave what he had to the Lord. Bible scholars across the centuries have wondered about the real meaning of this reading. One interpretation has been that most of the people actually brought food with them, but were afraid to let it be known, lest they lose it to the hungry crowd around them. But when the little lad came forward and gave his lunch to Jesus to share with everyone, his generosity shamed their selfishness, and they began sharing with one another. Once the spirit of caring and sharing took over, it turned out there was enough food for all, with some to spare. In fact, there were twelve baskets left over.

If that is what happened, I do not know. But I am convinced that it would work in our world today. Our world-wide problem, at least for now, is not that we have too little of the necessities of life; it's that we have too little sharing. There are those of us who are so afraid that we will lose our cherished possessions to those who have not, that we clutch them to our bosoms and keep them to ourselves. Who knows what would happen if a spirit of caring and sharing took over? In my mind there is not the slightest doubt that the needs of the world would be met, with twelve baskets left over.

In the book of Isaiah the prophet shares his vision of a time of peace and justice. The prophet describes it like this:

Then the wolf shall be the guest of the lamb, and the leopard shall lie down with the kid. The calf and the young lion shall browse together, with a little child to guide them. (Isaiah 11:6)

Underline that last phrase, because that is what we have in our Gospel reading today: a little child to guide us. In the midst of that great crowd of people, Andrew made a saving discovery: "There is a lad here with five barley loaves and a couple of dried fish." You and I need to make that same discovery in our world today. Let's keep our focus on the child, never underestimate the potential of a child, and follow their lead. "There is a lad here."

The Vine and the Branches

✝

"Those who abide in Me
and I in them bear much fruit."

(John 15:5)

What does it mean to be close to God? Jesus said, "I am the vine, you are the branches. Those who abide in Me and I in them bear much fruit, because apart from Me you can do nothing." Here we have two essential elements of Christian living: "abiding in Christ" and "bearing fruit." Many who follow Christ seek to major in one or the other, abiding in Him or bearing fruit. But Jesus says that both are critical. Notice how starkly He puts it: *I am the vine, you are the branches. Those who abide in Me and I in them bear much fruit, because apart from Me you can do nothing. Whoever does not abide in Me is thrown away like a branch and withers; such branches are gathered, thrown into the fire, and burned."* (NRSV)

I believe that many people today crave to be closer to God. Nothing else in today's world satisfies. This is serious business. As we just heard, without Christ we can do nothing. Abiding in Him is the source of our power to live the Christ-life. But neither can we say that we abide in Him if we bear no fruit. Abiding and bearing. Neither flourishes in isolation.

In her autobiography *Climbing Free*, rock climber Lynn Hill shares the peril she faced in May, 1989 while scaling the cliff face in France. As Hill reached the top of a 72-foot ledge, she leaned back into her harness to take a rest. Somehow her rope wasn't fully connected to her harness. When she leaned her weight on it, she fell backward into space. You can imagine how terrifying this was—falling through the air with nothing to catch her. Amazingly, she survived the fall.

As an expert in her field, Hill relied fully on her equipment. She had every expectation that her harness would support her full weight. Her experience illustrates the dangers of putting your faith in something that may fail. Many of us can appreciate that hard lesson. It was only a couple of years ago that experts were talking about a new economy—a stock market that would seemingly climb forever. And many trusting people put their faith in that market for their retirement. Some hard lessons were learned.

Many other people have learned even harder lessons after pouring their all into their marriages. They thought that marriage would last forever. But somewhere along the way, the harness snapped and now, much to their shock and despair, they find themselves falling. So where did they go wrong? My first guess is their priorities were a little off. To live as Christ tells us, we must always put God first. When God comes first He never fails you. He's always there with a support net, to love you. After God, our second priority is marriage, and with a Christ-filled marriage, the husband and wife can find even deeper fulfillment. The next priority should be the children, followed by jobs, career and so on.

Many people today crave to be closer to God. One reason is that other sources of security have let them down. Why put your faith in that which is not lasting? Physical health? Talent? Intelligence? Friends? Work? They are all important. They are all to be valued, but they all have one thing in common. Eventually they may fail.

Dr. Paul Brand spent most of his adult life as a missionary doctor in remote parts of the world. In a speech he once commented on various peak moments in his life. At age 27 he reached his physical peak. He had abundant energy and could take on any physical challenge. He said, "for some people, when they cross that peak, for them life is over."

At age 57 Dr. Brand said he felt like he had reached his mental peak. He was a famous surgeon working with leprosy patients in India. For many people, their mental peak marks the highest point of their lives. He repeated, "for some people, when they cross that peak, for them life is over."

Then, Dr. Brand commented that in his 80s he felt like he was reaching his spiritual peak. All his experiences in life were coming together to mature him into a wiser, kinder, more peaceful human being. He went on to say, "and I realize when I cross that peak, for me, life will not be over, it will have just begun."

Paul Brand discovered what it means to be connected to Christ in the same way that a branch is connected to a vine. In Christ we find a source of strength that never fails. We may face some difficult times, but these will serve only to root us even more firmly in his care. We crave to be close to God because in God we find the one reality that can never be taken from us.

But there is something else we need to see. Just as we depend on God, so does God depend on us. According to our lesson for the day, what happens when we abide in God? We bear fruit. We cannot separate these two: abiding in God and bearing fruit.

I have a fascination for strawberries, my favorite fruit. I love strawberry plants, and I have learned a powerful lesson from a strawberry plant. I was on my hands and knees one day in a garden pulling weeds, and I noticed something I had seen a hundred times before, but never caught the significance of it. It was the "runners" on the strawberry plants. I noticed that from the main vine of a strawberry plant a number of slender shoots extend like arms in all directions. These shoots are thin, green stems creeping along the ground, being pushed out by that mysterious power in the mother plant. After reaching out about six inches, the end of one of these runners will penetrate the ground and develop roots like the mother plant. Then the leaves of a new baby plant will shoot upward. All the while, before the infant plant is able to sustain itself, it received nourishment from the parents through the "runner." When the new growth is firmly fixed in the ground, the "runner" resumes its journey and reaches out another six inches, still nourished by the original clump of berries. Then the process is repeated. And while this one plant is multiplying, there are several others doing the same thing in different directions.

When I observed this process going on, I forgot all about the weeds and saw only that mother plant sending out its runners. This caused me to cry out, "O God, make me like those strawberries, reaching out in an effort to multiply and bring forth fruit." This is the logical culmination of being close to God—we bear fruit. What is the fruit we are to bear? It is life in the image of Christ—His love, His acceptance, His forgiveness, His compassion reflected in us. For example, it is simply impossible in the Christian understanding of life to be close to Christ without reflecting Jesus' love for the least and lowly.

Chuck Colson, former U. S. government official turned Christian author and columnist, has observed that when the Communists took over Russia in 1917, they did not make Christianity illegal. Their constitution, in fact, guaranteed freedom of religion. But they did make it illegal for the church to do any "good works." No longer could the church fulfill its historic role in feeding the hungry, educating the children, housing the orphans or caring for the sick. What was the result? After 70 years the church was largely irrelevant to the communities in which it dwelt.

That's the worst thing that can be said about a church – that it is irrelevant. If this church should disappear, would our community miss us? Or would they even notice our absence? A church that is joined to Christ as the branches are joined to the vine will be a church that invariably bears fruit. It is a church that is known for its love and its compassion. Of course, a church only bears fruit if the individual members of that church bear fruit.

A man wrote in Billy Graham's newspaper column sometime back and expressed his regrets: "I want to serve God, but I'm too old to go back to school and become a minister or missionary or something like that. Why didn't I listen to God years ago," he asked, "when I was much younger?"

Rev. Graham wrote back that the man had missed out on numerous blessings by not following God in his youth. But, Graham said, "It is never too late to serve God. And it isn't necessary to enter the ministry," he continued. "Every day you probably come in contact with people who will never enter a church or talk with a pastor and God wants to use you to point them to Christ." He charged this man with two tasks: to grow spiritually and to ask God to show him how to share his faith with others. In this way, he could serve God faithfully in the last years of his life.

We are never too old or too young to serve Christ. He is looking for people who desire to draw close to Him, and are willing to reach out to others in Christ-like love. So this is the challenge of today's lesson from scripture: Are you close to God? Are you bearing fruit?

A Bible scholar and pastor tells about a piece of wood that he keeps on his desk. He took this piece of wood from a vineyard in the San Joaquin Valley. It is a section of vine out of which grows a branch. The owner of the vineyard told him that if two people were in a tug of war using this section of vine, it would break; however, it would never break where the vine and branch are joined together, for that is the strongest point of the vine. A vine, according to a good teacher, is different from a tree. If you pull on a branch that goes into a tree it will break at the trunk of the tree—in a tree that is the weakest place. But in a grapevine that is the strongest point—where the branch is joined to the vine.

What a beautiful picture of our life in Christ. This is one part of our life that is unbreakable. Other things may fail us, but Christ will never fail us. It is because we are joined to Him that we can reach out in love to others.

My fondest memory of Father Arnold was when I was in kindergarten at Holy Name, and we got a new slide for the playground. It was during recess and Father came out to visit. Everyone was crowding around to watch him take the first ride down the slide. He had the biggest smile on his face, and everyone was cheering him on. This is one of my favorite memories because you could just tell Father was so delighted and happy to be around all the kids.

Becky Swing, age 16,
Graduate of Holy Name of Jesus School

Inclusiveness Versus Exclusiveness

*Thus Philip went down to
(the city) of Samaria and proclaimed
the Messiah to them.*

(Acts 8:5)

I would like to turn to the lesson from the Acts of the
Apostles and share a special message with you. Let me call it:
You are included.

When Carl Sandburg was the unofficial Poet Laureate of the
United States, a rookie reporter was assigned the task of interviewing
the great writer. The reporter did not want to mess up his big chance
at a real interview with a famous man. So he thought long about
the questions he would ask Sandburg. Here was the reporter's best
question: "Mr. Sandburg, what is the ugliest word in the English
language?"

Sandburg seemed surprised and pleased by the question. He
stroked his chin; "The ugliest word..." he paused for effect. The

reporter leaned in, pencil ready. "The ugliest word in the English language is the word 'exclusive.'"

He may have been right. Exclusive sounds like a good word, but only as long as you are included in the tight circle it guards. Do you enjoy the service and relaxed pace of an exclusive country club? Do you enjoy the benefits of an exclusive sub-division for your home? If so, exclusive may sound like a pleasant word. It protects your privacy. It guards your privilege. It allows you to associate with people of like station in life. But how does the word exclusive feel for those left on the outside? It feels like a stiff-arm in the face. It has the ring of a door closing and the sound of locks double-bolting from the inside. Exclusive says, "you are not welcome here." For this reason, God must not be very fond of the word.

Our text in the Book of Acts today shows another of God's efforts to redraw exclusive boundaries, to tear down separating walls. He sent the Gospel to the Samaritans. Remember that Samaritans were despised by the Jews. What does this mean for us? God includes people. All people. This is a difficult lesson for many of us. Like the Jews and Samaritans of the ancient world, we are taught racial and national prejudice from an early age. We are selfish; we learn first to love the face in the mirror. So we love most easily the faces that look like ours—our color, our language, our traditions, our flag.

But God is not so limited. He wants us to learn love by looking out of windows, not just by looking into mirrors. When will we learn that God is not the enemy of our enemy? God does not salute my flag. God does not prefer my race, or my gender, or my economic class.

A candidate for governor of the state of Georgia campaigned in the early 1960s on the platform of racial equality. He lost. Badly. One heckler interrupted his speech on a courthouse step with the question, "Where did you get those ideas of racial equality? Are you some kind of Communist?" The candidate calmly pointed to the steeple of the church on the courthouse square, "I got these ideas over there. I learned this at church."

It's not easy for us to love "Samaritans." We don't know why. But who are the Samaritans in your life? Who do you find it difficult to love? Who stretches the comfort zones of your world? How do you feel about God's passionate love for them? Would you go to share the Gospel with them if God asked you to do so? Peter and John did. And it made all the difference to the Samaritans. When the Holy Spirit fell on the Samaritans it was the same Spirit who fell upon them as fell upon the Apostles at Pentecost. My guess is that the Apostles needed to see that lesson in God's radical inclusiveness as much as the Samaritans needed to receive it.

But there is another lesson for us in this text: God's inclusive nature is often best learned by those who have felt excluded. Notice that the movement of God to the Samaritans was spurred by the persecution of the Church at the hand of local Jewish authorities. Christianity was seen as a heretical sect of Judaism by the authorities. As such, it was a threat to the purity of the faith. It had to be stamped out. The resulting persecution drove many of the Christians outside the comfortable and familiar surroundings of Jerusalem. And as they fled, they carried the Gospel with them. Jesus told them to carry the Gospel to Samaria and the outermost part of the world. Persecution forced them to do it.

Isn't it just like God to bring a good result out of an evil event? The authorities meant to eliminate Christianity, but their brutality spread it like dandelion seeds in the wind. The same phenomenon occurred in Communist Russia and China when those governments attempted to kill the Church. Decades later, after the collapse of Communist USSR, the Church still thrived. And Christians flourish under hostile conditions in China still today.

I have a story about a family with children, ages ten, eight, six and four. They lived in separate bedrooms along a single hallway in their parent's home. The oldest boy posted a sign on his bedroom door which read, KEEP OUT! If you have younger sibling you'll understand. The eight year old placed his own sign on his door, MEMBERS ONLY. He had a private club, of which he was the only member. The third son, age six, not to be outdone, created his own sign—NO GIRLS ALLOWED. You see, his room was right next to the youngest child, their baby sister—a girl! And the youngest child, the little sister of those three boys, wrote her own sign and posted it; WELCOME, ENNYBODY.

Only one of those doors leads to a church, and I'm sure you can figure out which one it is.

Thanks be to God!

The Active Christian and the Trials of Life

Temptation and Sin

Pain and Suffering

Get Away Satan!

✝

Then Jesus was led by the Spirit into the desert to be
tempted by the devil. He fasted for forty days and forty
nights, and afterwards he was hungry. The tempter
approached and said to Him, "If you are the Son of
God, command that these stones become loaves of bread."
He said in reply, "It is written: 'One does not live
by bread alone, but by every word that comes forth
from the mouth of God.'" Then the devil took Him to
the holy city, and made Him stand on the parapet of
the temple, and said to Him, "If you are the Son of
God, throw yourself down. For it is written: 'He will
command his angels concerning you, and with their
hands they will support you, lest you dash your foot
against a stone.'" Jesus answered him,
"Again it is written, 'You shall not put the Lord,
your God, to the test.'"

Then the devil took Him up to a very high mountain, and showed Him all the kingdoms of the world in their magnificence, and he said to Him, "All these I shall give to you, if you will prostrate yourself and worship me." At this point, Jesus said to him, "Get away, Satan! It is written: The Lord, your God, shall you worship and Him alone shall you serve." Then the devil left Him and, behold, angels came and ministered to Him.

(Matthew 4:1-11)

I'd like to share with you a story, today, about a church volunteer that we'll call Bill. Bill's church was in the middle of a stewardship campaign, and Bill was their biggest champion. He visited every family in the parish, made phone calls, and took notes. He took his job very seriously.

The name of an elderly woman was at the end of the list of church members whom he needed to contact. Bill decided to go out to her home and make a personal visit. When he arrived, he presented the case, explaining how the money raised from this campaign would go to support the parish. When he finished talking, the elderly woman said to him,

"Listen, I knew your grandfather, your father, and now you come along. You people are all alike. I've despised you for years, and if you don't leave, I'll break this broom over your head."

Bill left immediately. When he got into his car, he pulled out his notes and wrote down, "Doubtful prospect."

Well, in today's Gospel reading we are told that before beginning his teaching ministry, Jesus was tempted by the devil, after spending

40 days and nights in the desert. Like the volunteer worker, the devil presented his case to Jesus, only to discover that Jesus was a "doubtful prospect."

What does this temptation story of Jesus Christ mean to us? I believe there are two important lessons in the story.

Jesus Understands Temptation

First, I believe that this story helps us to see the humanity of Jesus. It shows us that Jesus understands temptation, because He too, was tempted. It is a good feeling to know that, when we are tempted, Jesus will say, "I understand."

There was a man who became an alcoholic and drank for 25 years. One day, a member of Alcoholics Anonymous came to see him. When this man walked over to the younger man, he spoke just two words. He said, "I understand." The younger man replied, "I've waited 25 years to hear those words." And then he wept.

"I understand." The temptation of Jesus Christ means that He can say those words to all of us.

Temptation Plays On Our Strengths As Much As Our Weaknesses

The second lesson that the temptation story of Jesus offers us is that, although we often think of temptation as a sign of weakness, temptation itself, is often pointing in the direction of our strengths.

It is easy to think of personal weaknesses that invite temptation. An alcoholic is tempted to drink. A gambler is tempted to gamble. A smoker is tempted to smoke. The lazy person may be tempted to idleness, and the sexy person is tempted to illicit sex.

I could go on and on. All of us have areas of weakness which cause us to fight daily battles against temptation. But, that's only half of the story.

In the Gospel today, we see the other half of the story. Jesus was tempted three times, and all of them were tests of his strength.

First, the tempter challenged Christ to turn the stones into bread. This was tempting Jesus to use his power selfishly. Next, the Devil told Jesus to throw Himself off the mountain and let God rescue Him. A major strength in the life of Jesus was His faith in His Father. Here He is tempted to use that faith to claim a personal exemption for Himself, as though God might make an exception for Jesus and not let Him get hurt—not allow Him to suffer. Finally, the Devil offered Jesus kingdoms of the world. Jesus had the power of a great vision. He dreamed of a day when God's will would be done on earth as it is in heaven. In this last temptation, the Devil handed Him a short cut—a short-cut to achieving his dream.

So you see, temptation can be where we are strong. In fact, I think it occurs as often in the areas of our strengths as it does in the areas of our weaknesses.

We all have weaknesses, we don't deny this. What I want to point out today, however, is that we also have power and strength. We can't deny this either. I'd like to focus on this power for a moment.

What are we doing with our power? How are we using it?

For example, if you are a young man, you may be handsome and have a great personality. These qualities give you power. What will you do with it? Will it help you or hurt you? Likewise, you may be a young woman with a beautiful face and shapely body. These two characteristics give you power. How are you going to use it?

Maybe you're a good student with a good academic record. This, too, gives you power. So how are you going to use it? Maybe you're older. A grown man who owns his own business. You've made a good living for yourself, and have others working for you. You do the hiring and the firing. That's power. So, how do you use it?

Now, some of you might be thinking that you're not handsome, not beautiful, not a good student or a wealthy employer. "What about me?" you ask. My answer is this, "We all have power." No matter how weak we may think we are, we all have power.

I know of a young man who has a terrible weakness. He is a drug addict. He can hardly get through a day without feeding his weakness. But that same young man has tremendous power. He is greatly loved by his father and his mother. That puts him in a position of strength. He uses that strength to cost his parents thousands of dollars and hundreds of sleepless nights. He has taken the power of love and used it to inflict untold suffering on those who love him.

Most of us are not drug addicts. We can be thankful for that. But all of us are loved by somebody. That's power in our hands. We can use that power to help or to hurt. To bring joy or to bring pain. Which will it be?

I'm convinced that more people have ruined their lives by misusing their strength than by giving in to their weakness. We need to take inventory of our strengths. Do we have many talents? Are we good looking? Are we smart? Are we good workers? Do we have many friends? Are we good money managers?

Next, we need to ask ourselves how we are using this power. Then, look to see how we match up against our model, Jesus. Today Jesus showed us how to travel safely on Temptation's Trail. On our journey, the Devil is sure to encourage us to take a detour that will surely lead to a dead end.

There is a story about a grocer who leaned over the counter and said to a boy who had been standing there for several minutes in front of the candy shelves, "Are you trying to steal some candy?" "No sir," the boy replied, "I'm trying not to."

Friends, all we can do is try—try our best to follow Christ, especially when we are tempted to do otherwise. I'd like to close by reflecting on a passage from Paul's letter to the Romans. It describes Paul's own struggles with his sinfulness and temptation. Paul writes:

"I do not understand what I do; for I don't do what I would like to do, but instead I do what I hate…"

"For even though the desire to do good is in me, I am not able to do it. I don't do the good I want to do; instead I do the evil that I do not want to do...

"What an unhappy man I am! Who will rescue me from this body that is taking me to death?

"Thanks be to God... Jesus Christ!" (Romans 7:15-25)

○

My name is James Renier, a proud alumni of Holy Name of Jesus School. As I look back on the many years that I had the privilege of knowing Father Arnold, I can't think of one time where I walked away from him and didn't learn something new about the Church, my Faith, or God. When I was in 6th grade, I received a sparkplug from him during a Sunday mass. This was his way of recognizing the people who were "sparks" in the church and in their faith. Since I received the sparkplug, my faith has greatly increased. I have come to fully understand the sacraments of the Eucharist, Reconciliation, and Confirmation and the impact that they have on me every day. Once I was confirmed I became a Eucharistic Minister and then a Head Eucharistic Minister because Father Arnold taught me the importance of serving others and spreading Jesus to people. Being a Eucharistic Minister allowed me to serve Jesus by giving his Body and Blood to the people. Because of Father Arnold's teachings, God is #1 in my life and always will be no matter what.

Jimmy Renier, graduate of Holy Name of Jesus School

Whatever Happened to Sin?

✝

"If we say, 'We are without sin,'
we deceive ourselves,
and the truth is not in us."

(1 John 1:6)

There's a story that I've told before, that fits well with the topic of sin.

There was a man who was hired to paint somebody's house. He wanted to get the job done quickly, so he didn't bother to read the instructions on the paint can, and he mixed the paint with water. Well, the paint looked okay, but a little cheap. He decided to go ahead and use it anyway, and he painted the house. That night there was a rain storm. The next day, the paint on the house was streaked and thinned. A voice from heaven came down to the man and said, "Repaint and thin no more."

Well, friends, today we are not talking about house painting. Instead, we are talking about sin. There are many three letter words in the church vocabulary: lie, cry, die, awe, law, bow, vow, and of course, sin. In my opinion, we don't hear enough about that one.

Back in the 1970s there was a famous psychiatrist, Karl Menninger, who was known nationally for his fire and brimstone talks about sin. He often asked, "Whatever became of sin?" He wasn't afraid to talk about it. In fact, he often quoted today's Scripture passage from 1 John.

In our culture today, we don't like to talk about sin. We talk about tolerance and acceptance. But what I say to you today is that if we don't talk about sin, we can't sensibly speak of Easter, of the Resurrection, of Jesus Christ, or even ourselves.

Sin Ruptures Relationships

So, what is this thing called sin? What is it all about? Well if we go to the Catechism, sin is defined as "an offense against God as well as a fault against reason, truth, and right conscience." The Baltimore Catechism tells us that sin is "breaking God's law."

What about the Bible? What does it have to say about sin? Well if we open the Bible up to Genesis and start reading about Adam and Eve, we learn that sin was not invented in Rome. This is not a recent phenomenon. Sin has been around for a while.

Sin goes back to the very first man and woman that God created. He created them in His image, and He deemed them to be very good, His most wondrous creation. And what did this most wondrous creation do? They turned their backs on God. God asked them not to eat the fruit of the tree, yet they did it anyway.

Sin is rebellion. It is a way to rebel, to revolt and to disobey. God's creatures said "No" to their Lord, and in doing so, they ruptured their relationship and intimacy with God.

Jesus considers sin a separation from God. Sin breaks the bond between God and others. The parable of the prodigal son is a perfect example of this. It isn't just a story of wasted wealth and sinful actions. No, the younger son broke the bond he had with his father.

When he returned, he said, "I am no longer worthy to be called your son."

Often, Sin Happens Because of a Lack of Love

Of course we don't go around telling God, "I hate you, so I'm going to fornicate." It usually doesn't work that way. So what does cause us to sin? Most sin happens when we don't love God, our neighbors, or ourselves enough.

Jesus said, "Come, you who are blessed by my Father. Inherit the kingdom prepared for you from the foundation of the world. For I was hungry and you gave me food, I was thirsty and you gave me drink, a stranger and you welcomed me, naked and you clothed me, ill and you cared for me, in prison and you visited me." (Matthew 25:34-37) Allowing people to go hungry in this world, that's a sin. Killing the unborn is a sin. War is sin.

Friends, holiness is having love for our neighbor. Charity is kind and patient. How can we say that we love the God whom we cannot see, yet we do not love the brothers and sisters whom we can see?

To conquer sin, we need love. We need to love God, love our neighbors, and love ourselves. When our day of judgment comes, God is not going to look at our mental credentials. Rather, He's going to look at our hearts. It's not about our IQ. It's about our "I do." "Whatever you do to the least of my brothers, so, too, you've done unto me."

Love Can Conquer Sin

Through His death and resurrection, Jesus destroyed the tyranny of sin. But, He did not destroy our ability to sin. Though sin no longer enslaves us, we are still tempted to sin. We are still free to sin. We still sin.

What return should we make to our Lord for His suffering? For His dying? For His saving grace? Why, that's obvious. Don't sin!

And how do we refrain from sin? With love. That's what we've been talking about. The answer is love. Rather than setting our eyes on sin, why not shake loose the love! As we know, love is stronger than sin.

However, we're not talking about a sentimental love, or a movie-screen type of love or a teeny-bopper love. Friends, we're talking about the kind of love that carried Jesus Christ to the cross. This kind of love can turn the other cheek. This kind of love can keep a marriage together. This kind of love can reach out to the homeless and the loveless and those who ail from everything from acne to AIDS.

As St. Paul said so beautifully in his letter to the Corinthians, "Love is patient, love is kind. It is not jealous, it is not pompous, it is not inflated, it is not rude, it does not seek its own interests, it is not quick-tempered, it does not brood over injury, it does not rejoice over wrongdoing but rejoices with the truth. It bears all things, believes all things, hopes all things, endures all things. Love never fails." Friends, when there is this kind of love, sin will come in a distant second.

Through love we will find holiness. And Holiness in Lent leads to Easter. Holiness in the crucifixion leads to Resurrection. Holiness in Christian dying leads to Christian living.

It is through this kind of loving that sin can be conquered, and the weight of guilt lifted. Let us love like Christ and sin no more!

****

Note: Fr. Arnold wrote an article for the Holy Name of Jesus bulletin many years ago related to this subject of sin. The following is that article.

Turtle Mentality and American Mentality

I would like to write about a dilemma that is happening to our American morality. The dilemma by which the twentieth century men and women no longer commit sins, but as they say, "experience life." Consequently, some nasty behavior has suddenly become quite virtuous.

Drugs today are an integral part of American culture. What is happening is that we are becoming so much at home with the problem that we are rapidly losing the ability to look at the root of the problem. The value of not having to rely on drugs is replaced by the value of helping people cope with drugs. Our concern now is how to help drug users live comfortably, rather than asking why people take drugs in the first place.

Or, consider sex. Recently, I watched a few programs on TV regarding abortion and sexual problems. The greatest portion of the program focused on the idea that a lack of proper birth control information is the main cause of our sexual problems. At first glance it may appear to be the right answer. It isn't. Because there are so many abuses of non-marital sex, people tend to say, "Let's be practical." Or, "Let's be sensible." Or even, "Let's be realistic." I would instead say, "Let's be honest." We have taken our moral standards and made the exceptions so humane that the original values are fast fading out. Why not raise our voices against the casualness with which we Americans are slipping into drugs, divorce, abortion and non-marital sex? It is this word, "casual" that is so critical. We seem to have adopted a morality of casualness. Why? Because we have been propagandized and sloganized into a morality of expediency. Talks of restraint, self-control or discipline are seldom referred to when mentioning immoral behavior. We seem only to be concerned about the after-the-fact. I call this, turtle morality.

Do you remember the old story about the little boy who found a turtle and made it his pet? One day the turtle suddenly rolled over on to its back and died. The boy was heart-broken. He could not be consoled. His mother called his father who raced home from the office and tried to console his grief-stricken son. Finally, the father said, "Look, son, here's what we'll do. We'll have a little funeral ceremony, and you can invite your friends." At this, the boy stopped crying. "Then, we'll put the turtle in my silver cigarette box (the boy was interested), and we'll get some ice cream and cookies and have a party afterwards." The boy was smiling from ear to ear at this point. Suddenly, however, as soon as the father finished speaking, the turtle flipped over on his legs and began to walk away. "Oh, daddy!" exclaimed the boy. "Let's kill it!"

That's the turtle mentality. The original value is lost in the attraction of the kindly assistance. Everyone is so taken up with the helping hand that they elevate their tragedy into virtue. The original incident of the turtle's death is no longer important. Someone once called this the "filter mentality." "Enjoy the smoke but not the cancer. Have the sex, but not the baby."

We need to call sin what it is—SIN. When we see sin, we have a tendency to quickly call it by various phrases: "misguided," "ill," "high," "tension," "release."

Sin isn't disappearing, awareness of it is. Sin isn't changing, but sensitivity to it is. The famous psychiatrist Karl Menninger said it well when he stated that, "The modern world has lost its sense of sin." We need to be aware of this turtle mentality. We live in a country where opinions measured by Gallup or Harris Polls can easily become the standard for right and wrong. We live in a country where ethical standards can easily become the same as therapeutic compassion. We live in a country where more energy is being spent on adjusting to the unfortunate wrong situation than upholding the original moral dictate. There is an indifference to sin. We must be careful that we don't fall into benign humanitarianism. As Christians, we must take a stand on the ground that separates human compassion from religious conviction. This is not reactionary conservatism. This is following the teachings of Jesus and preached by the Catholic Church. We need to be aware of what this creeping expediency is doing to the world. We need more Christians to preach and teach as well as to help remedy bad situations.

God bless you. Have a good week.

Where Do We Go From Here?

Suddenly a leper came forward and did Him homage, saying to Him, "Sir, if you will to do so, you can cure me." Jesus stretched out His hand, touched him and said, "I do will it. Be cured."

(Matthew 8:2-3)

Friends, today's Gospel reduces suffering to one simple little statement. It happens when the man with leprosy comes to Jesus and says, "If You will to do so, You can cure me."

I would guess that thousands of people, including myself and many of you, have said something similar to "If You will do so, You can cure me." I've prayed that way. I've prayed about problems with school and church. I've pleaded "Lord, come on, You can handle it." I've asked Him to take the problems from me.

In our reading today Jesus answers the leper, "I do will it, be cured." That's great, but we all know of many tragedies that don't turn out that way. I know people who have prayed well and hard, but their marriages weren't saved, the diseases weren't healed, or the family wasn't saved from bankruptcy.

When life deals us a disappointing hand, we may stop and ask, "Where do we go from here?" People respond to disappointment in various ways. Some people give up on God. Unfortunately, for those who give up on God, or want to be rid of God, banish him, it won't solve the problem. We're still faced with a cross to carry and the question, "Where do we go from here?"

Others, rather than trying to banish God, will doubt God. Or at least, they doubt His care and concern. Doubt can happen to any of us. It even happened to Jesus. While on the cross He said, "My God, My God, why have You forsaken Me?" If you take that question at face value, it means Jesus felt that God had failed Him. Anybody who takes God seriously will wonder at times, "Where is He?" I want you to know that doubt is not the opposite of faith. It's part of faith. There are many mysteries in our Catholic faith, and suffering is one of those mysteries. We may not know why we suffer, but we do know that suffering can bring us closer to God as we learn to depend on him for the strength to deal with it. In addition to leading us to a richer spiritual life, suffering can make us better people, more sensitive and understanding toward others. Also, suffering can make us humble. Suffering can be powerful. In fact, we were redeemed through Christ's suffering.

And yet, we continue to ask ourselves, "Where do we go from here?" Friends, through faith, we must recognize that God has a purpose, a plan for our suffering.

The primary purpose of God in this world isn't to make life easier and more comfortable for us. In fact, most of us know that commitment to God may lead to suffering. But look at Christ. He stayed committed. He knew about the pain and suffering He was about to endure but He didn't focus on just Himself. He prayed three times to His father, "Not My will be done, but Yours." And that's our answer, too. If we recognize a higher purpose, we will have a rugged faith that will help us through the times of doubt and suffering. As we practice and live our faith, we will be fortified. We'll have a reserve—a build-up of faith—to support us through the tough times.

And a tough time will come no matter how tight our controls, no matter how much we plan, no matter how rightly things are going. A time will come when there's nothing we can do to change the situation. A time will come when something we've worked hard for is destroyed. A time will come that we are given burdens we cannot bear. A time will come when we are overwhelmed with anger and disappointment. At times like these we can choose to give up, and give in to fear and resentment. Or we can grit our teeth and keep going, no matter what, but feel crushed by anger and despair during the whole ordeal. Or we can pull up that rugged faith, allow that faith to calm us, bring us back to center, and place our burdens where they belong—at the feet of Christ—and trust Him to do what we cannot do for ourselves. What He will do or how He will do it, we may not know, but we can know, most assuredly, He will meet the need. He may not take the burden from us entirely, but He'll provide us the strength we need to carry on, and grow in our faith.

Where do we go from here? Friends, I think our answer is this: We can choose to become bitter in life, or we can choose to become better. Those of you who have been parishioners here for a while have heard me preach about becoming better, not bitter, many times before. I knew it was important, but it was really driven home when something happened in my life, and I learned for myself what a difficult thing this can be. My brother, Otto, who was also my best friend, died suddenly when he was just 52 years old. He was also a priest and taught at St. John's in Collegeville, Minnesota. He was out jogging one night and had a fatal heart attack. I can't begin to tell you the loss I felt, and still feel today, at not having my brother. It was then that I had to face my anger at God for taking someone so young, who offered so much to so many, and who meant so much to me. I had to make a decision about whether to hang on to the anger that would lead me to bitterness, or I could cling to my faith and with help from Jesus, carry my cross of grief and longing. I chose to become better, not bitter.

We all will, at some time in our lives, be faced with that choice. It may even happen more than once. And each time we ask: Where do we go from here? Friends, we must go to the cross of Christ. Jesus tells us "Unless you take up the cross and follow Me, you can't be My disciple." He's telling us each to make the commitment to accept our own cross and to help others carry theirs. Recognize that there is a higher purpose—as Jesus said in His prayer to His father, "not My will, but Yours." We must make a conscious choice to bear our crosses, endure our suffering, and ask for strength from God to help us do it. We need to look for ways we can help others with their crosses and suffering. And we must trust God. Where do we go from here? We go to Christ so that we can become better, not bitter.

What I admire most about Father Arnold...

There is so much I admire. He gave me so much. One thing I will forever remember is: if there was something out of place on the floor, Father Arnold would pick it up. One day as he was bending to pick up one of my messes, I offered to pick it up for him. His reply was "Oh no, I always say a prayer for whoever dropped this." From that day on I often left something in his pathway. Now when I pick something up, I pray for that person. So many lessons I learned from him... so much love he gave so freely.

Diane VanValkenburg, Director, Faith Formation, Holy Name of Jesus

Don't You Care?

✝

Your sons and daughters were eating and drinking wine in their eldest brother's house; and behold a great wind came up across the wilderness and struck the four corners of the house, and it fell upon the young people, and they are dead"

Job 1:18-19

On that day, when evening had come, He said to them, "Let us go across to the other side." And leaving the crowd, they took Him with them, just as He was, in the boat. And other boats were with Him. And a great storm of

214

wind arose, and the waves beat into the boat, so that the boat was already filling. But He was in the stern, asleep on the cushion and they woke Him and said to Him, "Teacher, do you not care if we perish?" And He awoke and rebuked the wind and said to the sea, "Peace! Be still!" And the wind ceased and there was a great calm. He said to them, "Why are you afraid? Have you no faith?" And they were filled with awe, and said to one another, "Who then is this, that even wind and sea obey Him?"

Mark 4:35-41

Both of our readings today focus on coping with stress and suffering. They have a common setting—a storm. In the reading from Job, a terrible storm sweeps over a house and kills all ten of Job's children. In the other, a storm comes up when Jesus and the Apostles are in a boat on the Sea of Galilee. Jesus is asleep, and the Apostles worry about their survival. Both stories are about "hanging on" in the midst of stress.

In our lives today, we certainly have the weather storms spoken of in the readings. However, the "storms" we deal with may have more to do with things like:

Kids growing up right

The atmosphere at your job

Finances at home

Loss of friends

Dealing with alcoholism or addiction

When these things happen, we might feel, like the Apostles, that our "boat" is being tossed about in the sea. Friends, the best thing we can do when the boat is tossing is rock with it! This means accepting that there are areas we cannot control. Realizing this and letting go can lead us to submitting our will to that of God. This submission can be a really difficult process for many of us.

What struck me about the Book of Job was how tough it was for Job. Job was a wealthy, religious, good man. He was also very successful—he was a cattle man with many huge herds. But he lost it all, his ten children and all of his wealth, and was considered cursed by many. A whole series of catastrophes occurred that took everything he had. Even his wife turned on him. She got out, left him. She jumped out of the boat when it started rocking! And then she turned on God as well. She told Job not to waste his time with religion. Then Job's three friends told him that maybe Job deserved the suffering as punishment—they accused him of sinning! Job knew he had not sinned and kept his faith and he eventually got through all of his trials. He stubbornly clung to his faith even when those closest to him suggested he give it up.

In the reading from Mark, Jesus and the Apostles were crossing the Sea of Galilee when an unexpected storm came up and the boat was getting swamped. They were terrified, and there was their leader, asleep! They woke Him and asked Him, "Don't You care?"

We, too, when we find ourselves in a storm-tossed boat, may wonder if God is paying any attention to us and ask, "Don't You care?" Don't You care, God, that I have a malignant tumor and would leave three very young children motherless if I die? Don't You care that my child is on drugs? Don't You care that I can't pay all my bills even though I work hard day after day?

Sometimes in our helplessness, we feel like children. I read a story a while ago about a little girl who stood with her mother in a line in front of the gas chambers at the Belzec concentration camp during World War II. She didn't understand what was happening, but she could see how distressed everyone around her was. As they drew closer, she tugged at her mother's sleeve and said, "Mama, why are we going in there? It's dark, and I've been a good girl."

She didn't understand it. There are times when we've each probably felt like that little girl, on a smaller scale. We've been good! We've done everything the "right way." Why isn't life working out the way we think it should? A storm is raging all around us, our little boat is tossing around with waves crashing over the sides. And we cry out, "Jesus, don't you care?"

Or maybe it's more like this: there we are cruising through life, dealing confidently with everything that comes by. Some days even leave us feeling like Superman or Superwoman. All of a sudden, a big storm blows in, the boat starts rocking, and we find we are only Clark Kent after all. Then what? We turn to God. When we feel inadequate to deal with life's pressures, we are comforted by the promise that God is with us. And we know that somehow we'll get through the ordeal. That's how it's supposed to be, right?

Some of us know that's not always the case. Sometimes we call out to God and experience nothing, only silence. And like those disciples in the boat who find their master sleeping while they quake in terror, we wonder, "Is God asleep?"

Silence between two people can be uncomfortable if it goes on for a short while, but when it goes on a long time, it can break your heart, particularly when it's God's silence. When we turn to God for comfort and hear only silence, we may ask, is He really there? What a bleak, hopeless feeling that can be. But could it be that God speaks even in the silence?

This is probably one of the most difficult things to grasp as we suffer and hope and expect an answer from God: the idea that God may be speaking to us even in the silence. Could it be that God is expecting us to use that time for some purpose? That time of silence can be a time of self-examination. It can be a time of reflecting on those things that are most important to us. Do we need His silence to think and then to confront our fears and the inadequacy of our faith as the Apostles in the boat did? Can we use this time to surrender to God's amazing love? Can this silence lead us to submit our will to God's will?

Some of us, when faced with this enormous silence from God, may fall into the trap of wondering if we deserve the pain and suffering in punishment for what we may have done. That's what Job's friends thought, and fortunately he didn't listen to them. Now, fortunately for us, Jesus reassured us that this is not the case when he said in the gospel of John, "He suffers not because of sin, but that the works of God may be made manifest." So rest assured that we do not suffer punishments, nor does God send suffering to our loved ones, because of our sins.

It was in great fear that the disciples woke Jesus their Teacher, and asked "Do you not care that we are perishing?" But Jesus got up, rebuked the wind, and calmed the sea. He turned to the disciples and asked them why they were afraid. He also asked, "Have you no faith?" The storm outside created a storm inside as well—a storm of fear. And that fear could have been calmed if they had come to grips with their doubts. And isn't that often the case with us, as well?

In the silence we may wrestle with all that we think is important to us. Then, all of a sudden, everything is still. We find that God has, after all, calmed the storm within us. We find that God has given us peaceful acceptance of a painful situation. We often find that it is then that we can marvel over what God has done, His great work.

We recognize that even when we thought God was sleeping, He was at work all along. He provided us with people who care, people to listen, to pray for us, to help and support us. And we found strength, within ourselves and within those same people who offered support in other ways. They help us hang on and stay in the boat!

We find that through our pain and suffering, our faith in God has changed, grown, and deepened. And like those fearful disciples in the boat, we are filled with great awe. I'm always amazed that sometimes people even reach the point of being grateful of the terrible ordeal they experienced, because it helped them move so far in their spiritual journey.

I hope we are closer to knowing how much indeed God does care for each of us. Don't wish away the storms, rather, trust in God to see you through them.

In Our Weakness,
We Are Strong

✝

... He said to me, "My grace is
sufficient for you, for power is
made perfect in weakness."

(2 Corinthians 12:9)

In our reading today, we learn that Paul was afflicted with a physical condition that caused him great pain. He begged God three times to alleviate His suffering, but God refused. He told Paul that His grace was enough, and in Paul's weakness, His power would reach perfection. It had to be tough for Paul to get an answer like that. And what does it mean, anyway, that power reaches perfection in weakness?

Maybe a story from Tim Galway's book, *The Inner Game of Tennis*, can help us understand. One cold snowy winter night when Galway was driving from Maine to New Hampshire, his car slid off a deserted country road. It was 20 degrees below zero, the car wouldn't start, and he had only a light jacket with him. He had no gloves, no phone, no map, and no idea exactly where he was. He began to run along the road but soon tired. Reality set in as he trudged along, with freezing ears, fingers, and toes. Galway thought, "I could die." At first he was frantic and panicky, but eventually reached the point of calmness: "Okay, whatever happens, I am ready." At that point, he saw a house nearby and was able to reach safety. Galway later reflected that when he reached the point of calmness, he felt a new power come into him. He found strength in the weakness that came from detachment, from letting go.

It's certainly hard for us modern Americans to understand the idea of power in weakness. An essential part of our character is to be in control. Books and seminars encourage us to 'pull our own strings,' 'look out for #1,' and 'win through intimidation.' We go through life aggressively because we believe that to be weak is to be at the mercy of others. We spend much time and energy denying our human limitations and avoiding any signs of weakness. Sickness, suffering, and death are the great enemies, which must be destroyed. But how? The modern answer is typically money, power, sex, or technological know-how. Because of this it can take us a long time to understand the cross, and to let go of the "I can do it." Until we let it go, we will find it difficult to believe that we need God.

The Scriptures offer us a different response for handling the pain of our human condition. In his second letter to the Corinthians, Paul reminds us that our humanity is not to be denied, but accepted. We will experience our share of human weaknesses and limitations. We will grow older, slower, grayer, and maybe a little heavier around the middle. We will become less agile or upbeat than we once were. We may experience chronic pain and illness. Suffering, depression, and loneliness could become constant companions. We may even identify with the lament of the writer of Psalm 102: "My days pass like smoke, and my bones burn like a furnace... I lie awake. I am a lonely bird on the housetop... I wither away like grass." (Psalm 102:3,7,11)

St. Paul offers us a message of hope, however, by reminding us that humans are more than just plain earthen vessels. We are earthen vessels that house the spirit of God! We are wonderfully made, a little less than the angels. Even though we may be afflicted, perplexed, persecuted, and struck down, we will not be overcome. The healing presence of God transforms all our hurts and brokenness into something meaningful. Our sufferings—accepted in faith and borne with patience—become a way in which we can manifest Jesus, proclaiming that life is stronger than death.

Jesus is the true vine, sent in the flesh to proclaim God's word of forgiveness and healing. Everyone who turns to the Lord in faith is given the grace to bear fruit that lasts. What is this fruit? The fruit of abiding in Jesus is love. This abiding in Jesus is especially important in our moments of weakness and suffering. It is so easy to despair and become a prisoner of our pain. We may want to withdraw from God and others. We could become more and more lonely and depressed. Our pain might consume our thoughts and feelings and narrow our everyday horizons.

We need not remain in the prison of pain. Look again to the Psalm 102 for inspiration. The psalmist, in the midst of affliction, searches for a meaning beyond the present suffering. He looks for a hope that endures, and so he turns to the Lord: "But thou, O Lord, art enthroned forever; thy name endures to all generations… it is the time of favor; the appointed time has come." (Psalm 102:12, 13)

This part of the psalm gives us a most attractive insight into God. The Lord will build up Zion. He will regard the prayer of the destitute and not despise their supplication. In other words, our God is a God who cares. He is not indifferent to the sufferings and prayers of His people. He is involved with His people and labors to save them.

The lament in Psalm 102 continues: "From heaven, the Lord looked at the earth, to hear the groans of the prisoners, to set free those who were doomed to die so that the name of the Lord may be declared in Zion, and His praise in Jerusalem, when peoples gather together, and kingdoms, to worship the Lord." (Psalm 102:19-22)

These verses tell us that the Lord is a compassionate and loving God. He requires that we be a community of love and healing. We are to be a people filled with hope, standing under the cross and journeying toward the empty tomb of Easter morning. We are to believe that this earthly existence is not the last word and to encourage each other with the hope of the risen Lord. This hope will sustain us in our present suffering and illness. It isn't an escape or an easy panacea to get us out of tough times. Rather, it is a source of power to help us endure them and be one with Jesus and His suffering.

The sacrament of Anointing of the Sick is a present sign of strength and grace. It is a sacrament of hope that directs us toward this vision in the Book of Revelation: "He will wipe away every tear from their eyes, and death shall be no more; neither shall there be mourning nor crying nor pain anymore, for the former things have passed away." (Revelation 21:4)

So when trials, hardship, and crosses come, remember there is strength in weakness, if you let go and let God's power take over. Hang in there and offer it up, but don't give up. It's easy to stop loving, to grow angry, and to become bitter. Instead, turn to God and become better.

I think there's no better closing to this homily than the words of a poem written by an unknown Confederate soldier:

I asked for health, that I might do greater things;

I was given infirmity, that I might do better things.

I asked for riches, that I might be happy;

I was given poverty, that I might be wise.

I asked for power, that I might have the praise of men;

I was given weakness, that I might feel the need of God.

I asked for all things, that I might enjoy life;
I was given life, that I might enjoy all things.
I got nothing I asked for, but everything I hoped for;
Almost despite myself, my unspoken prayers were answered,
I am among all men most richly blessed.

○

"For where two or three are gathered together there am I in the midst of them." Matthew 18:20

Father Arnold loved "gathering," and in that spirit of love we gathered. We gathered as a church, a staff, and as a family. He would often comment, "We are one family, the family of God." Our favorite memory is about gathering at one of the staff parties at the Bayrischer Hof in Montrose. Father knew how to have a good time and sooner or later everyone in the building knew it. You could depend on him to try the menthol snuff or pass around the boot of beer. Soon he was leading us all in the schnitzelbank song. By the end of the evening, there were people that were not even employed at Holy Name asking Father if they could join his table! Of course he said yes, because he believed "The more, the merrier."

Jodie and Paul Keefe, staff and family of Holy Name of Jesus

Life is Difficult

✝

Jesus said to them, "They need not go away. You give them something to eat."

(Matthew 14:16)

How many of you have heard about or read *The Road Less Traveled*, a book by M. Scott Peck? It begins with this simple sentence: "Life is difficult." Most of us would agree with that. After all, it's one of the reasons we're in church. We come here not only to praise and thank God, but also to ask for His help in coping with our problems.

Modern life moves fast, and things can change very quickly. This causes stress. Our challenge is to control that stress and not let it control us. This is easy to say and difficult to do in such a busy society. Many of us feel so stressed out, in fact, that we believe that there is more stress nowadays than there ever used to be. I don't think that's true.

Jesus certainly experienced stress back in the time that He walked the earth. Think about it. His cousin, John the Baptist, was slain by King Herod. The Pharisees harassed Him continually and the crowds would never leave Him alone. Then, in the end, His friends abandoned Him, and He died a painful death. Talk about stress!

Even in today's Gospel, one of the most beloved in the New Testament, there's stress. At the start of the reading, Jesus is trying to withdraw to a solitary place where He could rest. But, as always, the crowds follow Him, and He feels compassion for the people, heals the sick, and preaches to them. As evening approaches the disciples become anxious and suggest that Jesus send the crowds away so they could go buy themselves some food somewhere. Jesus tells them it's unnecessary to send the people away. He says, "You give them something to eat."

Of course there are many different lessons to learn from the story of the loaves and fishes, but today I'd like to focus on what it says about stress. The story illustrates two distinctly different approaches to stress—the approach of the apostles and the approach of Jesus.

First, let's look at the apostles. You probably haven't noticed how seldom the Gospels show them in a favorable light. We tend to make heroes of the apostles. After all, they were responsible for getting the church going. We'd probably be heathens if they hadn't been faithful to God's call! Yet the Gospels usually show the apostles with all their human weaknesses and difficulties. They often seem doubtful, suspicious, anxious, or frightened about one thing or another. In today's Gospel the disciples are once again stressed out. Five thousand men and their families have come to hear the master. They've hung out all afternoon, and now it's suppertime. What's to be done? There are no Golden Arches in sight.

We can identify with the apostles' anxiety. When extra people show up at dinnertime, we feel just as stressed as they were. What will we do? Food doesn't come out of thin air. At least not since Moses and the Exodus. Like the apostles, we look at the cloud instead of the silver lining. We live by fear, and not by faith.

Now let's look at Jesus, who remains kind, compassionate, and peaceful, despite being exhausted and continually dealing with so many problems. What's His secret to serenity? How does He handle the stressful dinner situation in today's Gospel?

With confidence

Jesus faced stress with confidence. When the disciples suggested that He send the hungry people home, Jesus said not to do that, but to "take care of them yourselves." He was a true leader who spoke with amazing authority. When He said, "You take care of it," to the disciples, He expected them to display the same type of confidence, to trust in God that things were going to work out. That's what faith is—a confident assurance concerning things hoped for and a conviction about things not seen. Jesus had that, and we can too.

You say, "Well, it was easy for Jesus. He was God's son." Friends, Jesus prayed, "Our Father..." Aren't we also God's children? Why do we allow our fears to drive us?

With calmness

The disciples were frantic because they found only five loaves of bread and two fish among the whole hungry crowd. Jesus, however, remained calm and simply requested that the loaves and fishes be brought to Him. He told the disciples to go and get everyone to sit down. It gave them something helpful to do. Sometimes the best thing we can do for people is to help them be still. Sometimes it's the best thing we can do for ourselves. Be still. Be still and know that He is God.

This reminds me of a story about a man sitting by a pond who accidentally dropped in a valuable coin. He poked around in the water for a while with a stick in an attempt to get his coin up from the bottom, but all that did was stir up a lot of matter, and soon he couldn't see anything. Not knowing what else to do, the man just sat there quietly thinking. A few minutes later he glanced down and saw that the water was clear again, and there was his coin in any easy place to retrieve. Sometimes the best thing you can do in a stressful situation is quit running frantically around. Sit down, or maybe kneel down. Compose yourself and commune with God.

With competence

When the disciples brought Jesus the loaves and fishes, He blessed the food and fed the people. He fed them spiritual food as well as physical food. He healed their bodies and their spirits. People flocked to Jesus because He did the job and did it well. He did what He could, and left it at that. He didn't let himself get hurried or frustrated.

You and I ought to do the same. One way to relieve stress is to become competent in areas that are important to you. For example, if being a parent is important, spend time with your children, read parenting books and magazines, attend parenting workshops, or become a part of a parenting group. Then you won't be as likely to feel threatened by your teenager's rebellious behavior. Another example is work. Do everything you can to succeed there. Organize, prioritize, and strategize so you can make your time count. Keep up with new information in your field. Do your best to get along with coworkers. Then, if you get a boss who is difficult to please, you'll be less likely to feel insecure. You'll be surprised how much stress you can eliminate from your life if you work hard at being competent.

With companionship

Jesus spent much time with His disciples because He wanted to train them to continue His work after He was gone. No doubt He also counted on them for friendship and emotional support. I think stress can be relieved by such support. We need good friends to keep us from coming unglued, so find some good spiritual people to associate with. I know that my own stress is lessened because I can count on a great staff here at Holy Name. Of course, Jesus' greatest companion was His father in heaven. No wonder He could deal so well with all the stress He had.

Friends, I think that we should look at what's going on inside us when we feel stressed. Most often, stress is not out there somewhere separate from us. It isn't caused by something external. Instead, it

228

comes from an internal thinking process that makes us view life in an 'ain't it awful' kind of way. Do you think this isn't true? Then why is it, when people have similar problems, some get stressed out and others don't?

This reminds me of a story about an American ambassador who was taking part in an important convention. He was having a hard time falling asleep because he was so worried about a presentation he was to give to several other dignitaries in the morning. He kept tossing and turning and thrashing about, until his wife finally intervened.

Wife: Let me ask you something.

Ambassador: What is it?

Wife: Did God govern the world before you were born?

Ambassador: Yes.

Wife: Will God govern the world after you die?

Ambassador: Yes, of course.

Wife: Then why don't you think he's governing the world right now while you're in it?

The ambassador thought about it for a minute, then rolled over and went to sleep.

Friends, stress is a part of life. Learn to manage it. Imitate Jesus. Meet stress head on with confidence, calmness, competence, and companionship, and use the fail-proof stress buster—prayer. It won't always remove what's causing your stress, but it will help you deal with it. Prayer restores calm, while relieving tension, headaches, and fatigue. Just read the Bible, and let the words slowly sink in. Say your old favorites. Or it can be helpful to simply repeat simple phrases like these: "Our Father," "Jesus is Lord," "Come, Holy Spirit," and "Hail Mary."

Yes, life is difficult. But with God's help, we can learn to handle the problems and stresses that come our way. Then our lives will have the quality and purpose that they're meant to have.

In the 1980's my son had graduated from Holy Name 6th grade and moved to Orono Middle School. I was on staff in the Religious Education program at Holy Name and he was not the most responsible kid on the block. He was in football and continually neglected to inform me of when practices were and when he would need a ride to and from practice.

One day in August we were frantically busy trying to get class schedules organized, teachers trained, etc. Steve called and said he needed a ride home from football practice. I had a meeting scheduled and simply couldn't leave so I told him if he couldn't inform me ahead of time so I could schedule such things he would simply have to walk home (about 5 miles to near Holy Name).

Clever young man that he was, he, of course stuck out his thumb. Much to his great good fortune, and my eternal embarrassment, Father Arnold picked him up.

Steve had just switched from hockey to football because we all felt football would take less time away from the family. Father Arnold and Steve had quite a conversation on that ride about the impact of sports on family life. In fact, Father used it in homilies several times. Steve also learned to plan ahead a little better.

Father Arnold has been a dear friend of our family. He has shared our joys and sorrows... and lots of laughs too. He walked us through the death of our parents/grandparents; husband/ father; through the struggle with cancer. I enjoyed many trips to Europe with him. He often shared our Christmas Eve dinner with us. We miss him a lot.

Kathleen Hansmann, Parishioner of Holy Name of Jesus

Finding Comfort in Jesus When Facing Suffering and Death

✝

Come to me, all you who are weary and find life burdensome, and I will refresh you... Your souls will find rest, for my yoke is easy and my burden light.

Matthew 11:28-30

Today is All Soul's Day, and you may wish to visit the cemetery to remember those who have gone before us. We devote our prayers today to our dead in hopes that they may attain Heaven if they haven't already. As Catholics we believe that if a person dies in less than perfect grace, but without mortal sin, the soul would go to Purgatory, to be given another chance. So we pray that God will be merciful, that God will grant forgiveness, and that He will welcome them into the eternal light of heaven.

This tradition comes to us primarily from the second book of Maccabees. In that book, many Jews died in a battle, and when their fellow soldiers went to bury them, they discovered that the dead Jewish soldiers were wearing amulets for a false idol beneath their tunics. Judas Maccabeus, their leader, ordered the remaining men to pray and offer suffering that the sin of the dead be blotted out. In doing so he made atonement for the dead that they might be freed from their sin. In the New Testament, there are two references in Scripture in which St. Paul mentions praying for the dead. From these came the tradition in the Catholic Church to pray for the deceased.

About a year ago, a well-known and beloved church leader died. The cardinal-archbishop of Chicago, Joseph Bernadin, died of cancer of the pancreas and liver on November 14, 1996. Cardinal Bernadin wrote a book before he died about the last three years of his life. It's a small but powerful book of personal reflections that he called *The Gift of Peace* (Loyola Press: 1997). In his book, Cardinal Bernadin describes two traumatic and fearful events that occurred in his last three years: the false accusations of sexual misconduct leveled against him, and his battle with the aggressive form of cancer that eventually caused his death.

Letting Go

Cardinal Bernadin's reflections during this very difficult time of his life give testimony to his faith, his hope, and his life. Today, as we celebrate the Feast of All Souls, and remember in a special way all who have died, especially our own beloved family members and friends, I think that the theme of Cardinal Bernadin's book is very appropriate. His theme is "letting go." He explains the theme at the beginning of his book as this: "By letting go, I mean the ability to release from our grasp those things that inhibit us from developing an intimate relationship with the Lord Jesus... Still, letting go is never easy. I have prayed and struggled constantly to be able to let go of things more willingly, to be free of everything that keeps the

Lord from finding greater hospitality in my soul or interferes with my surrender to what God asks of me... But there is something in us humans that makes us want to hold unto ourselves everything and everybody familiar to us. My daily prayer is that I can open wide the doors of my heart to Jesus and His expectations of me."

I Will Refresh You

His book of reflections show how slowly and surely the cardinal did let go of his work, his plans, his projects, and eventually his whole life as his illness progressed and caused him much pain. He presided at a communal anointing of the sick not long before he died. He quoted the comforting words of Jesus we just heard in today's gospel: "Come to me, all you who are weary and find life burdensome, and I will refresh you... Your souls will find rest, for my yoke is easy and my burden light."

The Cardinal followed this with these comments: "This is a favorite passage of mine, and possibly, one of yours also. It is so comforting, so soothing... Jesus practices what He preached. He was gentle toward the people He served and was humbly obedient to the will of His Father. He called us to love one another and laid down His own life for us. The 'rest' He offers us comes from His attitudes, His values, His mission, His ministry, His willingness to lay down His very life—in whatever circumstances we find ourselves.

"What makes Jesus' yoke 'easy'? A good yoke is carefully shaped to reduce chafing to a minimum. Jesus promises that His yoke will be kind and gentle to our shoulders, enabling us to carry our load more easily. That is what He means when he says his burden is 'light'. Actually, it might be quite heavy, but we will find it possible to carry out our responsibilities. Why? Because Jesus will help us."

Cardinal Bernadin continued with this: "Perhaps the ultimate burden is death itself. It is often preceded by pain and suffering, sometimes extreme hardships... But notice that Jesus did not promise to take away our burdens. He promised to help us carry them. And if we let go of ourselves—and our own resources—and allow the Lord to help us, we will be able to see death not as an enemy or a threat, but as a friend."

Death: Burden or Blessing?

As we remember and pray for all our departed brothers and sisters, it is important that we consider death today. Is death a burden or a blessing? An enemy or a friend? Is life a matter of hanging on to the bitter end or letting go and letting God do with us according to God's will? The answer to these questions does not come easily. I'm pretty sure the Cardinal would have chosen life over death if he had had a choice in the matter. But when his doctors told him that his condition was terminal, he chose to put into practice his theme of "letting go." The strength and courage for him and for all of us to "let go" come, of course, from our belief that even Jesus, especially Jesus, had to let go of His life. But it is His death that will make our death a blessing, not a burden: a friend, not an enemy. For as we heard in our second reading, "It is precisely in this that God proves His love for us: that while we were sinners, Christ died for us."

Jesus Christ, true God and true man, beloved Son of God, is no stranger to death. He died the most horrible, painful death possible so He could tell us, "I know exactly what you are going through. That is why I went through death for you."

Whenever we come together to celebrate this Holy Mass we come in contact with His death. For here we do what Jesus did "the night before He died." Here we proclaim, "Christ has died."

But of course, we also come in contact with the other side of death, which is new life. For here we also proclaim, "Christ is risen!" Here we meet and actually eat the body and the blood of the risen Lord Jesus Christ. Here we have the assurance that the Jesus who died for us is still with us. He is still in our midst to help us carry our cross, to make our burden light and to prepare us to meet death as the friend who will introduce us to life everlasting.

Seasons and Special Events of the Active Christian

✝

Advent and Christmas

Lent and Easter

Graduation

Wedding

Thanksgiving

Trinity Sunday

Funeral

Wake Up, Shape Up, Cheer Up, Hurry Up

✝

Four weeks of Advent
Excerpts from homilies and Bulletin articles

oday is the first Sunday of Advent, and as I look at the readings for Advent, in all three of the cycles I see that there are many words to describe the purpose of Advent—renew, rejoice, repent, resign, come, be prepared, and the list could go on and on. It seems to me that the special words are *be prepared*. It's clear from scripture—The Son of Man will come to judge. We need to be prepared.

The readings for the first Sunday of Advent call for us to wake up and be alert, so I like to call this "Wake Up" Sunday. The church has no idea when the Son of Man will come, thus the instruction to be watchful and alert. We can keep His first coming in mind as an assurance that He will come again. His birth in Bethlehem helps our belief in His return. How He will return is a mystery, even though the end is described in symbolic terms. We also hear that it may be as a "thief in the night" which makes it sound like there will be little warning. Some of the Scriptural writing sounds like it will be so sudden that there will be no time to repent. The book of Daniel says He will come as a judge. Either way, it sounds like we better be ready.

How then should we prepare? How do we know we are ready? How can we renew ourselves as followers of Christ? I don't think a lot of us will have the opportunity to show our faith in big ways. In fact the Christian life shouldn't be lived occasionally in just the big events. A steady living of our faith in the day-to-day ordeals, the daily cross, and self-denial, may well be the answer. Self-denial is the best preparation, particularly in the little things like the little favors for our fellow man. Self-denial is the proof or our earnestness in the faith, it requires going out of our way, inconveniencing ourselves in a spirit of preparedness, which can help us at the sudden and unexpected coming of the Son of Man.

Another important theme in Advent besides being prepared, is waiting, not exactly a modern virtue. We are into things being instant, from coffee, to relief, to happiness. We want it NOW. We seem to have an unwillingness or even an inability to wait. In the spiritual life, waiting with patience is a necessity. We need to sit quietly to hear the Lord speak. Close your eyes, sit quietly, and listen. Especially in this season when candles are so important, symbolic of the light of Jesus, sitting quietly in the light of a candle can really help us with this listening.

Wake-up to the need to be prepared, and then to renew your faith as you cultivate a calm, meditative, spiritual Advent journey.

****

There's a priest I know who on the first Sunday in Advent puts up an artificial tree and adds one ornament a day. It's a Jesse tree, which represents the ancestry of Christ, figures from the Old Testament. So, for example, he'll add an apple representing Adam and Eve; animals for Noah's Ark; a birch bark canoe for Moses who was found as a baby floating in the reeds. And all shaped somehow in the shape of a heart. When asked why they're all shaped in a heart, he says so you won't miss what Christmas is all about, it's about the love God has for us. If you don't put your heart into Advent, you probably won't find it on Christmas Eve. So hearts aren't just for Valentine's Day. Jesus comes from the heart of God to fill the hearts of all the people. What kind of heart does God ask us to put in the celebration of Advent? There's a little verse that goes like this: Yesterday is history. Tomorrow is mystery. Today is a gift, that's why we call it the present. It's a play on words in the present time and that's what we look forward to at Christmas. Four weeks from now, the day after Christmas, will our hearts be really filled, or will they be empty?

Second Sunday of Advent

As we look at the readings for this second Sunday of Advent, they are calling for us to Shape Up! You remember that last week we were called to Wake Up to a spirit of renewal in preparation for the coming of our savior Jesus. So now we need to reform and repent in order to shape up and be ready for Him.

The prophet Isaiah, John the Baptist and the Blessed Virgin Mary each give us models for our Advent spiritual journey. They each show a longing to be right with God, a spirit of repentance, and empathy. Looking at the prophet Isaiah, we see one of the best examples in the Old Testament of all who longingly awaited their Redeemer. Isaiah gives us this Advent prayer, "drop down dew ye heavens, from above, and let the clouds rain to just one; let the earth be open and bring forth the Savior."

Although John the Baptist didn't prepare us for the birth of Christ, he did prepare us for Jesus' public mission. John's life and preaching fit well in Advent as he calls for us to prepare for Christ. He is God's herald and the forerunner of Jesus. Just as John the Baptist called the Jewish people to repentance and conversion, so does he call us to "repent for the Kingdom of Heaven."

Advent is the time of conversion of heart. Without putting our hearts into our efforts to shape up, I don't think we'd get very far. John the Baptist gives us encouragement for genuine reformation of life when he says, "prepare the way of the Lord, make straight His path, every valley should be filled, every mountain and hill shall be made low and crooked shall become straight."

Like John and Isaiah, Mary is very much in our minds during Advent as we think of the coming birth of our Savior. The purpose of Advent is to prepare for receiving God's grace, and who could be a better model than Mary? She said "yes" to God and became a true Mother to Him. She completely turned her life over to God. God usually doesn't ask us for nearly as much as He asked of Mary. Shouldn't we be as willing as Mary?

Friends, Advent is about getting rid of the darkness and going into the light. Light came in the world and the darkness did not comprehend it. We have to make sure that when Jesus comes to us that the darkness is gone. Shape up! Use the examples of Isaiah, John the Baptist and Mary, to shed the darkness and invite the light of Christ in.

3rd Sunday of Advent

Today is what we call "Cheer Up" Sunday. Most of the readings for this Sunday in each of the three cycles are focused on joy and rejoicing. Today, the third Sunday of Advent, follows "Wake Up" and "Shape Up" Sundays, the first two Sundays of Advent. The readings for today tell us to "prepare our hearts and remove the sadness that hinders us from feeling the joy and hope that His presence will bestow."

What is the secret of Christmas joy? It's rejoicing in the Lord. The Lord is near—He is with us. Once this is a reality in a person's life, there will be joy. We hear at Christmas time, "Listen, I bring you news of great joy, a joy to be shared by the whole people." Joy in the Lord is forward-looking—the essence of our enjoyment is in the anticipation—Christ will come again to bring us eternal joy. God, who created this world with its goodness and beauty, created joy also. He is love, He is joy. Living in Jesus, living well, moral living—brings joy. It happens as a "result of being a Christian."

Humor is a virtue. Good humor can become a trait of character; we can become a joy to be around. Laughter brings people together. It can be a part of the glue of human communities. It can serve as a channel of grace. Humor testifies that Christian joy can shine brightly even in the darkest times.

Another theme that comes out of our reading for this Advent Sunday is prayer. As we work to prepare ourselves for Jesus, one of the most important ways to do that is through prayer. Talking to God in praise, thanking and asking is prayer. St. Paul wrote in his letter to the Thessalonians that we should pray and rejoice always and never stop. That's a marvelous way for us to be ready for Jesus.

Cheer up—have a joyous week

Fr. Daniel Durken from St. John's Abbey came up with the perfect way to describe how joy is the result of our relationship with Jesus.

Jesus

Jesus Others You

Doing things
for others
helps draw
you closer to
Jesus.

You

Prayer,
Meditation,
Reading

Let me explain how this works. In the vertical line, the "J" stands for Jesus. The "O" stands for nothing, and "Y" is you. It shows that nothing should come between Jesus and you. This calls for using prayer, meditation, reading and learning to deepen our faith.

The horizontal line is about loving others as yourself, doing good works, caring for the poor and disadvantaged, reaching out to others, touching them with our faith. "J" again stands for Jesus, "O" stands for others, and "Y" again for you. It means that doing things for others links you to Jesus, brings you closer to Him. Think of the Be-attitudes. Joy is the result of working on both sides of this angle.

4th Sunday of Advent

The fourth Sunday of Advent is what I refer to as "Hurry Up" Sunday. There's not much time left until Christmas—usually less than a full week, sometimes only a few days. Advent is a short season anyway, and this short week gives us our last chance in preparing ourselves for the coming of our Lord.

This week we see in the liturgical texts an emphasis on Mary. We say Merry Christmas to each other—maybe we should say MARY Christmas, that would be very correct Scripturally and liturgically. The Gospel says, "Mary set out proceeding in haste"—and greeted Elizabeth. When Elizabeth heard Mary's greeting, "the baby in her womb jumped for joy," and Elizabeth poured out her praise of Mary and the child of Mary's womb. The focus of the Gospel is on Mary. That makes a lot of sense to me.

Doesn't it make sense to say that the final four days before Christmas are Mary's days? Who better than Mary can help us focus during these last few days? Mary teaches us to prepare for Jesus through silence, prayer and resignation to God's will. During this last week, pray slowly the Hail Mary and let it touch your heart. Peace and peace-making can be the focus of today's prayer, especially as outside pressures rob us of our few peaceful moments.

I mentioned the Jesse tree that is decorated with heart shaped ornaments. We hang the final ornament today. It is a simple heart, the very heart of Jesus. The heart is the source of love, trust and joy that we have tried to put into our celebration of Advent.

The heart of Jesus was and is filled with strength, dedication and purpose. It was the "strength of the Lord" that enabled Jesus, our shepherd and savior to accept and do God's will: in His lowly birth, throughout His humble life, even unto His unjust death. It was the "strength of the Lord" that enabled Jesus to offer Himself for our salvation, both in taking our human flesh in the incarnation, and in sharing our human death in the crucifixion.

The Lord was Mary's delight because He was her strength just as He is ours. Mary knew that Jesus, God, had fulfilled her people's ancient prayer. The heart of Jesus was filled with all the strength of God: strength for preaching and teaching, strength for curing the sick and raising the dead, strength for living our human life and dying our human death. All that strength empowered Jesus to come to each of us, to accomplish God's will for us, to sanctify us, to be God's peace for us.

During these last four days try to do some special deeds. Do this so we can personally be closer to Mary and Jesus. Then remember our needy people—think of who is lonely. Mother Teresa said in regard to loneliness that "It could well be the most hurting problem." Write a few extra cards, make some phone calls, and seek peace and forgiveness.

Christmas is a gift from God that people cannot keep until we give it to someone else. Christmas is a feast of love. And this love must begin at home. No place is it more important than between spouses and between children.

Friends, He is coming, our Prince of Peace, so be sure you have peace in your heart with everyone. It's the peace of Christmas that should reign in our hearts. When you come for Christmas Mass, let go of the hectic and hurried preparations, allow the time you've spent in preparation to help you find the peace in your heart, and be ready to give yourself to the Savior who came to save us.

So, Mary Christmas, and remember Jesus loves you.

Father Arnold would like to acknowledge that the concepts of "Wake Up", "Shape Up, "Cheer Up" and "Hurry Up" Sunday, and the JOY configuration, originated with a fellow Benedictine priest, Father Daniel Durken, of St. John's Abbey in Collegeville, Minnesota, and Fr. Arnold thanks him for the insight which he so effectively shared with the parishioners at Holy Name of Jesus.

The following poem by Alice H. Mortenson is one that Father Arnold thought was particularly appropriate for "Hurry Up" Sunday.

Ready for Christmas

"Ready for Christmas," she said with a sigh
As she gave a last touch to the gifts piled high.
Then wearily sat for a moment and read
Till soon, very soon, she was nodding her head.
Then quietly spoke a voice in her dream: "Ready for
Christmas! What do you mean?
Ready for Christmas, when only last week
You wouldn't acknowledge your friend on the street!
"Ready for Christmas, while holding a grudge!
Perhaps you had better let God be the judge.
Why, how can the Christ-child come and abide
In a heart that is selfish and filled with pride?
"Ready for Christmas! You've worked, it is true,
But just doing the things that you wanted to do.
Ready for Christmas! Your circle's too small.
Why, you are not ready for Christmas at all!"
She woke with a start, and a cry of despair,
"There's so little time, and I've still to prepare!
Oh, Father, forgive me, I see what you mean;
To be ready means more than a house swept clean!
Yes, more than the giving of gifts and a tree,
It's the heart swept clean that He wants to see,
A heart that is free from bitterness-sin,
Ready for Christmas—means ready for Him!

– Alice H. Mortenson

Christmas: The Greatest Story of Love

The people who walked in darkness have seen a great light; upon those who dwelt in the land of gloom a light has shone. You have brought them abundant joy and great rejoicing . . . For a child is born to us, a son is given us; upon His shoulder dominion rests. They name Him Wonder-Counselor, God-Hero, Father-Forever, Prince of Peace . . .

(Isaiah 9:1-6)

*B*eloved: the grace of God has appeared, saving all and training us to reject godless ways and worldly desires and to live temperately, justly, and devoutly in this age, as we await the blessed hope, the appearance of the glory of our great God and Savior Jesus Christ. (Titus 2:11-14)

In those days Caesar Augustus published a decree ordering a census… So all went to be registered, each to his own town. And Joseph, too, went up from Galilee from the town of Nazareth to Judea, to the city of David that is called Bethlehem, because he was of the house and family of David, to be enrolled with Mary, his betrothed, who was with child. While they were there, the time came for her to have her child, and she gave birth to her firstborn son. She wrapped Him in swaddling clothes and laid Him in a manger, because there was no room for them in the inn. (Luke 2:1-9)

Christmas is all about love

Friends in Christ, the Christmas Story is about love, the greatest love story of all of history. God so loved the world that He sent His only begotten son, that whoever believes in Him shall not die, but shall live. God's son came not for condemnation but for salvation. So great is this story, that all of history dates itself from the birth of Jesus. We refer to dates as so many years before Christ or so many years after Christ. The whole world recognizes that there was something special about that love story about the birth of Jesus.

I would like to share tonight three ideas about this Christmas love story. The first idea has to do with tracing our roots. The second reflects on the idea of a Savior being born. And third, that this Savior is the light of the world.

Tracing our roots

Many people enjoy learning about their roots. With great curiosity some will spend countless hours going through old documents from as far back as possible to trace their family's history.

I meet people every year from the parish who have gone to Germany or Ireland to trace their roots.

Some people even hire a company to produce a genealogy for them. Many people enjoy learning whether they have a family crest. In addition, we enjoy hearing stories from the elders about relatives they personally knew, so the descendants can get a sense of what their ancestors were like. And, of course, grandchildren enjoy asking their grandparents what their parents were like when they were children.

Christmas is one of those special events that brings together members of the extended family. That's why many of you are here today, either coming home or visiting relatives. That's why many members of our parish are gone today. They wish to be with extended family. There is much love to share, many stories to tell, a lot of catching up to do, and just good old fashioned enjoying the holidays with one another.

This evening we have gathered in this church to do the same: to remember, to celebrate. Through the sacred scriptures we traced back not only the human lineage of Jesus, but we also traced back our Christian roots in Jesus. And so we gather to share these sacred writings. Each Mass, Christmas Eve and Christmas Day, has different readings giving us a chance to catch up with people we may not have heard from in the readings throughout the year.

Christmas is a fulfillment of all the accounts of the Old Testament prophets concerning the birth of the Messiah. Christmas is a promise of salvation given to us as a free gift for all who are willing to hold the infant Jesus close to their hearts. Christmas truly celebrates how divinity and humanity are combined, how heaven touches earth and how earth can touch heaven, how we can embrace God and how God embraces us. That's Christmas.

And so as we celebrate the birth of Jesus this evening, let's be grateful for our roots, our extended family through all the earth, a family which allows us to be brothers and sisters of Jesus.

In my 45 years as a priest, I have been blessed to spend every Christmas at home with my family—8 living siblings, their spouses and children, and my mother, who's 95. About a month ago I got the idea that maybe I was going to do this differently. It's getting hard for me with all the Masses and driving 90 miles there, then driving 90 miles back all in the same day.

So I wrote home about a month ago saying that I was going to come home the day after Christmas rather than on Christmas Day. Sister Jane in our family, who spoke here one time, is the one who keeps track of everybody in the family. I would decide which day and time I would be there for Christmas and then she would invite everybody at that time. When it got closer to Christmas, I called up Sister Jane, and I could tell by her voice that she didn't like my change of plan for Christmas. So I told her that I would, after all, come home on Christmas Day. She said, "I thought you'd change your mind." She not only keeps track of everybody, she seems to have almost prophetic insight into what will happen! So I'm going home tomorrow and looking forward to it.

A Savior has been born for us

Typically on this night, we focus on the miracle of that birth in Bethlehem nearly 2000 years ago. We appropriately worship the God who humbled Himself to dwell among us. We celebrate His coming. But perhaps the focus of our celebration should not be on the infant Jesus, but the salvation that the Christ-child brings to the world in His adult life. To celebrate Christmas is to know what happened. And what happened is that our salvation came in the form of this Savior born that Christmas Eve.

In our reading from Luke, we learn that a census was being done and that the census was taken during the reign of Augustus Caesar. Augustus Caesar reigned from 27 B. C. to 14 A.D., and historians refer to that period as Pax Augusta because there was peace during Augustus's reign. In fact, almost everyone in the world was at peace when Jesus was born. What a time for the Prince of Peace to be born!

Luke carefully uses titles like "Savior" to describe Jesus as one who rescues humanity from sin. Messiah in Hebrew, and Christus in Greek identify Jesus as the anointed one of God. Lord, the most frequently used title in Luke's gospel, is a tribute to the dominion of Jesus over all humanity.

But Christmas is much more than the celebration of the historic birth of our Lord. It's about God keeping His promise that He would save humanity. It's about God coming to us as our Savior. What a lesson for us to learn tonight: that it was through the grace of God that Jesus came to us and brought salvation. That it is because of this that Paul says in his letter to Titus that we have to live temperately, justly, and devoutly, as we wait in the blessed hope of him coming again.

Tonight we celebrate that Jesus was born for us; that our lives are different because of Him. Our hope of eternal life is assured. And together as true followers of Jesus, we can make certain there is good news of great joy and peace on earth.

The Savior is the light of the world

Finally, this Savior who was born to us, who lived His life for us, who died for us, is the light of the world. Isaiah speaks of a time when people who walk in darkness will see a great light, and that a child will be born to us, a son is given to us. And look at the wonderful titles Isaiah gives to that person who was born for us: the Counselor, and the Prince of Peace.

There is no better description of Jesus than saying that He is the light of the world. And there is no better symbol of Jesus than the candle. You know, if you darken this place, one light gives you sense of direction. We can use the beacon of the light of Jesus to keep us on the right track, to keep our focus on Him.

Did you ever notice when you get close to the light you can feel its warmth? It always reminds me of when the disciples were on their way to Emmaus. They didn't know they were walking with

Jesus. When they discovered they were walking with Jesus, they said, "Weren't our hearts burning within us when He spoke?" Our hearts, too, will burn from within when we speak with Jesus, when we're close to Him.

Have you noticed that when you really want to follow Jesus in a culture like ours you might get burned? There are so many cultural behavior patterns that lead us in a direction away from the light of Jesus. In fact, we might say that to follow Jesus is to go counter-culture. As Christians we may be called to be counter-culture and speak up about the wrong directions those cultural behaviors may lead a person. When you have the courage to be different than the culture, you might feel that you get burned by people. But when you get close enough to the light of Jesus, you'll feel the warmth of basking in that light, and your hearts will burn within you in a good way—like the disciples on the road to Emmaus. So when you have the courage to be counter-culture and you get burned, you're a real Christian!

In the Gospel of John we find that he describes Jesus as the light that shines on in darkness. He constantly talks about darkness as death, rejection that's sin, and the light that overcomes it. The message of Christmas gives us hope in Jesus Christ—the light of the world, a light which no darkness can extinguish. Even the major trials and problems of life cannot snuff out the light of Christ.

The greatest gifts

Every Christmas I go through all my cards and the last day before Christmas I pick one out for myself. I keep that one. I've been doing this for the 17 years I've been at Holy Name. This year I received 12 of the same card. You know what that means? There are at least 12 people who contributed to the Maryknoll Missionaries and received a card in return. That means at least 12 people gave something to Maryknoll in honor of this Benedictine pastor. Isn't that nice? I'll really treasure that. My greatest gifts are when people give to someone else in my name.

I have a little story that I heard from Paul Harvey, the radio commentator. It goes like this. A little boy, Michael, listened intently to the priest telling the story of Mary and Joseph and the birth of the baby Jesus. He heard how the time was near for the baby to be born and how there was no room in the inn for them to stay. They would have to make the best of the stable with the animals. At this point Michael nudged his mother and said proudly, "I'll bet when they heard who He was they made room for Him."

To this Paul Harvey added, "No Michael, we do know who He is… and we still don't make room for Him."

I have to share with you a letter tonight. I got this in the mail after a call from a woman in Brooklyn Park who says she goes to church here. Her husband left her a few days ago. She has four children, no car, and no gifts for her children. She had nothing for Christmas. She called up for help. I helped to make sure that she could stay in her apartment and found some gifts for her.

Here's a letter I received in the mail an hour after I helped her. "Please use our anonymous contribution of $400 to help those in need." That was the third time this week that I received a contribution to help those in need, and was able to help someone within the hour. God bless us.

In fact, I mentioned in a morning Mass this week that I had helped someone out, and after Mass someone came by with a donation. I asked if I could use that one for the one I'd already helped. No, the person said, it's for the next one. So I stay ahead of the game here.

But anyway here's the letter. "Enclosed is a contribution of $400 to use as you see fit. You can believe this. Just last week our children, they're around 4, 5, and 6 years old, were asking about the homeless you talked about. I explained to them that many times people come to you because they have no place else to go and that you help them. I told them that we were giving this money to you so that you would help those people. My children decided that next year they wanted to start saving their money for the homeless. We are going to New York soon and the children asked if they can give the money they save to the homeless in New York." Children six years old get the message!

The Minneapolis paper this week said there are 12,000 homeless every night in the state of Minnesota. Of those 12,000 homeless, 6,000 are children. Last year on Christmas Eve, about noon, I had two different families at my door, homeless, kicked out of their apartments. One had three children, all of which had pneumonia. I drove them to the Hennepin County hospital in downtown Minneapolis. For the other one I found an apartment. And that all happened between noon and the 3:00 Mass. Just before this Mass at 5:00, I went back to my answering machine and there were two messages which are still on there right now just in the couple of hours since today's 3:00 Mass.

Is there room at your inn?

Friends, there was no room at the inn when Jesus was born. And Jesus said, "you'll have the poor with you always." What are we willing to do? Two years ago we started having a second collection for the homeless. Last year the week of Christmas I spent from that collection, putting people who didn't have anything into homes.

Be kind to the poor. Look at what you have. Be kind when you're giving to the parish and be kind in the second collection to the homeless. I'll see they get it in less than two weeks. And with no expenses, no overhead!

I finally discovered why I get so many people in need. I'm the only one home! I'm the only one whose home is at the parish. Most priests don't live at the parish anymore. Ministers are married and don't live next to their churches anymore. I'm home; that's why I get them, I guess.

I promise you I will stay home, if for no other reason than that the poor can find me, because they need me.

The Heart of Lent
is Change

✝

When you give alms, do not let your left hand know what your right hand is doing, so that your almsgiving may be a secret. And your Father who sees in secret will repay you.

(Matthew 6:3-4)

I presume that even though we are beginning the season of Lent, it's okay to begin a homily with a lighter story. I'd like to tell you about a man with an open collar shirt who went into a restaurant. He was stopped by the hostess who told him that he must wear a necktie to get into the restaurant. So the man went out to his car and looked around for a tie. He saw some jumper cables. He took them and tied them around his neck in a fairly acceptable looking knot and let the ends dangle free. He went back to the restaurant wearing the jumper cables as a tie. The hostess carefully looked him over for a few moments and then said, "Okay, I guess you can come in. Just don't start anything!"

Well today I'm here to tell you that Ash Wednesday is the start of something. Lent, the season of the church year that leads us to Easter, is here already. Ash Wednesday comes early this year. It seems as though we just finished the Christmas season, so it looks like we are going straight from the crib to the cross. Out of the crib and onto the cross.

Traditionally, Lent has been a time of repentance and self denial. It's a time to take stock of our lives. And so, we ask ourselves some questions this evening. The main question I ask is this: When we look at ourselves, whether 40, 50, or 60 years old, how different are we than when we were half our age? If Lent is about change, if Lent is about transformation, if Lent is about being different, then how different are we now at say, 76 years old compared to when we were 38 years old? Are we more patient now? Are we more dependent on God now? If we had a grudge about something 20 years ago, do we still hold that grudge? When we were inclined to be judgmental before, do we find ourselves less inclined to being judgmental now? Friends, that's the heart of what I think Lent is all about. It's about change. Do we become different? Do we become more Christ-like? Do we let in more of Christ and less of ourselves?

Some people go to Mass week after week and year after year, and never change. Lent gives us the opportunity to break that cycle. Interestingly enough, a grain of wheat remains a grain of wheat unless it dies. There might be nothing worse than staying a nice, little grain of Catholic wheat. It could keep you from becoming the bread of Christ who died for us. This Lent, I challenge all of us to make a change. Today's Gospel gives us some good suggestions on how to get started.

Jesus tells us that doing acts of righteousness is important. It is through these acts of righteousness, that we can begin to change; however, we must be careful not to do these righteous acts in front of others. Remember, there is an important difference between righteousness and being self-righteous.

Almsgiving

The first act of righteousness that Jesus talks about in today's Gospel reading is giving to those in need. We are called to help the poor. Everything we have comes to us freely from God. Likewise, we should give freely to our neighbor. Jesus warns us, however, to keep our giving between God and ourselves.

Prayer

In addition to giving to the needy, we should take a look at our prayer life during Lent. In today's Gospel Jesus reminds us not to put on a big show with our prayers, but to go into a room by ourselves and close the door. I don't think many of us need to worry about being too public with our prayer life. But I think we do need to ask ourselves a tough question. Do we really, really pray enough? When prayer becomes a part of our lives, it can be a fascinating phenomenen. From the window in the office of the rectory, it is so wonderful to look out and see people walking into the Blessed Sacrament Chapel. When I come home at 10:00 at night, people are still going in. Sometimes I see a well-dressed businessman, spending time at holy hour. Other times I see a wife and her husband visit in the middle of the day. I see children with their problems, and I say to myself, what a powerhouse we have in this chapel here. Prayer. Have you ever stopped to visit Jesus in that chapel? Our parish provides this amazing opportunity. Prayer will put the focus of Jesus in you. How often do we pray? Can we pray more?

Fasting

The final act of righteousness that Jesus talks about in today's Gospel is fasting. Jesus tells us that we need to fast, but that we should not look somber while doing it. Fasting is an act of righteousness. It's an act of self control—a way of focusing totally on God and seeking His guidance and help. It is also an expression of sorrow and repentance.

We tend to think of fasting as going without food. Many of us have given up sweets during Lent. That's fine, if it helps you become closer to God. But as I've said before, don't give up sweets and become bitter. That's not the purpose of Lent. There are other ways of fasting. For example we can fast from an activity that we enjoy and use this time to spend with God. This, too, is fasting. When friends need to meet, they'll cancel other plans in order to get together. You can do that with God, too. Cancel the dinner, cancel the party, or turn off the television program and make Him the priority.

Friends, we are to celebrate Lent each year with acts of righteousness. Give to the needy. Pray. And through fasting, show God that He comes first in your life.

If we truly want to change, if we really want to become different, then we need to go straight to the nuts and bolts. Acts of righteousness will help us get there. We are here to start something tonight. We are here to start living during Lent in the way Christ wants us to live. We are here to make a change.

Disappointments, Disappointments, Disappointments

✝

When the great crowd that had come to the feast heard that Jesus was coming to Jerusalem, they took palm branches and went out to meet Him, and cried out: "Hosanna! Blessed is He who comes in the name of the Lord, the king of Israel."

(John 12:12-13)

We began the celebration today with Jesus' triumphant entry into Jerusalem, and the events surrounding His passion. This is why the day is appropriately called "Palm Sunday" or "Passion Sunday." Word had been spreading far and wide about Jesus. He was a healer, a teacher, and a leader. Jesus was becoming quite a celebrity as Holy Week began. And yet, as the crowd waved palm branches and shouted Hosannas, the shadow of the cross loomed in the background. Jesus passed by the crowds in the bright sunlight of adoration. However the cross loomed on the edge of night.

Can you imagine the emotions that surged in Jesus' chest as He rode the donkey into Jerusalem that day? He was not fooled by the crowd's adoration. He knew that public opinion was a fickle thing. One day you are a hero and the next day you're out of office. But Jesus knew what lay ahead for Him, and He did not welcome it. He knew that rejection, pain and death were patiently waiting for the week to play out. It was not the cup He would have chosen for Himself. Jesus had no martyr complex. He did not willingly seek to die. Jesus merely saw it as being obedient to His Father.

Can you imagine the disappointment Jesus felt as He looked into the faces of the people around Him that first Holy Week? Disappointment with the crowds who would shout "Hosanna" one moment and "Crucify Him!" the next. Disappointment with His disciples—one of whom would betray Him, one who would deny Him three times, and His three closest friends who could not even stay awake on the job while He agonized over the cup the Father had placed before Him. Can you imagine the hurt He felt for them?

Disappointments, disappointments, disappointments. Jesus was face to face with disappointment. He knew it would end like this, but it is still hard to stifle the will to believe, or to hope, that things might turn out better than expected.

Sometimes you and I have to learn how to handle disappointments, too. Disappointments at home, disappointments with friends, disappointments with the job, disappointments with the church. Disappointments, disappointments, disappointments.

I know of a priest who kept a sign on his office desk. During the first five years of his ministry, the sign read, "Win the world for Christ." During the next five years of ministry, the sign read, "Win five for Christ." After ten years, he changed the sign to read, "Don't lose too many."

Friends, life is hard. There are disappointments out there. There is a story of a man who received a call from an employment department in Florida. "We think we have a job for you," the caller said. "Can you pick lemons?" "Boy can I ever," the man replied. "I've been married five times."

Life is hard. There are hurts and there are many opportunities to make the wrong choices. Fortunately, life rests on God's shoulders and not our own. As Jesus knelt in the garden in prayer, He knew there would be no way of avoiding the cross. But He knew that God would ultimately be in control. When we remember that God is in control, we can endure.

I'd like everybody to repeat these three words after me. Disappointments, disappointments, disappointments. Everyone say it. Disappointments, disappointments, disappointments. We will all face disappointments. So, how should we handle them? Well, let's take a look at how Jesus did it.

First, Jesus suffered in submission. He let go of His will in the Garden of Gethsemane and responded to His situation with complete faith and trust.

When we are young and vigorous, we believe we will live forever. We are convinced that anything is possible. As years pass and we face life's many disappointments, we tend to see that anything is possible as long as God is a part of it. Jesus suffered in submission. He let go of His own will. He responded to a situation in total faith and trust. When there are disappointments, we, too, have to let go of our will for the will of God. That is how we become better and not bitter.

The second thing we should remember about how Jesus handled disappointment is to remember that Jesus suffered with the knowledge that His hurting could be used by God. His suffering was not meaningless. We may not know the reason or the purpose for our disappointment, but we do know that God can use them for His glory. This is not easy for us, nor was it easy for Jesus. The Scriptures tell us that in His suffering and disappointment, He was fully human. He hurt just as we hurt.

A mother was telling her young daughter about the passion and death of Jesus. The mother explained how upset the people were and how they wanted to punish Him. She described how they put a crown of thorns on His head, whipped Him, and finally nailed Him to the cross that they forced Him to carry. The little girl was quiet for a moment and then replied, "Mommy, that seems like they were a little hard on Him. Couldn't they have just sent Him to His room?" Well, that's nice, but that's not the way it worked out. He suffered and died, but He knew God could use His suffering and disappointment, just as God can use our suffering and disappointment.

Finally, the last point I want us to remember about how Jesus handled disappointment is this: Jesus suffered with the conviction that God is good and loving. Jesus trusted that His Father was listening to His prayers and sustaining Him. The presence of evil did not make Him question God's goodness.

Writer Shirley Nelson said that in her family, it was considered proper to hold in their feelings. Emotions were a very private thing, not to be shared with others. When Shirley's younger sister died in a tragic accident, the family kept the display of grief to a minimum. The sorrow, the anger, the questions and the depression. All of it was held in private. Only once did Shirley's mother give an indication of the inward pain she was experiencing. "I'm just thankful nobody can see my insides," she told Shirley.

Well, friends, God knows what's going on in our insides. If we could have seen Jesus' insides during Holy Week, we would have seen His hurt, His suffering. But more than either of these, we would have seen His love of the world, and His love of His Father in heaven.

Today we celebrate Palm Sunday. Passion Sunday. We celebrate in the bright sunlight, but are on the edge of night. Today we remember Jesus' submission to the will of the Father. Today we remember that all suffering, all disappointment can be used to the Glory of God. Today we acknowledge that, even when there is evil in the world, God is good and loving. Today, we commit ourselves to the cross. We commit to carry our crosses as Jesus taught us to do.

"Father Arnold lived God in every word he spoke. Sermons of his have impacted me since before I can remember. My father tells a story of how, one Sunday, Father was talking about the passage of how difficult it is for a rich man to get into heaven. "It is easier for a camel to pass through the eye of a needle," he said from the front of the church. Six years old at the time, I turned to my parents and asked them if we were rich. "Well," my dad replied in an undertone, "we're not poor..."

I'm sure Father Arnold wondered why the little red-haired girl in the front row began to cry during this homily.

His sermons did more than just guilt me into tears, however. He had that ability to bridge the age gap that very few grasp. We at Holy Name School regarded Father Arnold as an unchanging, unaging fixture that would remain in our lives forever. I distinctly remember asking him if he would preside at my wedding when I got married."

Mandy Inhofer

261

Embrace the Cross

Whoever does not carry His own cross and come after Me cannot be My disciple.

(Luke 14:27)

*I*n the passion story from Luke's gospel, Jesus speaks from the cross three times. First, Jesus says, "Father forgive them, they know not what they are doing." Next, Jesus speaks to the thief hanging beside Him. He says, "This day you shall be with Me in Paradise." The final words Jesus speaks from the cross are, "Father, into your hands I commend my spirit."

In today's gospel we read from the Gospel of John, whose account is slightly different than Luke's. In John's Gospel, Jesus' last words are, "It is finished."

Although the stories differ slightly, they are the same on one important point. In both stories, we see that Jesus died as He lived. He practiced what He preached. Although He suffered, He carried His cross and continued to be compassionate, merciful, and loving to the end.

Today our focus should be on the cross, not the crucifixion. The crucifixion was a single event. The cross, however, represents all life. There is no such thing as a cross-less Christ. Likewise, there should be no such thing as a cross-less Christian.

Before His crucifixion, Jesus told His disciples, "Unless you take up the cross, you cannot be my disciple." He did not say that you had to be crucified to be His follower. Few of us will ever be crucified; however, all of us are asked to embrace the cross.

What it Means to Embrace the Cross

Embracing the cross means to carry it as Jesus did. This is different from dragging it, putting up with it, or complaining about it.

This is never easy to do. As you know, we don't get to choose the crosses we are asked to carry. They simply come. Having said that, we don't need to create any crosses for ourselves or others. There are already enough to go around.

Without question, we will all have crosses to carry during life. How we choose to carry them determines whether or not we grow from the experience.

We will no doubt experience sorrow or grief because of the crosses. Friends, grief is not a problem to be cured. Rather, it's a statement that you love somebody. Carrying our crosses will be hard and painful, and we may need help along the way. Even Jesus had help carrying His cross.

It may take some time before we can truly embrace the grief, embrace the pain, and begin to grow. Some people never do. Some people, through their anguish, become angry—angry at God, angry at the world. Their anger eventually turns to bitterness. In bitterness, we do not find growth. We do not find life. It's our choice, and it can be a tough one to make. Do we become bitter because of the crosses that life has given us to carry? Or, do we become better? Whether or not we grow from our experiences is entirely up to us.

Crosses for the Christian to Carry

The true heart of Christianity is the cross. "Unless we die, we can never bear fruit, nor can we rise." There are some crosses that we, as Christians, must embrace:

The cross of discipleship

This is our constant struggle with the culture, with laziness, with the flesh. The struggle to follow Jesus, even when it's difficult to do so.

The cross of fidelity

This is fidelity to one's vocation, to our talents, and to know when to say "yes" and when to say "no" correctly.

The cross of ministry

Can we be both a leader and a servant? Jesus was both.

The cross of caring

Can we listen to those who need to talk? Do we make time to be with those who are in need?

The cross of responsibility to others

There are some who come for help that we would rather turn away. We are called to serve our neighbor.

Friends, we will face many crosses throughout our lives, and it will be our choice to decide how to face them. Will we embrace them or will we run from them? Will we carry them or will we drag them? Will we grow from the experience, become better, and live? Or, will we become bitter and die? It will be our choice to make.

On this day, Good Friday, as we remember how Christ, our Savior, suffered and died so that we might live, let us remember the cross. Let us remember, too, how Jesus faced the cross. Today, we salute the cross. We sing to the cross. We carry the cross. Let us embrace the cross.

During the veneration of the cross, as you each come forward to pray, you will be given a nail. This nail can serve as a reminder of the cross and of the example Jesus gave us in how to face the crosses of life.

Note: One of Fr. Arnold's favorite hymns is *The Old Rugged Cross.* We often sang this hymn on Good Friday. Following are the words to this song:

The Old Rugged Cross

Rev. Geo. Bennard

On a hill far away stood an old rugged cross,
The emblem of suffering and shame;
And I love that old cross where the dearest and best
For a world of lost sinners was slain.
(Chorus)
So I'll cherish the old rugged cross,
Till my trophies at last I lay down;
I will cling to the old rugged cross,
And exchange it some day for a crown.
Oh, that old rugged cross, so despised by the world,
Has a wondrous attraction for me;
For the dear Lamb of God left His glory above
To bear it to dark Calvary.
(Chorus)
In the old rugged cross; stained with blood so divine,
A wondrous beauty I see;
For 'twas on that old cross Jesus suffered and died
To pardon and sanctify me.
(Chorus)
To the old rugged cross I will ever be true,
Its shame and reproach gladly bear;
Then He'll call me someday to my home faraway,
Where His glory forever I'll share.

I have known Father Arnold since my days at St. John's in the late 50's but the major impact he had in our families lives really started in the mid-80's when our oldest son, Paul (SJU '85) died Thanksgiving Day of 1985 in a hunting accident. Our family attended St. Bart's at the time (still a Benedictine parish) and Paul funeral Mass was at St. Bart's with burial at Holy Name. Father Arnold gave the homily at Paul's funeral and I will never forget what he told us and that has impacted my life ever since..." Bob and Dixie, you now have choice to make, you can either become bitter about this or you can become better... the choice is yours." Naturally you don't remember everything about a homily so a week or so later I asked Father if I could get a copy. He didn't want to give me his rough and abbreviated notes but did suggest he would tape record the homily for me. What a treasure... to this day I carry the tape of my son's funeral homily in my car and once in awhile still listen to our good Padre's great message for our family. Another highlight of Father Arnold and the help of the Abbey monks is they helped arrange for the Johnnie fight song to be sung at Paul's funeral Mass... he so loved St. John's!!

My other story of Arnold the monk from St. John's is how the tape/video project got started. Less than a year later, October, 1986, our second son, Timothy died and since we were now members of Holy Name his funeral Mass was at Holy Name in what is now the Good Samaritan Center. Again, Arnold and with many other monks from St. John's concelebrating the Mass, Father did the homily and repeated his message of bitter versus better along with many other suggestions on how our faith in Jesus would see us through this additional trail. Shortly after this the new Church was ready and Holy Name really started to expand. The tape of Paul's homily was so meaningful to me that I started talking to Father Arnold in 1987 about audio taping his homilies. He would not consider it and no matter how many times I asked him he would not agree. I do not remember the exact date but I do remember the exact spot when he finally agreed. It was in the summer of 1997 and I caught him between the Rectory and the Church and asked permission again to audio tape. "Why do you want to do this, Bob," he asked and I replied, "Father there are the Gospel's of Matthew, Mark, Luke and John... I just want to record the ones by Arnold... for all of us!" He laughed and said, "okay as long as you don't sell them!" I agreed but didn't tell him I would give them away... We then secured a tape recorder, put it in the first usher's room of the new church and started the audio tape project of some daily and Sunday Mass homilies. As people heard about it we made duplicates and I know they were even sent around the country and overseas by parishioners to family members. Within a couple years Father agreed to having video rather than just the audio as I suggested a video of the entire funeral Mass with the homily, eulogies and songs would be good for the family. He agreed and even though the second funeral Mass we did the audio portion didn't work and the widow was disappointed (it did work for her funeral!), Father Arnold realized this was a very meaningful thing for the family and looked forward to giving the video to the family.

Since then most funeral Masses are video taped. With the installation of the video equipment I set out on a project of taping every daily and Sunday Mass of Father Arnold's for a four year period. It was a wonderful experience, many copies were made and thankfully video taping of the Masses and outstanding homilies of our priests and deacons continues. The gospel by Arnold may not be as well-known as the other four-but they have and will continue to make an impact on many of us.

Bob Labat, Holy Name of Jesus parishioner

To Be Continued

†

On the first day of the week, Mary of Magdala came to the tomb early in the morning, while it was still dark, and saw the stone was removed from the tomb . . . But Mary stayed outside the tomb weeping. And as she wept, she bent over into the tomb and saw two angels in white sitting there, one at the head and one at the feet where the body of Jesus had been. And they said to her, "Woman, why are you weeping?" She said to them, "They have taken away my Lord, and I don't know where they laid Him." When she had said this, she turned around and saw Jesus there . . .

(John 20:1, 11-14)

*F*riends in Christ, the title I have given to this homily is *To Be Continued*. You and I live in three dimensions of time. We have memories of the past. We have experiences in the present and we have aspirations for the future. It is a sad kind of life that is dominated by the past. And, it is a shallow person who lives only in the present. The more alive we are, the more we set goals and move toward them. And yet, out there in every person's future stands that inescapable reality we call death.

Today, I take it for granted that we are not morbid about death. We can even be grateful for it. It is a good thing that we do not live forever on this earth. It is merciful that older generations will die and make room for another generation. None of us would ever seriously ask to be spared death. When our time comes, we will be ready. In all of this, however, there is a catch. No matter when death comes, it will find us with an unfinished life. If death were the end of everything it would leave so many possibilities unrealized. If death were the end, it would mean that many seeds have been planted but never had time to grow.

Franz Schuber died when he was only 31 years old. He left behind his musical piece called *The Unfinished Symphony*. You and I are not great composers, but all of us will do that—we will leave some things that have not been completed. Life will get finished with us before we are finished with life.

The message of Easter concerns this vital matter. Jesus died in His early 30's, maybe 35 years at the most. He lived so beautifully. Everything he did could be described as good. But this beautiful life was interrupted by the cross. It looked like the end of Him and His cause. But on the third day, God raised Him up and He went right on living.

The life of Jesus in the Gospels is like a series of episodes we sometimes watch on television. Time runs out, but the story is not finished. A message comes on the screen that says, "To be continued." That, in effect, is what God wrote on the cross when Jesus died. And that is what He wrote on the tomb where Jesus was buried. The story was not finished yet. It would be continued.

The same can be said about your death and mine, and the passing of the ones we love. God is not in the business of ending His stories in the middle.

When William James, a great educator at Harvard, was a young man, he had little interest in eternal life. It did not matter much to him one way or the other. As he got older, it became more important to him. He thought and wrote about it more often. Someone once asked him, "Why?" William James replied, "because I'm just now getting fit to live."

Sometimes we feel that way about ourselves. We are just now learning to do it right, and it's not the time to end the story. It needs to be continued.

Consider this "To Be Continued" faith, as it applies to our friends. We don't often consider the impact of death until it happens to someone we love. Then, it becomes a matter of urgent concern. We question how someone we love could be taken away from us. We think about their potential and wonder if all of that promise is just thrown away forever.

Some of us have had friends who were physically handicapped during their lifetime. Their shot at life was limited at best. But the people who knew and loved them recognized the potential that was there. We've known some who made bad choices in their lives. It's easy to say, "what a waste." Only those who truly loved them understand what had been lost. And of course, others lived magnificent lives. They were caring and kind. Their living was like a symphony of love. Their death seems to make no sense, and leaves a terrible sense of loss.

That was the concern of those first disciples. In Christ they had seen the start of something wonderful. Then, suddenly, it all came to a screeching halt. Everybody believed it was over. The enemies of Jesus thought they had finished him. The Jesus movement which had started with such promise didn't appear to go anywhere. It just stopped, and that was the end of the story.

But friends, this story did not remain unfinished. In Christ God had started something, and He did not leave it unfinished. The red lights of Calvary that seemed to stop His movement turned to the green lights on Easter morning. And Christ kept on going, and He hasn't stopped since. He has been with us, and He has been with us alive. The cross could not stop Him. It was just part of the plan.

Today, on Easter Sunday, let us remember that God is not the God of unfinished plans. And that goes for you and me. God has started something in us—through Christ. He does not light candles only to blow them out. Friends, the Easter message is this: "To Be Continued." What God has started, He will bring to completion.

In the World,
Not of the World

✝

Holy Father, protect them that you have given me, so that they may be one as we are one. I have given them your word, and the world has hated them because they do not belong to the world, just as I do not belong to the world. I am not asking you to take them out of the world, but I ask you to protect them from the evil one. They do not belong to the world, just as I do not belong to the world. As you have sent me into the world, so I have sent them into the world.

(John 17:11, 14-16, 18)

*C*ongratulations—*ta tol!* That's the first word Jesus spoke after His resurrection. So it's appropriate to say that word now to you graduates. *Ta dah*, you made it, congratulations! *Ta dah*, also to you parents, teachers, friends, administrators, and other nurturers and supporters, you made it, too! Graduates, your growth process over the last four years has been gradual. Now, at long last, you are mature; that is, physically, emotionally, mentally, psychologically, and spiritually ready to handle the great gift of freedom. I warn you, though you probably won't believe me, that this newfound freedom may become a large burden on you. Despite the hassles, the high school environment is usually a relatively safe haven for young people.

So how should you handle your freedom? What kind of life ought you choose to live? Of course, many of you are planning to go off to college and seek some sort of degree—a BA, MBA, or maybe an MD. That's good. It's important to learn to use your talents wisely. Remember the Bible parables of the wise and foolish bridesmaids and the men given charge of the gold coins. But remember also, in life, that people don't usually want to know your IQ, but your "I do." Keep in mind how you're going to be judged in the end: "I was hungry, and you fed me." Or "I was hungry, and you ignored me."

Graduates, I'm telling you that you'll only be happy in life if you hunger and thirst for holiness. The world may value you more for what you do than for who you are, but in the words of Mother Teresa, we aren't called to be successful, but to be faithful. To help you in the faith department, young people, I'm going to challenge you to become three things.

1. Misfits

Often times, students and others in the parish give my name as a reference on their job applications. On occasion, employers call and ask me questions that pertain to the job candidate's character:

- Is this person honest? Reliable?
- Can you depend on him? Does he keep commitments?
- Does this person get along with others? Is he a team player?

The employer wants to know these things because it can be disruptive to an entire organization if one worker is irresponsible or cannot get along with those around him. Sometimes people like this are called misfits.

I'm always happy when I can answer yes to an employer's questions. People who are responsible and get along with others are easy to recommend. They are good to know and make life a little more pleasant for all of us. The world needs people like that.

Yes, it's definitely a good thing to be able to get along with others, but it's a virtue that needs qualification. A person shouldn't always just go with the flow or ride with the tide. In fact, in some ways, one ought to be a misfit.

In today's Gospel, Jesus speaks to His Father about this issue. His prayer—a good one for a graduate—makes these two points:

- Jesus was a misfit Himself.

To say that Jesus was a misfit seems sacrilegious; however, we don't mean that He was emotionally unstable, couldn't get along, or felt picked on or persecuted. Jesus got along really well with a wide variety of people, but He didn't get along with everybody. He was loved and admired by most, but hated and feared by some.

What made Jesus a misfit were these convictions:

- He believed in a God who cared for all people alike.
- He believed in the inherent value and worth of every person.
- Jesus' disciples are in the world but not of the world.

Graduates, I'm warning you. If you choose to be a follower of Jesus, it could make you a misfit. Many times your principles will conflict with the culture. It's tough out in the world. Watch that you don't compromise your values, especially your respect for life. Martyrdom will probably not be demanded of you, but if you speak up for your beliefs, you may lose some friends. Instead of giving in to peer pressure, try to practice peer ministry. Be a healthy-minded misfit like Jesus, and stand up for the lowly—the poor, the aged, the unborn, and those of other races, nationalities, and religions.

Remember to balance competition with compassion. Understand that many winners are not gainers and many losers are. It's better to fail with integrity, than to succeed through deceitful means. Integrity is more important than ever. You can be certain that you will encounter many problems and troubles in your life. Though today's culture doesn't help much, pick up those crosses and carry them, and choose to let them make you better rather than bitter.

2. Committed Catholics

Young people, I'd like you to really think about the kind of Catholic you will be, the kind of Christian. Will you be:

A cultural Catholic? Fifty percent of those who identify themselves as Catholic on questionnaires are Catholic in name only. They rarely go to Mass, maybe only on Christmas and/or Easter.

A habitual Catholic? Twenty-five percent of Catholics attend Mass out of habit, but are usually in and out very quickly. They don't participate in any community activities—social, educational, or service. Although they usually receive the sacraments, they are not really grafted onto the vine, or connected closely to Christ, and can easily fall off and be lost.

A committed Catholic? The remaining twenty-five percent of Catholics deliberately and on purpose choose Jesus and the Catholic church. They are the ones who are tightly connected to the vine. They are the ones who keep the church alive.

Committed Christians know Jesus personally as a friend. They live in consciousness of the Holy Spirit. The Greek word for Holy Spirit is *dynamis*, which is the same root word used for dynamic and dynamite. Committed Christians aren't the ones who call church boring. To people who say that church is boring, I say that the boredom is inside of them. If they were touched by the Holy Spirit, they'd be so alive that it would be impossible to be bored. To you graduates, I offer this advice: The Holy Spirit was behind the happenings at Mount Sinai and Pentecost, so be committed Christians and live in the Holy Spirit. Cheer up, liven up, go forth, and be witnesses. Don't copy our culture.

A second point I want to make about committed Christians is that they belong to and participate in a community—an atmosphere where faith is lived. This leads to ministry where love for people is the focus. Whether one counsels a student on drugs or a parent who lost a child, it's the ministry of Jesus in our midst. Always be sure to respect the gifts of others in your community. Realize that it's possible to belong to a group of Christians without being in Christian community. A truly Christian community will offer friendship, ministry, and a sense of hospitality, Benedictine values that you've learned something about.

3. Active Christians

Finally, I hope you'll all choose to be ACTIVE Christians, and I do mean A-C-T-I-V-E. So you can easily remember what that means, I've used each of the letters in the word ACTIVE to stand for an important quality or element of Christianity.

A stands for Awareness.

Pray for awareness, awareness of the good things in the culture, and also of the problems—violence, racism, family breakups, drugs. Keep your ideals but be compassionate—forgive people, including yourself, for messing up.

C stands for Courage.

Pray for courage, the courage to be truthful, to be different from others when it counts, to be in the world but not of the world.

T stands for Time.

Understand that your time is sacred. Think about what it means when you pray: "Give us THIS DAY our DAILY bread" and "NOW and AT THE HOUR of our death."

I stands for Individual.

Realize that most great movements, inventions, and discoveries were the result of the efforts of one person. Never forget that YOU are important to God and to the world.

V stands for Vigor.

Realize that how you live your life matters. Live it with vigor and enthusiasm. Be filled with the Holy Spirit. Be alive!

E stands for Example.

Follow Christ. Think about and imitate other good role models. Set a good example for others yourself. Be an ACTIVE Christian.

Let me close now with two quotes. The first one comes from the Reader's Digest: "Almost nobody listens to a commencement address, except perhaps a few parents engaged in one last effort to get something for their money." I think this is probably true. How many of you here today remember who gave your commencement address? How many of you remember anything said that day? No one? So graduates, that tells you exactly how important I am today!

****

No, it's really not important that you remember me, or the exact words I said. My mission today was to inspire you and increase your enthusiasm for the life ahead. I hope I've done that. I'll leave you now with this quote from Pope John Paul II, delivered on October 3, 1979, to 19,000 young people at Madison Square Garden in New York:

"*Dear young people, you and I and all of us together make up the church, and we are convinced that only in Christ do we find real love and the fullness of life. So I invite you today to look to Christ. When you wonder about the mystery of yourself, look to Christ who gives you the meaning of life. When you wonder about what it means to be a mature person, look to Christ who is the fullness of humanity. And when you wonder about your role in the future of the world and the United States, look to Christ. Only in Christ will you fulfill your potential as an American citizen and as a citizen of the world community.*"

A Covenant
Relationship

✝

...I have loved you with an everlasting
love, therefore I have continued my
faithfulness to you.

(Jeremiah 31:3)

Friends in Christ, a Christian marriage is much more than a legal contract. It is a sacred covenant that reflects the intimate relationship of Jesus to His Church and God to His people. It is intended to be:

One union

In marriage, a husband and wife join together as one—reflecting the relationship of the one true God to His people.

A faithful union

Just as Christ died for the church, the spouses in a marriage are to die to all others and to themselves so they can be there for each other. They bear with one another and suffer for each other. I've even heard of some men who go through morning sickness with their wives. Now that's intimacy!

A fruitful union

Jesus said that he came so we could have life and have it abundantly. One fruit of the richly shared love of a married couple is, of course, children. Another fruit of a married couple might be a welcoming home, one that is filled with hospitality and charity.

A final union

Jesus promised to be with us always until the end of time. In their marriage ceremony, spouses make the promise to stay together until the end of this life.

So the purpose of marriage comes not from a contract, but from a sacred covenant. A purposeful covenant-based relationship doesn't just happen all by itself, however. There are certain fundamental keys that can help a marriage grow in intimacy, and keep it together and doing well. The things I share with you today are those that I've learned in more than 40 years of marriage counseling.

Priorities

Most importantly, both individuals in a married couple must know and abide by the correct priorities in life. These priorities are:

1) God

2) Spouse

3) Children/family

4) Work

in that order. None of these key areas can be neglected without problems. The most serious problems will occur, however, if you don't live in a way that reflects this order of priorities. How can you tell how you're doing with this? Well, look at any troubles you're experiencing and determine if they're related to priorities that are out of alignment. Ask yourselves: How are we using our time and money? Where do we direct our attention, thoughts, and feelings? To figure this out, all you have to do is study your calendar and your checkbook. If you aren't living according to the correct priorities, then perhaps some changes ought to be made.

God Must Take Top Priority

In a covenant marriage, God takes top priority. Despite all the shining, sterling qualities that a husband and wife bring into a marriage, it is a sacred covenant too precious to entrust to two human beings. The 50 percent divorce rate is testimony to that. You need God in your marriage—the Father who fashioned you, the Son who died for you, the Spirit who lives on in you. God is always nearby, faithful for days without end. Remember, though, this relationship cannot be one-sided. You must also be present to God. His faithfulness calls for your fidelity. He must be as real to you as you are to each other. If He is, the odds are in your favor. If not, I tremble for you.

One concrete way you can make sure God stays a priority is by going to His house every week. Churchgoing has been found to be a big factor in keeping a marriage together. Wonderful studies have been done on this, some not even sponsored by religious organizations. Unfortunately, however, I'd say a good percentage of couples that I prepare for marriage (about 75 per year) are not churchgoers. They ask me if they're supposed to go, and I tell them yes and give a pep talk about religion. There are all types of Catholic churches. If you can't find Christ in one, you can find Him in another. Why would anyone not want to be a churchgoer? One of the great things about being a priest here is seeing so many young couples coming to church together. So if you're serious about making God a priority in your marriage, be churchgoers.

A Spouse is Second Only to God

The next priority after God in a covenant marriage is one's spouse. My role at your wedding is to be the Church's official witness. I do not marry you two—you are the celebrants of the ceremony. I do not make you man and wife—you are the ministers of the mystery. This means that you are channels of grace to each other. To maintain this relationship throughout a marriage, husbands and wives ought to be each other's best friends. Friends like each other. They seek each other out and spend time together. They want to know what is going on in each other's lives. They share intimate thoughts and feelings with each other. This is as important today as it ever was. Once in a while when I get introduced to a new couple or spouse, the husband or wife says, "Father, meet my best friend." When this happens, I know this is most likely a couple I won't have to counsel. Unfortunately, though, there are couples that are not best friends. They may live in the same house, but actually share less than five minutes a day of intimate time. Can you believe that? Spouses, stay in touch with each other. This is very important. You need to work on it constantly.

Something that makes it difficult for a husband and wife to stay close is that they may not understand and work around the differences that exist between men and women. One important difference is in styles of communication. For example, say there's a couple where one spouse works and the other stays home with the children. Here's how the conversation might go if the man stayed home with the kids and the woman just came home from work:

Wife: "How were the kids today?"

Husband: "Fine."

Wife: "What happened around here today?"

Husband: "Nothing. How was work?"

Wife: "Well, here's what happened at the meeting this morning,... talk talk talk. Then at lunch I heard that Amy's getting married, talk talk talk... My client's son plays soccer in the City League just like Johnny. They ought to play each other soon... talk talk talk."

Here's how the same conversation might go if the roles were reversed. That is, the mother was home with the kids all day, and the father just got home from work:

Husband: "How were the kids today?"

Wife: "Well, it's been quite a day. Billy was missing for a half an hour this morning. I had no idea where he was. I nearly called you, then he showed up. Guess where he was... talk talk talk. Then this afternoon Janie fell down and scraped her leg again... talk talk talk. And Johnny has something to tell you... talk talk talk."

Husband: (Silence) or "Hmmm."

Wife: "How was work today?"

Husband: "Fine."

Men often (not always) tend to talk in one-syllable sentences. No communication, no sharing, no intimacy, at least not in the mind of a woman. Women, on the other hand, may talk with a lot of words (not always)—a style of communication that a man finds difficult to follow or fathom. Intimacy can be difficult if this is the situation. Spouses, beware of your communication differences and learn to compromise. It's especially important that you do everything possible to remain intimate with each other in today's busy culture.

Besides being friends, spouses should also be lovers. Our culture's notion of love, however, is not really the gospel notion of love. Real love is patient and kind, sees and does no evil, and looks to the good of the other. When I was at Benilde-St. Margaret's High School, a girl once asked me, "How do you know when you're in love?" I replied, "When your boyfriend asks what would you like to do, where would you like to go, how would you like *me* to show affection in a way that is pleasing to you, then you might be seeing the start of love."

Husbands and wives, be affectionate with each other. It's horrible when married people are starving to death for affection. Here's what I get in counseling: "My spouse is too busy to show affection," or "I am too tired to show much affection to my spouse." Too busy for affection? Too tired? Can you believe it? Spouses, tell each other how much you care for each other. Show each other. This is very important. The reason you're here today is because you've shown each other your love and affection. It's up to you both to make sure that things stay that way.

Next Comes Family

In a covenant relationship, children and family come after God and spouse. Young couple, children are a blessing. With children, the poor are rich; without them, the rich can be very poor. Parenting is not easy, however. It's a demanding and lifelong responsibility. Together, young couple, you must provide children with everything they need to grow and thrive. Notice, I didn't say that you must give your children everything they want. After all, the more people get what they want, the less they will want what they get. No, you must give your children what they need. That is, give them love, security, example, and self-worth. And don't forget discipline, and by that I mean gentle correction. Help them come to know the greatest argument against misbehavior: it simply doesn't work. The very best thing that you will ever do for your children, however, is to love each other.

Where Work Fits In

Finally, I need to talk to you about where work fits into married life. In our culture, work is considered to be very important. For many people, it's even a big part of their identity. That means that if you're not careful, work can move up in priority without anyone in a family even realizing it. I don't mean to say that work isn't important, but if it displaces God or spouse or family in emphasis, it can cause problems in a marriage. Too often this actually happens, and the result can be broken hearts and lives and dreams. In all my years as a priest, I've never heard of anyone on his or her deathbed who says, "I wish I'd spent more time at the office."

Another important idea related to work and marriage is that both spouses need to appreciate each other's contributions, whether they come from working inside or outside the home. You need to acknowledge that both spouses work even if only one leaves the house and collects a paycheck.

****

Friends, one of the greatest treasures you can give each other is to say "I do" without regrets. Throughout your married life, you need to keep reminding yourselves what it is that you do treasure and then protect those things. If you treasure your marriage, you will constantly work on it. Keep the right priorities. Maintain your friendship, share love and affection, and appreciate each other.

Thanksgiving

And let the peace of Christ rule in your hearts, to which indeed you were called in the one body. And be thankful.

(Colossians 3:15)

*S*omeone once said that if the only prayer you ever say in your life is a thank-you, it would suffice. Friends, that person was right. To be a Christian is to be thankful. But what exactly is thankfulness, and why is it so foundational to our spiritual life? To whom and for what ought we be thankful? How do we experience and express our thankfulness?

Thankfulness is a feeling or expression that springs from a special type of remembrance. It comes from remembering and truly appreciating all the blessings we have, not just with our heads, but also with our hearts.

To whom should we be thankful? Three Scripture texts can help us understand the answer. The first one is:

I give thanks, O God, that I am not like the rest of men . . . (Luke 18:10)

Do you know who said this? It was the Pharisee who was praying in the temple at the same time as the lowly tax collector. This Pharisee was an important, self-made man, just like some of you around here today. There's nothing wrong with being competent. However, don't make the mistake of the Pharisee when it comes to being thankful. He congratulated himself, saying he was thankful to be so worthy, so much better than others, especially the tax collector on the other side of the temple.

We as a nation can be like that, too, you know. We are very proud to be such an independent, self-made country. The trouble is we focus so much on consumerism or our personal success that we forget God. We forget that to whom much is given, much will be required. In our self-gratification, we lose the meaning of true gratitude.

I thank my God every time I remember you...
(Philippians 1:3)

This second Scripture reference certainly brings us a step closer to real thankfulness than the Pharisee's thank-you prayer. It's very good to appreciate others and their efforts, and not just focus on our own worthiness. In fact, every married couple, family member, or friend ought to try to remember and use these two phrases often: "Thank you" and "I'm sorry." Otherwise there's danger of taking each other for granted. That's true also for our nation. We have countless conveniences and blessings that we don't even think about. If you don't believe me, just consider the start of your day:

- Wake up—alarm clock developed by a Swiss inventor
- Throw off the sheets—made from Egyptian cotton
- Walk to bathroom—floor tiles created in Italy
- Use sink, shower, and toilet—porcelain developed in China
- Get dressed—clothing made in Southeast Asia
- Eat breakfast—dishes made in England
- Drink coffee—grown and harvested in Brazil

Yes, we as a nation ought to have a deep sense of gratitude because many of our conveniences come from the efforts of others.

Father, I thank you . . . (John 11:41)

This third Scripture reference takes us to the highest level of thanksgiving. When we recognize the true giver of all gifts, when we are filled with a continuous desire to thank Him for everything, when we are willing to be guided by His Holy Spirit, then we have reached the summit. This is what we want to strive for.

To fully experience true thanksgiving, you must:

1. Recognize something as a gift.

2. Acknowledge your dependence on the giver of the gift.

3. Express your appreciation or gratitude.

Once you express your gratitude, the gift-giver becomes the recipient of your thankfulness, and a circle of giving and receiving is completed. What a tremendous cycle this is! It works for individuals and for groups or even nations.

Giver
of Gift

Receiver
of Gift

Receiver
of Thanks

Giver
of Thanks

For example, parents give things to their children, and if the children are appreciative and express their gratitude, the parents then become recipients of thankfulness. Another example: People give of their time, talent, and treasure to the parish. The entire parish benefits from these contributions, and those contributions are recognized at an appreciation ceremony. The contributors then become recipients of the parish community's gratitude.

This giving-receiving circle is such a simple concept, you'd think it would be easy, but it's not. Maybe it's because there's such a strong emphasis on independence in our country. Some people never learn to recognize the gifts they're given. Others find it difficult to accept or receive gifts from anyone. Still others find it hard to acknowledge their indebtedness to those who give them gifts. And finally, there are the ones who never seem to be able to say thank you.

Saying thank you isn't that hard. There are many ways to show gratitude to God. You can exclaim about the beauty of nature that surrounds you. You can say prayers of thanksgiving for your many blessings. You can help out in your neighborhood or school. You can make good use of your personal gifts in your work. You can strive to improve conditions in the world.

Here are some gifts to be thankful for:

Creation

God speaks to us in the beauty of nature, given to us for our enjoyment. We are filled with delight and express our thanksgiving.

Life

We are made out of love for love. Life is a special gift that comes from God's unconditional love for each of us.

Special people

Don't take anyone or anything for granted. Remember, you never miss water until the well runs dry. Pray always for your spouse, children, family, and friends.

Special events and occasions

Joyous gatherings with people we love are occasions for gratitude. Wholesome celebrations—weddings, birthdays, family reunions, neighborhood picnics, festivals, etc.—naturally lead to feelings of thankfulness.

God's forgiveness

The opportunity to continually obtain pardon for our sins and start over allows us to develop and share the gifts and fruits of the spirit with others.

Pain and struggles

Wait, did I say pain and struggles? Yes, we ought to be thankful even for these because they can give us insight.

Freedom

On Thanksgiving Day, we remember our Pilgrim fathers and mothers who journeyed and toiled to make this land one of freedom. We remember those people who served in our armed forces, especially the ones who died or were injured. We remember all the others who helped create and improve our country. Finally, we also thank God for all the people who today continue the work of building and developing and furthering the ideals of the United States.

Friends, live thankfully. Thankfulness is the way of a follower of Jesus. To help you remember, I'll leave you with this short prayer:

"Count your blessings; name them one by one,
and it will surprise you what the Lord has done."

Our environments form us, creating indelible marks. Some of us are fortunate enough to have been placed in nurturing environments. Such was the case for me coming to the community of Holy Name of Jesus in 1989. Initially I was struck with an overwhelming sense of welcome. This Benedictine virtue seemed to be the hallmark of this community and one made manifest the first time I met Fr. Arnold Weber, OSB.

In St. Benedict's Rule for Monasteries, Chapter 2 speaks about, "What Kind of Man the Abbot Ought to Be." I always thought it to be a good instruction for Fathers both in clergy and family. I especially like these statements found in Chapter 2: "…that they be found to be about good works and humility—love all equally—listen well with an open heart—correct that which is needed and affirm and encourage others to advance in virtue."

Living the Rule was a natural for Fr. Arnold, a holy and humble man who served as my pastor, priest and mentor for more than 15 years. Over those years, as I listened to his homilies and watched him pastor his parishioners, I learned how to be a better wife, mother and minister to the people with whom I journey.

It has served me well to remember and ponder the wisdom in the kernels of truth he has given us. Some of these will be familiar catch phrases to those who listened to a man willing to share his personal journey in faith through homilies and conversations.

"Accept them as they are!"
"What are you going to do: get bitter or better?"
"Well that didn't go so well—What did you learn from it?"
"Remember, the faster you go the slower you'll get there. (This one works really well on icy winter days.)"

For me, Father Arnold is and has been the rock of common sense looking out for the common good.

Jean Roozendaal, Director Adult Faith Formation, Holy Name of Jesus

Trinity Sunday

✝

For all who are led by the Spirit of God are children of God. For you did not receive a spirit of slavery to fall back into fear, but you have received a spirit of adoption. When we cry, "Abba, Father!" it is that very Spirit bearing witness with our spirit that we are children of God, and if children, then heirs, heirs of God and joint heirs with Christ — if, in fact, we suffer with Him, so that we may also be glorified with Him.

(Romans 8:14-17)

*A*uthor Liz Higgs wrote about a conversation she once had with her young daughter Lillian on the subject of religion.

Liz: "Who rules the universe?"

Lillian: (without hesitation) "God does."

Liz: "What about Jesus?"

Lillian: "He works with God."

Liz: "What about the Holy Spirit?"

Lillian: "He works on the weekends."

Obviously, Lillian didn't have a clear concept of the Trinity. But who does? Let's face it. The concept of the Trinity—God as Father, Son, and Holy Spirit—may be a little abstract for us. That's probably a good thing. If we could explain God with a pat formula, He would not be God.

When Teddy Roosevelt was president, he had a favorite political story that he liked to tell about a senator who was accused of not supporting the Monroe doctrine. In his defense, the man said, "I believe in the Monroe doctrine. I support the Monroe doctrine. I would die in defense of the Monroe doctrine. I just don't know what it is!"

Maybe that's how we feel about the Trinity. We accept it and believe it, and we are devoted to it, even if we aren't quite sure what it is. A theologian once said, "The Trinity is a doctrine that, if a person doesn't believe in it, he may lose his soul. But if he tries to understand it, he may lose his mind."

The writers of the New Testament made no attempt to explain the Trinity. In fact, they never even used the word trinity. They simply spoke of God in three different ways throughout the text— God the Father, God the Son, and God the Holy Spirit—and let it go at that. Today's scripture is one of the few places in which all three persons of the Trinity are mentioned together.

Friends, even if we don't understand how it all works, it seems to me that the Trinity tells us, at the very least, these three things.

1. God, by nature, is a loving, involved father who reaches out to us, His children.

People who don't believe in the Trinity may think of God as a remote unapproachable being who causes world events but has no interaction or involvement with the people. Aristotle, for example, believed in this idea, and called God the unmoved mover. Other people who have had no relationship or poor relationships with their human fathers might also have trouble relating to God as a father.

But most of us can understand quite readily the joy of being able to call God Abba, which means Daddy. We can feel what it means to be children of a father who is lovingly involved with his family, who provides for them, cares for them, and shares with them.

Jesus helped us to know that God is not somewhere far removed and sealed away from us, unavailable or uncaring. He told us that God has actually counted every hair on our heads! Think about that radical view of God for a moment. It is one of intimate closeness and deep caring. What better news can we have than that?

2. God became one of us, an actual human.

God knew that we needed to see the life of faith in human flesh. He loved us so much that, in and through His Son, He became human. Jesus was a real human being. All those who knew Him saw Him first as a man—an incredibly remarkable man, but a human being. The Word was made flesh and dwelt among us. He pitched His tent next to ours, moved into the neighborhood and lived with us in order to be our teacher, model, and savior. Eventually, Jesus' close companions recognized that He was also God, beginning with Peter, who proclaimed, "You are the Messiah, the Son of the living God!"

The New Testament writer John proclaimed the Gospel Good News. He said, "In the beginning was the Word, and the Word was with God, and the Word was God." (John 1:1) The Good News is not that Jesus gave us great ethics. It isn't that He taught us some theology. The Good News is that God became a part of human history in and through His son Jesus, the Galilean carpenter. Never again could anyone think of God as just an abstraction.

3. God is with us always.

Ever since Christ's ascension back into heaven, God has come to us in the form of the Holy Spirit. This reminds me of a story. Once there was a Sunday school class where the children were told to pick the Bible character they would most like to be. One little girl chose Mary, the mother of Jesus, and another chose Esther because she was a queen. One boy chose Joseph because he was Jesus' daddy. Somebody else chose King David because he was strong and brave. Another kid chose Jonah because he went for a ride in a whale. But one quiet boy chose to be Lo. Everyone told him there was no character Lo in the Bible, but the little boy didn't believe them. He said, "Oh yes, there is! Jesus said, 'Lo, I will be with you always.'"

That little boy was right about one thing. God is always with us through the Holy Spirit. God the Father abides in heaven. God the Son lived in Galilee 2000 years ago. Here on earth now, God walks with us daily through the Holy Spirit, which forever lives with us and within us as our contemporary, helper, guide, and friend.

Friends, most Christians, though they don't really understand the Trinity, believe that God has revealed Himself to us in three persons: God the Father, creator and provider; God the Son, model and example; and God the Holy Spirit—powerhouse companion who jumps out of the stands and helps us run the race to the finish line.

Just like you, I can't really explain the Trinity or who God is. But if anyone asks me where He is, I will answer in terms of the Trinity.

First, I will say: "God, our almighty Father, the creator of heaven and earth, is in heaven." Then I will say: "Jesus Christ, His only Son, our Lord, is in history." Next I will stretch out my arms and say: "God the Holy Spirit is here with us in this world." I will put my hand over my heart and say: "God is here living inside of me, just as He lives inside of you." That's what the Trinity tells us about God.

Father Arnold's Prayers to the Trinity

To the Father: Abba, Daddy! and Our Father!

To the Son: Jesus is Lord! and My Lord and my God!

To the Holy Spirit: Come, Holy Spirit!

○

Thanks, Dear Friend, Servant Leader!

Fr. Arnold Weber is one of kind. A little larger than life. Certainly the epitome of the "old school" of ministry and priesthood. Servant leader, yet, always contemporary. That is a rarity. To be grounded so well in the ancient sources of spirituality, ministry, and scripture. You broke open the Word to us in marvelous and relevant ways. Just as you used to break open the sod from the farm of your youth to bring forth good things.

You were quite a teacher too. Maybe that was one of your strongest points. Willing to take the time to prepare, and reflect on the simple lessons of life to share with the 'little ones' and the 'big folks' as well. You loved to use the teachable moments to preach the Gospel of Jesus. How did you do it? You must have stayed close to your roots and family life. You knew that the great mysteries of life are always relational and grounded in the family.

A sociologist as well. You prided yourself in that discipline and read extensively to keep abreast of the modern trends of society. Grounded in a modern discipline yet full of the ebb and flow of humanity even from ancient times. Human nature doesn't change much even over your eighty years. Religious trends always caught your attention to keep you informed about how to speak to modern dilemmas.

Person of prayer certainly. A leader of prayer for so many occasions of life transitions; a grave side service for the forgotten, a huge celebration for the elite, the Sunday celebration full of hope for the week, a child's prayer for the kids at faith formation classes, wedding celebrations and anniversaries of folks you baptized. Wow! It has been a long time of serving. This could only have come from some real time in private prayer.

Prophetic too, not unwilling to challenge the rich and powerful yet comfort the afflicted. Calling a spade, a spade no matter the consequence or whether it was politically correct. I am sure you suffered and were lonely at those times as well. And then this horrific scandal of the priesthood and Church leadership of our time just as you were about to say your good-byes. That really must be hard after all you did to help folks feel good about their Church. There is the mystery of good and evil even in our time, dear friend.

It must be hard to have such an active mind and spirit when the body starts to fail and you can't do what your soul races ahead of you to do. Yet, you've carried enough crosses for this lifetime so, rest now, my friend. Enjoy the solace and comfort of that monastic community and mystical prayer life in full rhythm with the seasons. Yes, there is a season for everything under heaven. So, too for you. For all, there is a homecoming, which is bitter sweet.

And lastly, thank you for all those wonderful conversations together about how to do ministry and service better. It was a joy ministering with you these past fifteen years. As you captured so well in the saying on the entrance to the Church: "This is what God asks of you. Only this, to act justly, to love tenderly and walk humbly with your God!" (Micah 6:8) You certainly have been one of the wonderful things of God.
Thank you, dear Friend!

Bill Rose, Pastoral Care Director, Holy Name of Jesus

Responding to Grief

When Mary came to where Jesus was
and saw Him, she knelt at His feet and
said to Him, "Lord, if you had been
here, my brother would not have died."
When Jesus saw her weeping, and the
Jews who came with her also weeping, He
was greatly disturbed in spirit and deeply
moved. He said, "Where have you laid
him?" They said to Him, "Lord, come
and see." Jesus began to weep. So the Jews
said, "See how much He loved him!"

(John 11:32-36)

*F*riends, when leaving the home of someone who has died or is dying, I often ask: "How can our human minds ever grasp death? Especially, how can we understand a death that comes too early—the death of a child or teen or young married person with spouse and children?" They are here one moment and gone the next. Breathing, thinking, speaking, caring, and then gone, leaving a vast empty hole in the heart of a family or friend.

When death arrives, all diversions—career, new houses, new cars, plans for entertainment, even work for noble causes—vanish for those who have lost someone dear. Only people remain—family, friends, and the church. They alone can see and respond, even if only imperfectly.

No training can fully help someone respond perfectly to those who have lost a child, spouse, parent, or friend. Other family members are also feeling a loss, and may have trouble being as supportive as they would in other circumstances. Friends may feel inept when they visit a house of sadness, then return home to a world that is disturbingly unchanged. Even church staff people that deal often with death never become experts at it. Clergy people may feel as awkward, hesitant, and taken aback as everyone else.

As frustrating and inadequate as family, friends, and the church can be, they will usually rally to respond as best they can when death occurs. Most of the time they are a lifeline to the grief-stricken, and a great source of hope and strength. They will give what they can. It might be lasagna or hugs. It could be a listening ear. It could be a song, a special remembrance, childcare, or a shoulder to cry on. They will stop their own lives to attend the funeral and honor the life lost.

Jesus created circles of caring like this when He traveled around with His disciples. In doing so, He redefined the meaning of love, grounding it in mercy and forgiveness. He taught that love extended beyond the boundaries of family, that people are bound to each other through their relationship with God, not simply through shared biology or history. One of His two commandments was that people care for each other. A lot of the time, that commandment is far from the minds of most people. We get stuck in selfishness, enmity, and infidelity. Church folk are often no different than others when it comes to this.

Maybe that's why death brings out the best in us. Not because we are morbid or enjoy suffering, but because the down-to-earth rituals involved in care-giving help us be who God made us to be. When we hold someone's hand and stare at the wall wondering what to do next, we become more fully human ourselves. When we prepare and deliver food for the funeral luncheon, we put our own agenda aside and live for someone else. When we attend the funeral and pray for the repose of the soul of the departed, we join with all the other faithful in celebrating his or her life. And when we hug the sorrowful and listen to their anguish, we become like Jesus himself.

Section Seven

Biography
and Photo Album

✝

Father Arnold Weber, OSB

Fr. Arnold Weber, OSB

✝

Go Now to Love and Serve the Lord

By Don Prisby

*S*everal years ago, during a period of studies in the Holy
Land, I had a unique opportunity to journey upon the road
to Emmaus. In the mid-August desert heat, my walking companion
and I set out to walk from the site of the Last Supper in Jerusalem
toward the small town of Emmaus, approximately seven miles to
the west. Our intent was to mirror the events of the story in Luke's
Gospel (Luke 24:13-35). Not surprisingly, in our enthusiasm,
zeal and naiveté, we eventually grew uncertain of our location.
Plodding along a strip of sand through the low-lying desert shrubs,
we stumbled upon (of all people) a shepherd, resting with his flock
of sheep and goats under a generous shade tree. Pointing down the
trail, the shepherd assured us that we were on the right path. With
direction and new confidence, we continued our walk.

It was not until several years later that I realized the significance
of that encounter. My companion and I, like the two disciples
in the Biblical story, were lost on the road to Emmaus. In like
manner, we met a shepherd along the way who gave us critical

direction. Likewise, on our own faith journeys, we often find ourselves immersed in the immediacy of life, yet we long for greater direction. We celebrate liturgy with its meter, music and ritual, yet we are not always aware of the meaning of those gestures. We live in neighborhoods, go to work, or are part of a parish, yet may not fully appreciate the value of community. We see the less fortunate around us, yet wait for an invitation to reach out. We hear Scripture or Church teachings, yet we need to have their nuances explained to us. Today, as in every age, we can easily get lost—lost in the allure of the fast track, lost in the hopes and tragedies of relationships, lost in our commitments, lost in our accomplishments, lost in our toys, and lost in the frenetic rush of life. At defining moments we may cry out for direction on the journey. As we travel down our own respective roads to Emmaus with the eyes of faith, perhaps we are lucky enough to find a trusted friend along the way to help. Just as my classmate and I discovered a shepherd on the actual road to Emmaus, perhaps God sends us shepherds to give direction through our own harsh and bewildering terrains.

It is 2005 now, 20 years after my "adventure" in the Holy Land. My vehicle is pointed north along a cold and snowy Minnesota road. I travel upon a ribbon of asphalt, cutting through the mist of a colorless December morning. The dense fog hangs over the patch of white fields on what is an unusually warm winter dawn. As I travel further north, I pass towns called Saint Michael, Saint Augusta, Saint Cloud, and Saint Joseph. Town by town, the urban growth of businesses and residential development loses its grip on the humble simplicity of rural living. Eighty miles north of the anonymity of the Twin Cities is the campus of Saint John's University and Saint John's Abbey, where I am scheduled to spend time with Rev. Fr. Arnold John Weber, OSB. I am not lost on this day, but am eagerly anticipating an encounter with another shepherd, one who has broken bread, provided direction, explained the Scriptures, transformed lives, pointed to the poor and helped reveal the transcendent in the imminent for people on thousands and thousands of faith journeys.

Arriving early, I spend some time in preparation for our meeting in Saint John's Abbey Church, an architectural wonder which resides above Lake Sagatagan, adjacent to Saint John's Abbey. The church's massive gray concrete bell banner draws me under and into the cool, dark chapel. There is a palpable silence as I kneel on the hard wooden kneeler, and the heavy stillness envelopes me. The restlessness of the city and my journey is quieted. A monk moves amid the shadows of the sanctuary, placing candles on the altar, adjusting a book on a table and silently moving through his routine, perhaps in preparation for community prayer or Mass. The time has come for me to greet Fr. Arnold.

I enter another building, the Great Hall, which is the original Abbey Church established in 1856. There I learn that Arnold John Weber, hailing from the neighboring town of Saint Martin, was ordained a priest at the age of 26. I find a spot to sit amid a welcoming arrangement of comfortable sofas and tables to wait for my host.

The door leading from the heart of the monastery opens and Fr. Arnold emerges, shuffling toward me, clad in neat casual slacks, a plaid button down shirt and a light winter jacket. He is now in retirement at the monastery and at eighty years old, his firm handshake and the sparkle in his eyes still express vitality and promise. "Let's have lunch in Saint Joe," he suggests. After a slow and steady walk to the car, we travel together to a restaurant in the town of Saint Joseph, home of the College of Saint Benedict, the all-female sister school of Saint John's University.

Arnold John Weber was born on October 21, 1925, the second of 12 siblings born to Bernard and Louise Weber. Their home was a 120-acre farm in the heart of Minnesota. It is a family farm which is run today by Arnold's brother. The community of Saint Martin was then as it remains today—a rural town of mostly

German immigrants, sturdy people rich with potential. The Weber family, sharing a vibrant German Catholic heritage, nurtured a strong work ethic and love of the Church in their children. While two of Arnold's siblings died young (a sister shortly after her birth and a brother at age 11), two of the sons, Sylvester, who was known as "Otto" (now deceased) and younger brother Arnold were called to lives as Benedictine priests. Four daughters, Evelyn, Mary Ann, Angeline and Theresa, became Benedictine nuns. Two other Weber daughters, Alice and Elizabeth, married, and two brothers, Jerome and Raymond (now deceased) chose lives dedicated to the family farm.

Arnold was educated in a one-room schoolhouse by his grandfather, Nicholas Weber. In 1940, upon reaching high school at the age of 15, Arnold's father decided to send him to Saint John's Preparatory School. At that time, Arnold was already attracted to the possibility of becoming a priest. While his father knew that sending Arnold to Saint John's Prep would assure that Arnold would continue to grow in his faith, he almost certainly knew that it would be a gateway to life beyond the farm. This was quite a sacrifice for the father of such a strong son.

Arnold completed his studies at Saint John's Prep in 1946. He continued his formation in the novitiate at Saint John's Abbey. He was ordained a priest on June 7, 1952, at the age of 26. Arnold would continue his studies and his service to the Church by completing a Master's Degree in Sociology during five successive summers of study at the Catholic University of America in Washington, D.C. He would spend 18 years of service at Saint John's Abbey in various roles as prefect, professor, athletic coach, retreat director, and vocation director. From 1970 to 1972 and then again from 1977 to 1980, Fr. Arnold served both as Religious Education Director and Administrator at Benilde-Saint Margaret's High School in St. Louis Park. While nearing the end of this first term at Benilde High School, Fr. Arnold was assigned briefly to Holy

Name of Jesus in Wayzata. Although the parishioners of Holy Name quickly fell in love with Fr. Arnold, his first term at Holy Name lasted less than a year before he was asked to serve as Pastor at Holy Rosary in Detroit Lakes. He served as pastor of Holy Rosary Parish from 1972 to 1977. In 1980, at the age of 55, he was assigned by the Abbot to return to Holy Name of Jesus as pastor, where he would remain for 23 years. In September 2001, at the age of 75, Fr. Arnold stepped down as head pastor of Holy Name of Jesus. He remained in residence at Holy Name until 2003, when he was called to come back home to the monastery in the rolling hills of Collegeville, Minnesota.

At lunch we place our order and get reacquainted. I look across the table at a man who embraces life, loves the church, is a leader, directs people in service to the poor, embraces the values of Vatican II, is known throughout the diocese, and now resides quietly within the walls of the monastery where his life of Benedictine service began. Being here in this peaceful, resource-rich yet humble rural land reminds me of an insight I had during a trip to Assisi, Italy. I remember thinking how likely it was that such a humble yet strong man as Saint Francis of Assisi would come from a land of rolling hills, vineyards, earthen buildings and rural ethic. I feel the same sentiment as I sit across from this great and humble man, who is fruit of the strength of family and farm and who is seasoned with the experience of service, care for the poor, and pastoral and academic curiosity.

For most who have known Fr. Arnold and certainly for those who were part of his pastorate at Holy Name of Jesus, his most memorable attributes are his appreciation of Vatican II, his passion for liturgy, his encouragement of the laity, his unwavering respect for all life, and his love of the poor. There was hardly a day when Fr. Arnold was not preaching about the unearthed values expressed in the Vatican II documents and how those teachings were applied not only in the liturgy but in the call of the Church, especially in the call of the laity. Equally, one could not miss his passion for helping the poor and his innate ability to connect a wealthy Western Twin Cities suburban parish to the less fortunate found in the local neighborhood, the inner city, the nation and the world.

Under his brilliant leadership at Holy Name, people were invited and mobilized, funds were raised and communities transformed by liturgy and social justice. Today, organizations like the Hammer Residence, Ascension School, Interfaith Outreach, Mexican orphanages, the poor in Guatemala, Sharing and Caring Hands, Mary's Place, and seminarians in Uganda are still being helped by this parish of 2,800 families. In addition, under Fr. Arnold's leadership, Holy Name was one of the two highest financial contributors to the Archdiocese of Minneapolis/Saint Paul.

Fr. Arnold's authentic care for others is expressed in the love that he has for children and the invitation he extends to them to love and serve the poor. This is perhaps most purely expressed during the offertory at Mass. Before the collection baskets are passed, the children are invited to come forward and share their food donations with the poor. Watching the children, some so young they are just learning to walk, come streaming forward, so eager to share what they have with others, is a lesson for us all. Arnold's love for the poor was also evidenced on his own front door at the rectory, where the finish was literally worn off by the tape holding countless envelopes of money, left for those in need.

In addition to his love for the poor, this is a man who could lose his voice in an impassioned plea to help the unborn, the elderly, the handicapped, and those who society has deemed to be of little or no value. Fr. Arnold possesses a respect for life that is firm and offers no gray area on the subject. He often quoted Mother Teresa of Calcutta and Pope John Paul II when he spoke of the current "Culture of Death" that permeates our society. His heart genuinely aches for the loss of life and potential, especially when it comes to the lives of the unborn.

A firm handshake, a focus on the needs of others, an ability to mobilize and inspire, and an invitation to get involved are all hallmarks of this dedicated priest.

As I reflect on the brief yet rich encounter I had with Fr. Arnold at lunch, I recall his thoughts on several subjects.

Principles of Life

How can we contextualize such a life? What are the principles that call and inspire Fr. Arnold in this life of teaching and service? Certainly they include the values contained in the Benedictine Rule of Life—the values of community, prayer, humility, work, the consecration of the ordinary and hospitality. And of course they include the Benedictine mantra, "In omnibus glorificetur Deus", translated to English, "That in all things God may be glorified." Also included are the Benedictine vows of conversion, stability and obedience. Of all the Benedictine principles, Arnold believes that, "hospitality is our greatest call." He notes emphatically that, "people need to be welcomed as though they are Christ themselves, especially the poor."

Arnold was also guided by other principles—such as those expressed in the Second Vatican Council. Among those, Arnold notes that the Vatican II call for, "full, active and conscious participation in the Liturgy" is the most significant. Speaking as though there are many more fields to plant and harvest, Arnold explains, "We need to go deeper into the value of the Vatican II teachings. Vatican II was not about rearranging the chairs in the sanctuary (referring to the liturgical reforms). We need to see how the Council called all people by virtue of their baptism into full participation in the church. We have a long way to go and there is still division in the church."

"We heard your voice"

Our lunch arrives and Fr. Arnold is gracious to answer my many questions though his meal sits before him. As we converse, a couple in their late 50's approaches the table. "We heard your voice, Father, and wanted to come over to see you," they said, looking delighted and surprised at this unexpected opportunity. I later learned that this was a couple he had known years ago from a parish. I am amazed at his memory as I watch him engage the couple in conversation about each of their children. This encounter reminds me of how people must have been attracted by the voice of Jesus in the equally rural and simple environments of Galilee, Cana, Nazareth, Jericho, Capernaum and others. The story of the encounter with the shepherd on the road to Emmaus comes to mind again.

The Liturgy

Fr. Arnold expresses that the celebration of the liturgy is intrinsically linked to service to those outside the community. He says, "The Mass concludes with the exhortation, 'the Mass is ended, go in peace to love and serve the Lord.'" He tells me a story about a gathering, where one little girl remarked that her favorite part of the Mass was the part that says, "The Mass is ended, go in peace to love and serve the Lord." He chuckles across the table, "The adults laughed, but they didn't get it. They were interpreting the little girl as saying her favorite part of the Mass was that 'it was ended.' The little girl's favorite part of the Mass was that we can now go and serve the Lord."

The Poor and Less Fortunate

"The poor are in the Scriptures," he cries. "One can hardly read twenty verses of Scripture in either the Hebrew Scriptures or the New Testament without finding reference to the poor. To be a people of the Word is to be a people for the poor." When he arrived at Holy Name in 1980, there was a promising initiative for service to the poor brought forth by one of the deacons and some of the lay leadership. Over the 20 years of his pastorate, that effort grew to over 100 programs serving the young and old, the poor and needy, those with special needs and the unemployed all over the city, country and world. He insisted, "I never ask people to give until it hurts, but to give until they love to give."

The Universal Longing

Considering his lifetime of preaching and service, I ask Fr. Arnold to share what he believes is the universal desire in people. He responds, "People want to be needed. They want to be in community." He points to the breakdown of the extended and nuclear families, and the feverish pace of life. "People need and want to be together." He explains that his most joyful preaching is with communities who respond as community. His favorite preaching experiences are at community events or at holidays when families and communities are reunited. His most challenging homilies are funerals, particularly funerals of suicide victims. Overall, he emphasizes that our constant challenge is, "to welcome and not to be so judgmental." About the Church, he remarks, "we are not in the judgment business, we are in the mercy business."

God's New Mission

"What an encounter I'm having," I thought as I pushed my meatloaf and potatoes around on my plate. "Father, can you tell me what your life is like right now?" I asked. He responded, "I spend it meeting with people like you who come up to visit me." Going a bit deeper I asked, "Father, we believe that God has made us in His image and likeness, and that He has a unique call for each of us. Your life has been long and rich. Can I ask you… what is God's call for you now?" Without hesitation, he looked down at his shaking hands, a result of Parkinson's disease. He also suffers from Type II Diabetes. "My call is to suffer now. I want to live the rest of my life embracing my suffering. I feel now that I am constantly dying (referring to the pain in his legs and feet and uncontrollable shake in his hands.) I feel now that God is giving me a taste of my own medicine and that I am truly called to be 'better not bitter.'" I detect a tear in his otherwise joyful blue eyes. He notes that he currently meets with the elderly and advises them that, "it is okay to pray as Christ did at the end of His life, to truly pray 'Father, into your hands I commend my spirit.'" He also quotes Saint Augustine, who said, "Our hearts are restless until they rest in thee." I ask him, "is there suffering in retiring to the quiet of the Abbey after such an active life?" He responds, "No, I am truly coming home." With a smile now, he continues, "However, living here was a bit frustrating at first because the monks pray so slowly—but I am getting accustomed to that." I sense that he is at home now in this place that nurtured his budding vocation and where he spent the first eighteen years of his life as a priest.

Home to the Monastery

The plates are cleared and we walk back to the car across a parking lot covered with wet slush and patches of ice. The ride back to the monastery includes an exchange of ideas, an update on the activities at Holy Name and a quick drive around the campus. Upon arrival, we enter the campus as though we are going through the front door of his home. He eagerly shows me the Institute for Ecumenical and Cultural Research, the Episcopal House of Prayer, the offices of Liturgical Press, the beautiful lake behind the monastery and the modest cemetery where he matter-of-factly states, "That's where I will be some day."

Were Not Our Hearts Burning?

As we approached the red brick facade of the monastery, tucked into the evergreens on the rolling hills above the forever fields, I am aware that I have just spent time with a great shepherd on a December day of his life-long faith journey. In the scriptural account of the Road to Emmaus, Jesus explained the deeper meaning in the Scriptures. Jesus and the two disciples broke bread over a "Eucharistic" meal. The disciples gained insight on living and were

311

led to see God in their midst. Reluctantly, I say goodbye to Fr. Arnold in the Great Hall and he generously places a warm loaf of bread from the Abbey kitchen in my arms. Heading home, I think about authenticity, commitment, and love for others. I consider the strength of family, community and conviction. I recall a day spent with an ordinary man from an ordinary town whose extraordinary life reflects the life of Christ. I recall a day spent with a man whose actions are consistent with his words, a man whose heart beats for the Church and for the people of God—all the people of God.

"Were not our hearts burning when He spoke to us on the way and opened the Scriptures to us?" exclaimed the two disciples in the Emmaus account. Most assuredly, our hearts burn within us today as a result of the life, deeds and words of this true shepherd, Fr. Arnold John Weber. He has given us words that challenge, assure, re-orient and clarify, words that call us into community and guide us along the road of faith, words that compel us to "go now to love and serve the Lord."

Photo Album

Arnold John Weber. Born October 21, 1925

The Weber family practiced their Catholic faith. Arnold's younger brother and four of his sisters went on to join the consecrated life as Benedictine priests and nuns.

Arnold attended St. John's Prep School in Collegeville, MN before joining the seminary.

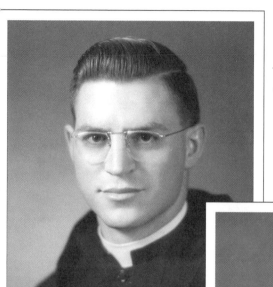

Fr. Arnold spent the first 18 years of his priesthood at St. John's.

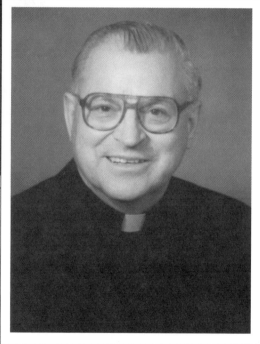

In 1980, Fr. Arnold was assigned to Holy Name of Jesus in Wayzata, Minnesota where he would remain for 23 years.

Testing out the new playground equipment at Holy Name of Jesus School, Fr. Arnold was the first to go down the new slide.

Fr. Arnold played an active role with the youth at Holy Name.
Participating in Vacation Bible School each summer was just one of the
many ways he participated.

While Fr. Arnold was Pastor at Holy Name, the parish grew in numbers. Many young families were moving into the area and choosing Holy Name as their parish. It was common for Fr. Arnold to baptize more than 200 children in any given year.

Fr. Arnold was one of the first priests in the Archdiocese to invite women (young and old) to serve at the altar.

Fr. Arnold's love for his vocation as priest is matched only by his love for Christ.

Whether directing traffic on Wednesday nights during the faith formation programs, or socializing outside the parish boundaries, Fr. Arnold always enjoyed being with the children of Holy Name.

*Fr. Arnold used to say that "dead churches don't need expansion
programs." Holy Name was very much alive.*

"Are you going to preach to me or are you going to help me?"
Those words, spoken to Fr. Arnold by a woman facing eviction, are the
words that started Arnie's Door.